About the Author

Denise Linn's personal journey began as a result of a near-death experience as a teenager. Her unique experiences at that time set her on a spiritual quest to study the traditions of many cultures including her own Native American heritage. Over the last 25 years she has studied with a Hawaiian kahuna (shaman), Reiki Master Hawayo Takata, a Shiatsu master, a Pueblo Indian medicine man, the Aborigines in the Australian bush, the Zulus in Bophuthatswana, and she has been adopted into a New Zealand Maori tribe. In addition, Denise lived in a Zen Buddhist monastery for over two years.

Denise is an international lecturer, healer and writer. She regularly gives seminars on six continents, appears extensively on television and radio shows throughout the world, and has authored five self-help books.

SIGNPOSTS

The Universe is Whispering to You

Denise Linn

RIDER

LONDON · SYDNEY · AUCKLAND · JOHANNESBURG

First published in 1996

1 3 5 7 9 10 8 6 4 2

Copyright © Denise Linn 1996

Published in 1996 by Rider,
an imprint of Ebury Press, Random House,
20 Vauxhall Bridge Road, London SW1V 2SA

Random House Australia (Pty) Limited
20 Alfred Street, Milsons Point, Sydney, New South Wales 2061, Australia

Random House New Zealand Limited
18 Poland Road, Glenfield,
Auckland 10, New Zealand

Random House South Africa (Pty) Limited
PO Box 337, Bergvlei 2012, South Africa

Random House UK Limited Reg. No. 954009

Papers used by Rider Books are natural, recyclable products made from wood
grown in sustainable forests. In addition, the paper in this book is
acid-free/recycled/chlorine free

Typeset by SX Composing DTP
Printed and bound in Great Britain by Mackays of Chatham PLC, Kent

A CIP catalogue record for this book is available from the British Library

ISBN 0-7126-7449-7

This book is lovingly dedicated to
DAVID, MEADOW AND MARIKA
for bringing joy into my life.

Acknowledgements

With loving gratitude to:

Judith Kendra, my editor, for her thoughtful feedback.

Joseph Winterhawk Martin, Credo Mutwa, Claire Brown, Ken Colbung, Lily Kauler and Sarah Broadhurst for their contributions to this book.

Contents

Introduction

In every moment the universe is whispering to you. There are messages for you carried on the winds. There is wisdom for you in the morning songs of the birds outside your window and in the soft murmurs of an ebbing sea. Even ordinary everyday events in your life carry communications from the realm of spirit.

Right now as you read this paragraph, you are surrounded by personal messages from the world around you. Whether you are conscious of it or not, you are always encircled by signs. Of course your night hours are filled with signs which appear in your dreams; however, no less valid are the signs that encompass you in your waking life. Signs are powerful indicators which can give you understanding about yourself, and insight about direction in life. They can also reflect what is occurring in your subconscious mind, beneath your conscious awareness.

In times past, people knew how to understand and interpret these portents and omens. In fact, the entire destiny of a tribe and even a nation was often decided by signs. However, as technology expanded, people become more and more isolated from their connection to the earth and their inner wisdom. Most lost their ability to listen to the secret messages around them. They lost the ability to see the signposts giving personal guidance in every moment.

It is now time to regain this lost ability. Our planet is changing very quickly and in the face of this rising tide of change we need to remember how to taste the messages in the wind and how to listen to the gentle voices in the clouds. This ability is going to be increasingly important in the years ahead. As we hurtle into the twenty-first century, there is an accelerated awakening of planetary consciousness. We are entering a time of signs and omens. There has never been a more powerful time in the linear history of our planet to step into our magnificence. Signs can show us the way. It is now time to relearn how to listen to the whispers of the universe.

My journey into the realm of signs and portents began when I was very young. In fact, I can't remember a time when I didn't watch for signs. I always felt that there was a deep connection between all people and all things. Even as a young child I intuitively recognized that there was a vast interconnected system of the universe deep within me, where all permeations of life resided. And I listened to the signs around me that emanated from that deep inner source. I believe that my Cherokee heritage is partially responsible for this perception of life, for native people throughout the world follow signs and believe in omens.

However, I also believe that my interest in signs can be credited to my upbringing. I grew up in a family where a very close family member was mentally ill for a period of time. This family member was paranoid schizophrenic, which often made life very difficult. However, every burden in life carries a hidden gift, and I gained a great gift living with her. She saw the entire world through signs. All occurrences had meaning and significance for her. Every event was connected to every other event. Often her perception of reality seemed entirely random and irrational. There is a fine line between the mystic and the insane. Every once in a while I would slip beneath the veil of the illusionary normal world and enter her world. When I saw the world through her eyes, remarkably, everything did have meaning. I recognized that many seemingly unrelated factors and occurrences would lead to a particular event, and horizontal analysis could link any event to signs surrounding *and even preceding* the event.

While still a teenager I had a traumatic near-death experience that further gave credence to the validity of signs. When I was thought to be dead, I entered a realm where I experienced a profound unity with all things. My experience was so meaningful that when I recovered my health, it started me on a quest to discover more about the hidden dimensions within life. My journeys led me to Native American tribal traditions, including my own Cherokee tribe (I'm an enrolled member of the Cherokee Nation), I also spent time with the Maoris in New Zealand, the Aborigines in Australia, and the Zulus in Bophuthatswana. I trained with a Hawaiian kahuna learning ancient Hawaiian healing techniques; trained in Reiki (Japanese system of channelling energy) with Hawayo Takata and organized the first Reiki courses for Westerners; trained and taught shiatsu (Japanese form of massage that utilizes pressure points) and lived in a Zen Buddhist monastery for several years. Every experience I had deepened my respect for portents and omens. It is from my lifelong experience of observing the signs in the world around me that this book is based.

Many examples are used in this book, which I have gathered from people who have attended my seminars. Giving lectures for over twenty-five years in six continents, I have been honoured to hear some remarkable personal stories. I have attempted to recount them accurately, although some have been edited for brevity and, most likely, some have settled a bit in my mind over the years. As I don't know all the names of those who have shared stories with me, I have used pseudonyms in some of the examples and I have used first names throughout for the sake of continuity. Several of the stories have been changed to protect the privacy of the person who told me the story.

Within each of us is the ability to read the signs. This book assists you in regaining your innate capacity to listen to the whispers of the universe so that you make decisions and choices that will empower you and your family in the times ahead.

1   How Signs Work

Although a full understanding of how signs work cannot be fully captured within the confines of the written word, it is possible to provide an underlying perception of the dynamics of signs and their corresponding symbolism. Signs capture abstractions of the human condition and create a bridge between the realm of spirit and the realm of form, as well as revealing the connection that exists between seemingly diverse objects. They can also reflect our feelings and reveal our fears. The study of signs spans the ages, therefore signs are best understood in the context of their religious, cultural, historical background and the soil from which they arose, as well as how they operate in your life. Fundamentally signs have two functions. They serve as messengers of important information about your present circumstances and even about your future. They also act as reflections of where you are in your life.

Messenger Signs

Messenger signs can come on the waft of a candle's smoke, or the gentle murmur of the wind, or in a dream, or from the thousand swirls of consciousness around you. These kind of signs can give you direct messages from spirit. They can give you guidance about your spiritual development or they can come in the form of a warning regarding future events. They can also give you a deeper understanding of the relationships and situations in your life.

One day when Rick was leaving for work, his front door was jammed. He had to throw his entire weight against it to get it open. Then, as he tried to open the garage door, the opener malfunctioned and he had to open the door manually. As he went to get into his car, the car door lock was obstructed and he had to struggle to get it open. Realizing that the universe was trying to tell him something, he sat in his car in silence for a few minutes. In the stillness, as he tuned in to his intuition, he felt that the signs were telling him not to leave home just at that moment. So he got out of the car and went back inside his house. As he walked around his home, everything seemed in order. However as he entered a basement bathroom, he was aware of a slight smell of smoke. Some bathroom tissues, which were in close proximity to an electric heater, had started to char. If left unattended, they most certainly would have burst into flame. Rick then realized that all the difficulties leaving his house had been messenger signs warning him of danger.

Thomas was about to enter into a partnership on a boat ownership. Just prior to the signing of the agreement he had a dream about his new partner. In his dream he saw the man looking friendly, but as he looked closer he saw that the warm countenance was, in fact, a mask. In the dream, the partner-to-be took off the mask and Thomas saw that his true face was devious and untrustworthy. Thomas recognized that his dream was a messenger sign that things were not as they seemed, so he stepped away from the partnership. In subsequent years, his dream proved to be prophetic and Thomas saw the wisdom of his decision.

Both these stories are examples of messenger signs which are always surrounding you in every moment. These signs do not always signify some grand and magnificent future event or warn you of some devastating and dangerous occurrence to come. Sometimes, and most often, they are gentle little messenger signs telling you things like, 'Love yourself more today,' or 'Remember to pay the gas bill,' or 'You are wonderful.' Learning to hear these gentle nudges can make your life so much more balanced and harmonious.

Reflection Signs

Another function of signs in your life is as reflections of your inner state of being. For example, those who think the world is full of lonely people and only see lonely people wherever they go, are most often lonely people themselves *even if they are not consciously aware of it*. All the lonely people they see in the outer world are signs or reflections of their inner loneliness. What you are aware of consciously is such a small part of what is actually occurring within your subconscious mind. However, the signs around you are always giving you clues to the deeper reality within you.

Sarah was sitting on a park bench for her lunch break. An old dog sidled up to her and looked at her with dark pooled eyes. Sarah's heart went out to the dog and she shared her sandwich with him. Like attracts like, and Sarah felt much sadness and sympathy for the dog. She said, 'Oh, you poor downtrodden thing. You look so unhappy. Everyone is taking advantage of you, aren't they?' After Sarah got up from the bench, an old man sat down to eat his lunch.

Once again the dog scuttled up for a handout. The old man said, 'Come here, old boy. Hey, you're a real fighter, aren't you? You've shown 'em. Nobody was ever your master. That's a good boy.' Sarah and the old man would both swear to the reality of their perception of the dog. And in both cases the dog was a reflective sign. The dog was a sign reflecting to Sarah that *she* felt downtrodden in life and that everyone was taking advantage of her. The old man had been a rebel all his life, so the dog was a reflective sign mirroring that *he* felt he was up against the world.

A very sad example of a reflective sign occurred when a pregnant woman asked me about something that had been perplexing her. She kept seeing dead animals: a dead bird, a dead mouse and a dead raccoon, and wanted to know what they were signs of. I replied that usually when death appears as a sign, it is a powerful indicator of renewal and rebirth; for life must end in order to begin again, just as winter precedes the spring. That made sense to her at the time; however she later wrote to tell me that the doctors had found that her foetus was not viable, and hadn't been for a long time. The dead animals that she was seeing were a reflective sign that the unborn child within her was no longer alive. Synchronously, she also did begin a completely new spiritual cycle in her life as a result of her baby's death.

Reflective signs can also give an inner view of deep emotional processing occurring within you. If there is an old karmic pattern that is just about to surface, it will first appear in your life as a reflective sign. If there are old childhood issues that are ripe to be resolved and healed, they will appear in your life first as reflective signs.

Samantha's father left home when she was a young girl and never returned. She suppressed a child's natural inclination to grieve over the loss of a parent. Instead she offered a shoulder for her mother to lean on and she seemed to cope with the situation very easily. She never allowed herself to process the myriad of emotions that she felt as a result of the loss. As an adult, though memories of childhood and her father were hidden in the far recesses of her mind, she often had difficulty with relationships. She would enter a relationship and then her partner would abandon her. This negative relationship pattern occurred again and again, and true love eluded her. Just after Samantha's thirty-fifth birthday, she began seeing and hearing things that reminded her of her past. Twice she walked down a city street and saw someone who looked exactly like her father. There seemed to be a surfeit of articles and documentaries in the media about parents abandoning their children. No matter in what direction she turned, the universe gave her signs that stimulated memories of her own childhood abandonment. These signs were indicative that the pain that had been buried so deep within her was rising to the surface to be released. As a result of the myriad of reflective signs stimulating memories from childhood, Samantha went into therapy and eventually healed and released her fear of abandonment. Within a year, Samantha began a loving (and lasting) relationship.

Reflective signs are valuable because they allow you to be aware of the underlying reality present in your life, and this self awareness leads to wisdom and ultimately peace. It is important to be aware of your subconscious emotions because, if left unattended, they can perpetuate illness and physical and emotional difficulties.

Why Signs Reflect your Beliefs

The visible realities surrounding you are symbols of your inner invisible world. Everything around you, every situation you encounter, every experience you have is filled with signs regarding your life. In order to understand this, it helps to know the underlying dynamics of why this occurs. To comprehend why signs work, it's valuable to understand how beliefs work, because the signs in your life emanate from your beliefs. A belief is a thought or a perception that you consider to be a fact or a reality. Beliefs are very powerful. They determine the way you think, feel and behave. In fact, they determine the fabric of your life. They can literally create the circumstances of your life and your personal signs emerge directly from your beliefs.

We all have conscious and subconscious beliefs about ourselves and our life around us and sometimes they are at odds with each other. The beliefs that specifically dictate the quality of life, however, are our subconscious beliefs, which are generally so deep-seated that we're not even aware of them. They affect our perception of reality just as tinted glasses allow only certain colours to reach our eyes. For example, a man's conscious belief might be that men and women are equal in their ability to drive vehicles; however, *subconsciously* he may believe that men are superior drivers. His conscious mind may not even know what his subconscious mind believes. Yet he subconsciously selectively sees only the reckless drivers who are women, which validates his subconscious belief.

Our subconscious programming directs the way we see the world around us and also prescribes the way others see us. This programming comes from the way others related to us when we were children, from decisions that we made in past lives, as well as from the collective consciousness of the society in which we live. If you are not sure what your subconscious beliefs are, just look at your life. Your life is an absolute projection of your subconscious beliefs about yourself and life.

Perhaps you've heard the expression, 'You are what you think.' This doesn't mean only what you *know* you think consciously. It also refers to what you *don't know* you think (your subconscious beliefs). A young girl being repeatedly told that she is clumsy is an example of how subconscious beliefs begin to develop. The child's critical faculties are not advanced enough to reject this negative programming, so her subconscious accepts the idea of her being clumsy. This belief of clumsiness begins to become a part of the girl's reality so that she begins really to feel that she is a clumsy person. *Whatever is expected tends to be realized,* so the child grows up constantly being clumsy. Her inner programming is so deeply imbedded in her mind that it becomes part of her 'ground of being'. When a subconscious belief becomes part of your ground of being it doesn't seem like a decision or belief, it seems like the true reality.

Our inner core beliefs can be likened to gravity. Gravity is so much a part of our ground of being that we don't have conscious awareness of the many pounds of pressure that are being exerted on every square inch of our body at every moment. Gravity is such a fundamental part of what we take for granted as reality that we almost never think about it. Core beliefs become so much a part of our view of ourselves and the world that we don't even know that they are beliefs. They are glued or imbedded into our personal energy field. And these subconscious beliefs continually coalesce into form in the manifest world. As your energy projects from your body in undulating waves all around you, it projects your beliefs into the world. Beliefs act as magnets, pulling to you situations and people that are congruous with your subconscious beliefs. This means that your personal world is created or manifested by the core beliefs that exist in your subconscious mind.

Here is an example of the way that core beliefs work. If you have a subconscious belief imbedded in your personal energy field that people can't be trusted, this subconscious belief is constantly projecting from you; this occurs even when you are feeling *consciously* very trusting. The emanations from your energy field will draw people into your life who aren't trustworthy. So if you constantly have people in your life whom you can't trust, this is usually a sign that either you have a subconscious belief that people can't be trusted, or *you* are not trustworthy or, more likely, that you don't trust yourself.

Sometimes people will attempt to adopt new beliefs and this will be effective for usually only a short period of time because the power of the subconscious mind is so strong. (A method to begin to reprogramme the subconscious mind to develop more positive beliefs is discussed in Chapter 3 'Surrounding Yourself with Signs'.) The signs in your life constantly reflect your subconscious beliefs about the world around you. If you want to discover what is occurring within the depths of your being at any given time, just look and listen to the signs around you.

Why Signs Reflect your Focus in Life

Signs can also help you be aware of what you are focusing on in life. For example, if you buy a yellow Volkswagen, suddenly you might see lots of yellow Volkswagens where previously you didn't. You might even be led to think that there is a sudden spurt in the sales of yellow Volkswagens, but actually you see more Volkswagens because you have put your focus on these cars. The universe around you is a sign of your focus.

We live on a busy corner in Seattle. Our house is close to the street (about twenty feet away). One day my husband casually mentioned that 200 buses a day pass our home. I was shocked. We had lived in our house for two years, yet I had never heard or seen even one bus pass. Even though huge buses constantly rumbled by our home, I had no focus on them, so I never saw or heard them . . . for two years! As unlikely as this sounds, it is true. However once my husband shifted my focus to the buses, I began to see them and hear them all the time.

Why Signs can bring Messages from the Future

Since the beginning of civilization, people have received accurate signs regarding the future. Ancient predictions have been fulfilled, dreams have correctly foretold the future, and every day people have received clear premonitions about the future. Questions about how this can occur have fascinated philosophers and scientists for centuries. The pivotal point in understanding this phenomenon is the examination of the nature of time. In the day-to-day world, the space around us is measured by height, length and breadth. However, scientist Albert Einstein declared that space and time were inseparable and together they were what he called a space-time continuum. He declared that both time and space were elastic and they both expand and contract, and in fact can warp themselves into four-dimensional curves. Hence time can loop back upon itself. Though this sounds confusing, in the realm of sophisticated mathematics it is completely logical. And to those who live in native cultures the cyclical nature of time is as natural as the air that they breathe.

An example of the malleable nature of time is the fatal maiden voyage of the *Titanic* in 1912. Phenomenal similarities occurred between the real *Titanic* and the fictional ship *Titan* whose sinking was chronicled in the novel *Futility*, by Morgan Robertson in 1898. The similarities are uncanny. In the book the *Titan* was an unsinkable ship with passenger capacity of 3,000 (more than had ever sailed on one ship), that collided with an iceberg during an April voyage in which many lives were lost because she didn't carry enough lifeboats. He wrote: 'She was the largest craft afloat . . . unsinkable, indestructible, she carried as few [life] boats as would satisfy the laws . . .' This is the exact scenario that occurred in real life fourteen years later for the *Titanic* ocean liner, which sank in mid-Atlantic. Many of the technical details also concurred between the two ships.

Morgan Robertson was one of many people to receive signs prior to the sinking of the *Titanic*. Though there were common themes, each person who received a sign about the sinking of the great ship was given a different aspect. Every person's psyche is unique, so it may be that when signs from the future present themselves they are seen from varying angles and points of view, just as present events are seen from various perspectives.

Signs bringing messages from the future can be likened to a time overlap, or a fold in time, where you have a window into the future. Scientists call these windows in time 'cosmic wormholes', from the idea that a worm can take a shortcut by boring a hole through an apple rather than going around it. Whenever you receive a sign from the future there is a reason; it may be to prepare you for future events or it may be to help you avert disaster. Whatever the reason it's important to listen to these portents of the future.

Where Signs Come From

Signs from the Collective Consciousness

The signs that appear in your life come from many different sources. Some signs originate from what is called the 'collective consciousness'. It was the well-known Swiss psychoanalyst Carl Jung who brought attention to this subject. According to Jung, the unconscious mind contained two parts: the personal unconscious, which contains the memories of an individual's entire experience; and the collective unconscious, which was a receptacle for the experience of the entire human history. He felt that the unconscious mind contained layer upon layer of information from all humanity's past, and all human beings shared in this collective consciousness. Jung based his belief on the fact that certain symbols are used universally around the world. In addition, part of his proof was the repetitive occurrence of certain symbols in his patients' dreams and their drawings. Jung believed that within the collective unconscious exists a number of primordial images or archetypes that take the form of intuitive knowledge or even universal apprehension. He thought that these archetypal images were particularly likely to occur during sleep, because when the conscious mind is off guard, the archetypes can then emerge.

Some of the signs that appear for you may indeed be from the collective unconscious. For example, the cross is a universal symbol from even the most primordial times. It has been a symbol of the cosmic axis between heaven and earth, the union of opposites, and all aspects of God. The cross has represented the merging of all existence on the horizontal and vertical planes, as well as the infinite expansion in all directions that denotes eternal life. It was also thought to represent the four elements that comprise the world, united in the cosmic centre. And of course, in the present day, the cross represents Jesus, the life and the resurrection. So if a cross appears to you as a sign, it can be one of the universal signs that exists in the collective consciousness that connects us all.

When thousands of people for hundreds of years focus on a sign or a symbol, an etheric energy is generated around that sign that exists in the collective consciousness. Anytime someone focuses on a particular sign, they are locking onto that force that has been created through the years by others who have used that same symbol.

Signs from your Culture, Society and Religion

Some signs come from your culture, your society or your personal religion. For example in some cultures black cats are signs of bad luck and in other cultures they are good luck signs. If you live in a culture where black cats are bad luck, *even if you don't believe in superstitions,* you very well might encounter bad luck because you have tapped into the cultural collective consciousness of your society. The signs of your culture can appear to you, even if you don't believe in them, because they are ingrained in the psyche of society.

Signs from your Heritage

Your heritage can be a source of your personal signs even *if you are not aware of what those ancestral signs are.* It is not uncommon for someone who has been removed from their heritage or adopted into another tradition to retain a subconscious alignment with the signs of their heritage. There is great value in researching the signs of your ancient heritage, for often this can give you powerful clues for understanding the signs that appear in your life. Everyone's ancestors originated in native cultures where signs were used to dictate the daily circumstances of life.

John was born in China, but as a baby he was adopted by an American missionary family. Growing up in the midwest of the United States he always had an affinity for grasshoppers. He would catch them and then would lie on the ground to observe them more closely. As he grew older he associated grasshoppers with good luck. He mentioned this once to his adopted father and he said, 'No, grasshoppers aren't symbols for good luck. They symbolize irresponsibility and improvidence and indolence,' and he told John the fable of the grasshopper and the ant. However, grasshoppers continued to be a good luck sign for John. Later in life, he had occasion to visit China and he was delighted when he found that, in his birthplace, grasshoppers were considered to be signs of good fortune.

It is valuable to examine how heritage signs are used in other cultures for this can assist you in understanding your own. In my travels throughout the world I have had the opportunity to spend time with native peoples and learn about their signs. In New Zealand I was invited to spend time on a Maori marae with the Teranaki people. In time, I was honorarily adopted into their tribe. The Tohunga (spiritual leader and medicine man) of this particular tribe is a remarkable man named Joseph Winterhawk Martin, who had been groomed since early childhood by the elders of the tribe for his position as a leader of his people. He was kind enough to share some of his tribe's signs with me.

The Owl

'When the owl flies over a house at night or calls three times we know it is telling us of the passing of a loved one. If it appears in a window ledge or sits on a post or gate outside your house we say to the owl, "If you bring sad news take it away and if it is good news stay with us and talk to us."'

The Wind

'We listen to the wind's sound and this can tell us of sickness, death, people coming to visit us, Mother Earth's changes and moods, good news, changes with the seasons and our own moods.'

Clouds

'The formation of clouds may tell us things of ourselves or those around us.'

Water

'The rivers, streams and lakes can tell us many things by observing the way they flow. The mood of the water, the colour and the flow; these are all sacred to our people.'

The Rainbow

'If the rainbow blocks our journey by going across the road in front of us, we will not go underneath it as it tells us of danger ahead.

'If the rainbow is cut in half, we are going to have a fight with someone.

'If there are two rainbows, one either side of you or your car, these are the guardian rainbows clearing the way for a safe journey.

'When a rainbow is pure white with no clouds in the sky, it is called Uanuku and we will be visited by the people of Tuhoe [magical beings who live in the mists].

'If it is a small coloured rainbow, it is a blessing from our ancestors and the Creator.'

White Heron

'This is our sacred messenger. It is said that we should see this bird only once in our lifetime; some are lucky and see the white heron many times. This bird is a good omen to our people. Feathers of this bird are worn by Chiefly persons or a gifted person such as a holy person.'

Moths

'Moths tell us if it's good to go fishing and to collect seafood.'

Sharks

'If we are in the sea and a white shark appears close to us, it tells us someone is in the water that should not be there or a female is in her moon time. [If] the sea becomes rough, this tells us it's time to get out and go home.'

Flax

'Feeling the base of the flax bush can give us a daily reading of the weather. This was common for the children to do daily for the grandmothers. Watching insects also enables us to quickly know the changes of Mother Earth.'

Another tribe that I had the good fortune to spend some time with was the Zulu people in Bophuthatswana. The most honourable Credo Mutwa, a revered Zulu Sangoma (healer and medicine man) said, 'We live by omens and we die by omens.' These are some signs that the present-day Zulus pay attention to.

Birds

'Birds that fly near you and then turn and fly to the left are not a good sign. The Zulu will then turn to the other side. Two or more birds means much joy; one bird means much sorrow.'

Pigeons

'Three pigeons means guests are coming. Six pigeons flying means falling in love or being kissed. Seven pigeons flying means a letter or a good message. Many, many pigeons together means a wedding is coming.'

Fish-eagle

'It's bad luck to find a fish-eagle or even their feathers, or any fish-eating bird. It is an omen of death. Even their call is a sign of death.'

Blue Crane

'These birds are a sign of self-sacrifice and heroism.'

Owl

'This is a good sign to Sangomas, but a bad sign for ordinary people. It is a bird of mystery. The Great Earth Mother has both an eagle and an owl on her shoulders to advise her by telling her what to tell the people. The owl is associated with the Great Mother.'

Crow

'The crow is not a bad sign. He is good luck and the cleaner of the world.'

Rhino

'If a rhino crosses your path, life is going against you. If a rhino is going the same way as you, your journey is blessed by Great Spirit.'

Walking

'If you go for a walk and people don't greet you it is a sign that you must purify yourself.'

In addition to telling me some of his tribe's signs, Credo also said his people have always used the signs to foretell events. He told me some of the ancient Zulu prophecies that have come to fruition:

Invention of the Telephone

'People will talk over wire thinner than the queen's necklace.'

First and Second World War Tanks, Bombers and Submarines

'Great wars will come with metal elephants with trunks of death, and metal birds dropping eggs of death . . . and metal canoes that would go under water.'

Surrogate Mothers

'Women will grow a child in their womb that is not theirs.'

DNA Fingerprinting

'You will look at a piece of skin and see mother and father.'

Heart Transplants

'Baboon's heart will beat in a human.'

Ken Colbung, (Nundjan Djiridjakin) spiritual leader and senior male clan leader of the Australian Aborigine Bibulmun Tribe generously shared some information about signs. Ken said that aboriginal lives are governed by signs. Though they have many in the natural world, one universal sign is the willy wag tail bird (djitti djitti) which is the prime bird messenger of the gods. They watch this bird's actions to see what the gods are telling them.

Ken further explained that signs are used by the Aboriginal people as a way to communicate with each other because they often live great distances apart. They are 'like a telepathic telephone. It's imporant when a sign comes to stop whatever one is doing, to hear the message of the sign. Examples of the kind of messages that one might receive are: "I'm sick, please come to me" or "Uncle is speared and needs your help".'

Here are some of the Aboriginal signs which tell you someone is thinking of you or trying to reach you:

'Whistling or ringing in the ears means an elder brother or someone with clan authority is thinking of you or trying to reach you; throbbing in the upper arm indicates your parents; heart throbbing indicates your mother's brother; throbbing in the groin or thigh indicates your husband or wife, and throbbing in the calf means an elder sister or brother is thinking of you. In addition, a cracking sound in the nose can mean a visitor or a big event is coming.'

Though the exact signs vary from tribe to tribe throughout the world, almost all tribes gain messages by listening to the wind, watching the clouds and watching flowing waters. Some tribal signs are based on practicality (e.g., 'If you see a shark, it's a sign to get out of the water') and some are unique to the area (e.g., Rhino crossings). Though signs vary and the same sign can mean different things in different cultures, the importance given to signs in native cultures is the same worldwide.

Signs from your Family and Personal History

Some of your signs can come from your own family and even from distant relatives, sometimes passing down through generations.

Some of your signs will appear directly as a result of your own personal history. If you had a brush with death because you were thrown off a horse as a child, horses might be a sign for you of danger. Therefore, anytime you are in danger, your inner self might tune in to images of horses as a way to warn you. Yet someone else might associate horses with the qualities of strength or grace or freedom.

Signs from Past Life Memories

Every experience that you have ever had from previous lifetimes is lodged in your subconscious mind. Included in these submerged memories are subconscious recollections from signs that were important to you in past lives. For example, in most cultures the rainbow is a great sign; however, in some African cultures the rainbow is not always a good sign, for it can foretell the end of the rainy season and the beginning of the drought. So if you've had a past life in that particular African tribal area, you might have a residual memory of rainbows signifying the end of abundant and fertile times. Therefore in your present life, a rainbow would appear as a sign of coming lean times, whereas for almost everyone else, it is a wondrous sign. To this end, it is valuable to explore your past lives to discover what signs were important to you then.

Signs from our Peripheral Awareness

Sometimes your signs will reflect your peripheral awareness. This means that there are always things occurring around you that you are not consciously aware of, but nevertheless your subconscious mind is recording everything in your environment and this information is often reflected back to you in the form of a sign.

Sandy stopped at an all-night petrol station to buy a chocolate bar because she was staying up late studying for an exam and had a sugar craving. As she was walking through the small convenience store she tripped and knocked over a can. When she knelt to pick it up she saw a picture of a skull and crossbones on a can of insecticide poison. The image of the skull and crossbones seemed to sear into her to the point where it made her feel so uncomfortable that she left the store immediately without buying a chocolate bar. The next day she read in the paper that the convenience store had been robbed at gunpoint just about the time that she was there. Though she wasn't consciously aware of someone sinister in the store at the time, her subconscious mind sensed danger and nudged her into tripping into the can of poison with the sign of danger that, fortunately, she acted upon.

Signs from Angels and Guides and Spirit

The most wondrous signs we receive are from our guides and guardian angels and spirit. These signs defy definition. They come from a realm beyond collective consciousness, your culture, your heritage and your past. They touch your soul like a leaf falling softly on the still pool of your consciousness with ripples growing outward in ever-expanding circles. They are divine signs.

In the Bible there are numerous references to these divine signs. In Genesis 9:11–13 God said, "'I establish my covenant with you, that . . . never again shall there be a flood to destroy the earth." And God said, ". . . I set my bow in the cloud and it shall be a *sign* of the covenant between me and the earth." This Bible verse (Revised Standard Version) refers to the concept that the rainbow is a sign from God promising that the earth will never be destroyed by flood.

Divine signs are real. Angels are real. Guides are real. The spiritual realm is real. Now is the time for the realm of spirit to manifest for humanity. From the archangels to your guardian angel, who is your personal comforter and friend, to your guides and cherubs who bring joy and laughter, right now they are bridging our physical reality with their pure spiritual energy. There are some ways that you can tell when signs come from the heavens rather than another source. Often in conjunction with a heavenly sign there is a warm expansive feeling in the centre of your being, accompanied by an infusion of love. Sometimes when a divine sign appears, the colours of your environment will seem richer and more vibrant, almost as if lit from within. In addition, often there can be a 'knowing' that occurs in conjunction with the sign that your life is unfolding exactly as it should, that your life is guided and that you are perfect just as you are. These celestial signs occur in many forms and they are important signposts on our path in life.

2 How Signs Appear in your Life

Signs are always around you and they manifest themselves in a myriad of forms. In fact, there is never a time in your life when you aren't surrounded by signs. Though most signs appear visually, they can present themselves through smell, sound or touch or they can appear as a hunch, an intuition, or even in a dream. For those individuals who are raised in native cultures, signs usually appear in natural forms such as in the clouds or in the movement of animals, but to people raised in Western cultures they can appear in manmade as well as natural forms. Here are a number of ways that your signs may appear for you.

Through Other People

Everything around us has energy and that energy responds to our expectations. Whenever you consciously (or subconsciously) project a question or a concern into the universe, people who cross your path in life will often have a sign or message for you. Sometimes people will mysteriously appear in your life who have an answer for you. Every person in your life is there for a reason. You couldn't see them otherwise, they would take another path. Often, however, we don't hear the messages because we rarely listen to what is being said. When someone is talking we usually spend almost all the time thinking about how we are going to respond, rather than purely listening. If you go beneath the surface, every conversation has the potential of deep meaning. Beneath the words are deep, powerful and personal signs.

If you stop and really listen to the people who come into your life, you can hear remarkable wisdom and you can be given life-changing information. Even talking casually to strangers, such as when you are waiting for a bus, can garner amazing messages. This works because there are two parallel universes. There is a normal mundane universe and there is an underlying mystical universe. Although these realities can look the same, when you shift your focus from the ordinary reality to the non-ordinary reality (such as when you quiet your mind and really listen to someone) you can gain great wisdom.

Anyone can shift from one reality to another just by conscious listening. This means when someone is talking, listen . . . without thinking of how you are going to reply. Don't spend time recounting your past or projecting your thoughts into the future. Just keep listening. Be in the present . . . right now . . . right now . . . right now. You can get very high doing this because usually when you really listen, after a while you will begin to hear signs, inner truths and personal messages being spoken beneath the words that are said out loud.

Charley was heading towards the Isle of Wight from London and his journey included a long train ride from London down to Portsmouth where he could catch a ferry to the island. He was tired and was hoping to have a seat to himself and was delighted when he found himself seated alone. However, just before the train was scheduled to leave Victoria Station a large, lumbering man, breathing heavily from the exertion of the walk, waddled along the aisle and plopped down next to Charley. Charley lowered his eyes and turned his head towards the window in an effort to avoid the portly gentleman.

As soon as the train pulled away from the station, the man began to talk to Charley about inconsequential matters. Charley began to feel more and more irritated. Then he remembered that 'There are no accidents,' and 'Every person you encounter has a message for you.' So instead of occupying his mind with disgust and distrust, he quieted his mind and began to listen. As soon as Charley began to really listen, the conversation turned from politics to farming. The gentleman began to talk about his years as a child growing up on a farm. He talked about how wonderful it was to work the land. He kept saying, 'When you support the land, the land will support you.' Charley was astonished, for when he was growing up his father, who was a farmer, always used to use exactly the same expression. Though Charley had grown up on their small family farm, when he was eighteen years old he left to go to work in the city. It was always his father's greatest wish that Charley would work on the farm, but Charley had not been inclined to do so because he felt that farming was a hard and financially unrewarding life. Charley was now in his mid-forties. His father had died recently and the farm had been left to him, and he was just in the process of selling it.

As he began to really listen to the seemingly rambling words of the man seated next to him, he was flooded with wonderful images of his own life on the farm as a young man. Yes, he had worked hard, but there was a richness of spirit that had been missing since his move to the city. When the gentleman got off the train after several stops, Charley sat in stunned silence. He felt a certainty about his future life path begin to grow within him. In that moment sitting on the train heading to the Isle of Wight, he made the decision not to sell his father's farm. He decided to quit his city job and try to make a go of the farm himself. He said it was a decision that he has never regretted. Charley took the time consciously to listen to the signs and hence was able to hear and decipher the messages that were being given to him.

The universe responds to our inner yearnings by mysteriously bringing people into our life to answer our questions and help quell our conflicts. Every time you follow your intuition, your personal vibration intensifies. This can be likened to turning up the volume on a stereo. The more your personal vibration is intensified the more you will pull people into your life who carry messages for you. It is a universal law.

The people around you can also be signs of relationships that you need to resolve. If someone enters your life who looks remarkably like someone whom you had difficulty with in the past, this can be a sign that it is time to resolve that past relationship either with therapy or by communicating with them. Sometimes a past relationship can be too painful to resolve in person, particularly if the individual is unruly or hard to communicate with, or if they are not still alive. However, if someone looks or acts exactly like a difficult individual from your past (except that they are kind or friendly etc.) this is a sign that the relationship is in the process of being healed. The unresolved past relationship is helped when new emotional patterns are created with the new look-alike person. As you are able to relate to the new look-alike individual in a positive way, this promotes clearing the negative energy between you and the original person.

Whenever you think of someone, often it is a sign to call or contact them. By adopting this habit, you may be surprised how often the person you contact will have a message for you or will have been thinking about you. Even if you don't always know why you needed to contact that person, the more you follow your intuition the more balanced and in tune you will be.

Arnold was walking through Central Park in New York and he passed someone who looked exactly like Leonard, an individual he had gone to school with thirty years earlier. He took his casual encounter as a sign to contact Leonard, with whom he had lost touch and hadn't talked to in almost as many years. When he tracked him down Leonard said, 'Hey! It's great to hear from you. I've been trying to find you. We are having a school reunion in a couple months and everyone wanted you to be there. Thanks for calling.' By listening to the signs Arnold was able to reconnect with old and valued friends.

Conversations

One of the most potent ways that signs appear is in the conversations of other people and sometimes even in your own. If you take the time to really listen to what is being said around you, you will begin to hear the most remarkable personal messages.

Overheard Conversations

Often signs will appears in conversations of others that you happen to overhear. Carol was waiting in a queue in the grocery store when the women ahead of her began to talk about bulging tyres and the danger of tyre blowouts on the motorway. Carol never looked at her tyres and never even gave them any thought. However, since the conversation impressed itself on her mind, when she went out into the car park to put away her groceries, she looked at her tyres. She was astonished to find a large ballooning spot on one of the front tyres. She drove directly to a garage and the service man told her it was lucky that she had come. The tyre was so thin that she could easily have had a blowout, and even a serious accident, if she had been on the motorway.

Casual Conversations

Sometimes signs can appear to us in our own casual conversations. Josh was talking with an old friend from college whom he hadn't seen in a long time and the subject of mountain climbing came up. Without any forethought, Josh said, 'I've decided to take up mountain climbing.' He was surprised that he had said those words because, until that very minute, he had never considered mountain climbing. He decided to heed his own subconscious advice and enrolled in a mountain climbing course and subsequently became an amateur mountain climber.

Signs can also present themselves in the casual conversations of others. Sharma was at a dinner party sitting very quietly, not taking part in the conversation. She was partially withdrawn because she was contemplating a very big decision in her life. She was not in a committed relationship, and she was over forty . . . and pregnant. No one at the dinner party knew that Sharma was pregnant, in fact, only her doctor knew about it and he was urging her to consider a termination because of health risks to both Sharma and the baby. Remarkably, during the course of the conversation the subject of pregnancy for single women over forty came up. Though Sharma didn't participate, there were so many positive comments shared that Sharma took the conversation as a sign to keep her child. Her pregnancy went well and she is now the happy mother of a healthy boy.

At every moment, within the environment surrounding each of us, there is so much more occurring than is available to our conscious mind. On a deeper level, we are subconsciously aware of the thoughts, feelings and energy of those around us. Our conversations will often reflect the silent dialogues occurring within the thoughts of those around us. For example, during a lecture in South Africa where I was teaching a diploma course, I wanted to make sure that we had all the names on the certificates correct so I said, 'Please let us know your exact name. I know you have already registered under one name but, for example, if your name is Louise and you are thinking of changing your name to Jean Louise let us know, so your diploma is accurate.' My example was a seemingly random one. Yet during a break in the lecture, a woman came up to me and introduced herself as Louise and said just at the time that I had given the example of the name change, she was contemplating changing her name from Louise to Jean Louise. My random comment was, in fact, registering and repeating someone else's thought. Even our seemingly random comments may be a response to invisible inner dialogues of others. In addition, the conversations of those around you may be responding to *your* inner thoughts and needs.

Conversational Slips

Another area of conversation that will present signs to you is in the conversational slip or what is commonly called the Freudian slip after the famous psychoanalyst who decreed that there were no accidents in our seemingly accidental slips of the tongue. These slips can occur either in your own conversations or those of others. Particularly pay attention when you (or someone else) means to say one thing and yet says something else.

George was a stockbroker who was going through a difficult period financially. One afternoon he was at his son's softball game where he was yelling to encourage his son. However, almost every time when he meant to yell, 'Watch the ball!' he said, 'Watch the *bull!*' instead. George wasn't aware of this slip, but his wife mentioned to him the fact that he was replacing the word 'bull' for 'ball'. Suddenly George realized that this supposed slip of the tongue was actually an inner message that he needed to keep a sharp look at the stock market and watch for a 'bullish' market. He told me that this sign helped him make some financial decisions in the following days that began to turn around his financial difficulties.

Expressions

The expressions that you use in your everyday conversations can also contain signs for you. Carole constantly used the expression, 'I can't stand it.' It's interesting to note that Carole had back problems and her consistent use of the word *'stand'* was a sign that she was having trouble *standing*. Coincidentally, she also was an individual who was unwilling to make a *stand* in life. As soon as she realized what her continual expression was telling her, she began to make progress both with her back problems and with her willingness to *stand* up for herself in life.

It's also particularly important to pay attention to the expressions that you use infrequently. Often those that pop up on the spur of the moment are valuable signs. Teresa was in the middle of an animated conversation when she used the expression, 'It goes without saying.' This was an expression that she rarely used. However, the moment she said it, she realized that the phrase was a sign that she wasn't really saying what she wanted to say. So she took a minute to collect her thoughts and then said what she really wanted to say.

After a trip to Asia, Marvin began frequently using the expression, 'It was a real can of worms,' about situations in his life. He normally wouldn't have been aware of any connection between this expression and his life except for the fact that he later found out, during a doctor's visit, that he had picked up some parasites on his journeys. He realized that his subconscious was trying to give him a message because the 'can of worms' could be likened to the parasites that infested his bowels.

Your expressions can often contain important personal signs.

Someone who continually says, 'It pisses me off,' may have bladder or kidney problems. Habitually saying, 'I can't stomach this,' may be a sign of indigestion or difficulty in terms of digesting food. If we say, 'I could have died,' or 'I am sick to death of it,' we may subconsciously be expressing a death wish. The expression, 'It makes me irritable when . . .' can go in conjunction with skin irritation.

Random Thoughts

A very powerful way in which signs filter into your consciousness is through your seemingly random thoughts. Thoughts that have no rhyme or reason, that just seem to linger for a few seconds and drift away, often contain remarkable keys to inner quandaries. Every once in a while, catch a thought and examine it to see if there is a secret message for you.

Chuck shared his story with me. He lived near the Atlantic Ocean on the east coast of the United States. It was his habit to take a walk along the sea shore every evening before dinner. One evening during a particularly beautiful sunset he was aware of a random thought about a Red Cross course that he had taken years before. For no particular reason, he found himself reviewing the CPR resuscitation technique that he had learned.

We all have thousands of random thoughts every day which are normally dismissed after only a micro-second's review. However, Charles had an experience on the way home that gave credence to the idea that his so-called random thought about CPR was actually a sign. On his walk back from the beach, just a few blocks from his home, an elderly woman walking in front of him collapsed and became unconscious, seemingly from a heart attack. Without even a moment's hesitation, Charles rushed over and began to administer CPR. Charles felt that his random thoughts were a sign preparing him to be ready for action. The ambulance that arrived a few minutes later said that Charles' quick thinking had perhaps saved the woman's life.

Emotions

A potent sign-bringer (particularly for those individuals who are in touch with their feelings) is emotions. Your emotions can contain potent signs that can be a remarkable source of information. Anita was going on the ocean cruise of a lifetime. She had saved for two and a half years to pay for it and yet as the time neared and she was preparing for the trip, she felt emotionally upset. She went through every possible reason for her upset feelings. She ferreted out all the unsolved issues regarding her journey but she could find no reason for her emotions. Finally her emotions became so strong that she decided that they were a sign that the timing wasn't right for her trip so she transferred to another cruise. As soon as she made the move, the negative feelings that she had been having completely disappeared.

Anita had been at sea on her rescheduled cruise for only a day when she met a man on the deck of the swimming pool. Their casual friendship developed into a full-blown romance by the end of the cruise and within a few months they became engaged. Anita was very pleased that she had listened to the signs and she is now happily married.

Sometimes the emotions that you feel are actually a sign that someone around you is feeling those exact emotions. If you are in the same physical location as someone who is feeling strong emotions *even if you aren't aware of that person* you might feel their emotions *and even think those emotions are your feelings.* Emotions projected by another individual might feel like your own. For example, Lea was sitting at the dentist's surgery reading a magazine when suddenly and inexplicably she felt sad. She thought to herself, I'm feeling so sad. I must be sad about something in my life. She searched through her memory bank until she found an unhappy incident in her past. She remembered a time when she was a child and her father had left for a trip without saying goodbye. The more she thought about the incident, the sadder she became. When she went in to see the dentist her sadness quickly receded. As she was leaving the surgery, she overheard one of the dental staff talking about the other patient who had shared the waiting room with her. The patient's husband was leaving for a long tour of military duty and she had been feeling very sad. Lea hadn't consciously been aware of the other patient, but she had felt the woman's emotions and accepted them as her own.

An inexplicable arrival and departure of emotions can be a sign that someone around you is feeling very strong emotions. Of course, you won't feel their emotions unless there is something within you that resonates with their feelings. The emotions of others will travel straight through you unless there is something inside you (such as a similar experience), to which they can attach.

Sheena was leading a guided meditation in a darkened room when she began to feel very angry. She began to think of the reckless way the garage attendant had driven her car the previous day. She became angrier and angrier, in fact she became so angry that she was having trouble leading the meditation. Then suddenly her anger disappeared. Sheena wondered why she had become so angry at the attendant, when at the time she was only slightly irritated, and it hadn't seemed like a big deal. Later, during a break in the seminar, someone informed her that when she was leading the meditation, someone had entered the room behind her (she hadn't been aware of this individual coming into the room) who was very angry about a traffic jam he had been caught in. He stayed for a short while and then left. Sheena had intuitively felt the anger, claimed it as her own and found something in her life to lodge it on. She wouldn't have felt the emotions except that there was something in her energy field to which they could stick. When you feel emotions, take time to check into your inner wisdom to see if this is a sign that you have tuned into someone else's emotions.

Of course, emotions can come from many places. Sometimes your emotions can be an indication of resistance to personal expansion and inner growth. For example, someone who has difficulty making commitments in life might feel fear in regard to making a commitment to a relationship. For that individual, emotions aren't necessarily a sign to step away from the commitment but rather an indication of a blockage that needs to be overcome. Emotions can also be indications of the replaying of old psychological tape loops. An example is a person who feels fear whenever they see even the smallest spider because of a bad experience as a child. However, there *are* times when your emotions are giving you signs or messages from your inner wisdom or when your emotions are signs of the emotions of others. Watch your emotions for signs of the greater universe around you.

Judgments

Periodically the judgments that we attribute to other people (or judgments we have about others) are specific signs for ourselves. At the completion of my lectures, people often come to talk to me. I usually receive a variety of comments about myself and the seminar. It is a constant revelation how much these comments reflect the individuals who give them. For example, a woman approached me after a lecture and said , 'Oh, you poor dear, you look so very tired. You must go home and get some rest.' This woman had sloped shoulders and her every word seemed an effort. She looked completely exhausted. The next man to speak to me said, 'Wow! How do you do it? I have never seen anyone display more vitality and energy than you do! It's quite amazing!' This man exuded tremendous vigour and vibrancy. After almost every lecture I observe the same phenomenon. In each case, the judgments that these individuals made about me and the seminar were actually signs or messages from their subconscious that reflected their own personal reality.

If you make the judgment that the people you encounter in life are usually angry (even if you are feeling calm and peaceful) this is a sign that you have some unresolved inner anger. If you see kind and compassionate people all around you (even if you don't feel very compassionate) this is usually a sign that you are subconsciously emanating kindness. I know a man who always complains that everyone lies to him. Yet everyone who knows this individual would agree that he never can be counted on to tell the truth. His judgment about others is actually a sign about his own judgments about himself.

Another way to use judgments to decipher signs is to watch the judgments that *you* think others are making about you. Velma was in a car park and threw her sweet wrapper out of the car window. Out of the corner of her eye, she thought she saw a man watching her. She was sure he was judging her for littering. Consequently, she got out of the car and took her rubbish to a litter bin. As she did this, she commented to the man that she was cleaning up after herself. From his nebulous reply she realized he hadn't even seen her litter. Velma had projected her own morality onto the man.

What you think others are thinking about you can often be very clearly a sign about what *you* are actually thinking about yourself. If you think that someone doesn't like something about you, it could, in fact, be that they actually don't like that particular attribute, but it could also be a sign that the perceived judgment is also a judgment that you have made about yourself.

Eric was giving a lecture and was just starting to embark on a controversial subject. Just at this point in his talk a woman in the front row began to turn her head side to side as if to say, 'No, Eric. Don't talk about this topic right now.' He thought that she was making a negative judgment about the direction that his talk was taking. Upon quick reflection Eric realized that she was right. It wasn't a good time to bring up that particular subject. Later he went to thank the woman for getting him to change the course of his talk. She seemed puzzled by his comments. Eric said, 'But you kept shaking your head side to side.' She said, 'Oh that! I have earrings with little bells in them and I was shaking my head side to side to hear the bells.' The judgment that Eric perceived that another was making about him was actually a sign that he needed to alter the course of his lecture.

Peripheral Vision

Have you ever had the experience that you thought you saw something out of the corner of your eye, only to look and notice that it wasn't what you thought it was, or that what you saw wasn't actually there at all? This is often one way your higher self has of getting your attention and delivering you a sign.

Martina was at a shopping mall when she thought she saw a cat out of the corner of her eye. When she turned to look there wasn't anything there. A few minutes later, she again thought she saw a cat out of her peripheral vision, but it was only the reflection of a store display. As she kept thinking she was seeing cats she wondered if there was a sign that had something to do with cats. Suddenly, she thought about her own cat that had just had kittens, and realized that she had locked the mother cat out of the house, separating her from her new kittens. Though she had planned on being gone all day, she wasn't far from home so she quickly returned to let a somewhat desperate mother cat respond to the meowing of her hungry kittens.

Sometimes peripheral signs emerge audibly as well as visually. You might think that you heard something that was never actually said, but this too can be a sign to pay attention to. Grant was talking to Bob about his car and Bob said, 'Grant, there is a small tyre in your garage.' However what Grant thought he had heard was, 'Grant, there is a small *fire* in your garage.' They both laughed when they straightened out the misunderstanding. Normally they would have completely forgotten about it. However when Grant returned home there had been a small fire in his garage during his absence. He realized his misunderstanding about what Bob had said, in fact, was a sign that his garage was actually on fire. We often mis-hear what others are saying and don't give any thought to it, and though not every slip of the tongue is necessarily a sign, sometimes there are potent messages hidden in what we *think* we hear and what we *think* we see.

Songs you sing to yourself

Have you ever found yourself singing a song to yourself when, perhaps, you aren't even conscious that you were singing? If this occurs, take time to listen very carefully to the words that you are singing, for often within the words are signs that have filtered up from your subconscious mind.

Robert had been singing a song to himself for a few days without ever realizing it. He found himself singing the words, 'Walk right in, sit right down, baby let your hair hang down.' When he paid attention to the words of the song, he felt that it was a sign regarding his forthcoming appointment. Robert was approaching an important job interview and he had planned on dressing formally and presenting himself as professionally as possible. However, he felt the words of the song were a sign to be more casual, confident and open in his approach. So instead of wearing a suit and tie, he wore a casual jacket and walked in to the interview with a confidence that said, 'You would do well to hire me.' He 'walked right in', 'sat right down' and figuratively 'let his hair down'. He was hired on the spot. At a subsequent time, he was told he had been hired because his employer liked his informal, let's-get-right-down-to-work attitude. In other words the lyrics of the song had given him a sign that enabled him to be seen to the best advantage during the interview.

Dreams

Somewhere in the window of your memory as you sleep hover elusive moments just out of conscious reach. They are so real that you can sense them waiting there. In response, you reach out to touch them only to find they quickly slip beyond your grasp and vanish. These moments are beyond the world of form and illusion. They dwell in the midst of the crack between two worlds and if you can only catch them, they are one of the most powerful sources of personal signs. Though there are currently many differing opinions about dreams, throughout history they have been used as a source of signs and messages from beyond.

Present day scientists believe that dreams are only neurons spontaneously firing in the brain, downloading the brain's unneeded information. Psychologists feel that dream symbols are the secret keyhole through which spontaneous productions of the human psyche pour into consciousness as a way of keeping emotional balance and releasing the suppressed difficulties of waking life. However, ancient dreamers believed that dreams contained valuable signs and messages. They stepped through the mysterious veil in the night to listen to dream messages and then carried back precious signs that sometimes changed the destiny of individuals and nations alike. They believed that their nightly visions came from external forces such as God, angels, nature spirits, gods and goddesses, various entities and the spirits of their ancestors.

Whether the signs that appear in your dreams come from an outside source or from your own higher self, it is important to listen to them carefully. Michelle dreamed that she was in the middle of a thick forest wearing armour. She was protected by the thick metal, and she couldn't move to get out of the dark forest into the sunlight of a nearby meadow. She couldn't see anyone in the meadow but she heard a voice say, 'Take off the armour. Come into the meadow and play with me.' When she woke up she felt as if she could still feel the heavy cold metal on her body and during the day she kept thinking about the armour.

The armour in Michelle's dream was an important sign. Armour is protection. It will appear as a sign when there is something or someone from which you are trying to protect yourself. Michelle was very involved with the Parent /Teacher Association at her children's school. When she first joined she enjoyed contributing to the school; however, as she kept accepting more and more responsibilities she felt overwhelmed. She wanted to say 'no' but always said 'yes' to every task she was asked to do. Consequently, she felt enmeshed in a situation where she didn't have personal boundaries and she felt she needed to protect herself emotionally. She armoured herself against her family and friends and wasn't enjoying life, or playing and having fun. When Michelle recognized the signs in her dream were telling her that she should let go of her emotional armouring and enjoy her life more, she began to delegate responsibility at the Association . . . and she therefore had more fun.

Dreams can also give you valuable signs about your body and your future. Michael dreamed of a wide open field in the middle of which was a huge beating heart. As he watched, the heart got bigger as if it were a balloon under tremendous pressure. It slowly began to lift laboriously into the sky as the pressure increased.

Suddenly the heart burst into hundreds of pieces. Michael awoke with a start from his dream. He felt certain that his dream was a sign regarding his health. Michael was young and in excellent health and didn't ever feel the need for an annual physical examination. However, he was sure that his dream was a sign to have a check-up for his heart so he made a doctor's appointment. During the examination the physician said, 'It's a good thing that you've come in to see me. Even though you feel healthy, your blood pressure is dangerously high and could have caused you extreme difficulty.' The doctor put Michael on medication until his blood pressure reached normal levels. It's important to note that an exploding heart in a dream might not always be a sign of high blood pressure. It could, for example, be a sign of an emotional overload, hence the expression, 'My heart is about to explode.'

Printed Words

Watch the printed words around you for signs. Especially watch the words that keep reappearing in your life. Printed words that are personal signs can appear in posters, magazines, newspapers, on the sides of trucks or vehicles, on licence plates, on tee-shirts or on television. Of course, in modern life we seem to be surrounded by a multitude of printed words. However, the words that are your signs will either keep repeatedly appearing to you, will seem to jump out at you or will linger in your mind.

For example, Kerrie lived in a city apartment and worked in a nearby, downtown office building in a large city in the United States. Every morning as she walked four blocks to work, she thought about asking for a pay increase. Her resolve always disappeared by the time she reached her office. She had been contemplating asking for a rise for a long time, but her co-workers told her that she would never get it because she hadn't been at the firm long enough. On her morning walk she passed retail stores that were closed and had 'Closed' signs in the windows. However, one morning as she walked to work, for some unknown reason, almost all the shops had forgotten to turn over their signs the night before and Kerrie passed shop after shop with signs in the window saying 'Open' even though the shops were closed.

As Kerrie contemplated how unusual it was that so many shops had forgotten to turn over their signs, she realized that the 'Open' signs were messages that the path ahead for her was open. She felt that the time was right to ask for the rise because the universe was saying 'open' to her. She walked straight into her boss's office and asked for a rise . . . and was given one on the spot. Her boss said that her timing was exactly right because they were just in the process of an office re-evaluation and change. She was told that if she had asked for a rise earlier she would have been turned down.

Radio, Television and Movies

One of the most common ways that signs appear is through radio, television and movies. The words of a song on the radio, the theme of a movie or a few pertinent words from a newscaster sometimes can contain signs that can change your life forever.

Andrew was driving home from work when a song came on the radio. The words of the song he heard were 'Jean, Jean, you're young and . . .' When he heard the words he thought of his mother, whose name was Jean, and he began to cry. He hadn't seen his mother in many years due to a rift in the relationship and he almost never consciously thought of her. However the repetition of the name Jean seared images from his youth with his mother into his brain. Instead of dwelling on the injustices he had suffered as a young man, he thought of when he was a small happy child and his mother was a loving mother. He thought of gentle and tender times. Andrew felt a deep longing and he knew that the words of the song on the radio were a sign that he needed to make contact with his mother again.

It took a few weeks to find her for she had moved twice, but Andrew felt strongly enough about the sign that he persevered. He flew to visit her in her home in Indiana. She was old and withered and she was no longer the dominating tyrant that he remembered from his youth. Her body was frail and weak. Her voice quivered like aspen leaves in the wind rather than the brash machine-gun staccato voice that he remembered.

'Andrew,' she said, 'I'm so glad that you have come. There are so many thing that I want to explain to you before I die.' They talked long into the night. He said that a lifetime of resentment seemed to melt by the coming of dawn's light as he began to understand why his mother had treated him so harshly. Andrew returned home feeling a lightness of spirit and a joy in his heart. Within a year his mother died, but Andrew felt complete and much lighter because of the time that he had spent with her. The signs had led him to his mother and she had opened his heart and led him in to find peace within himself.

Movements within the Natural Environment

In every culture human beings have gained signs from observing the movements of the natural environment around them. From the way that animals migrate, to the location of a lightning strike, to the formations in the clouds, nature in her ever-changing forms constantly provides signs. Even if you live in the city you are still surrounded by nature. The actions of the squirrels, the pigeons, the crows, the clouds, and the winds are all ways in which movements in nature will provide you with signs, even though you live in an urban area.

Gerald's wife passed away after a long illness and Gerald was in a state of very deep grieving. Though it had been two years since her death, he was still very sad and depressed. He told Callie, his neighbour, 'I really miss her but what gets me down the most is thinking that death is the final end of Ruby. I just want to know that she is okay and that she didn't cease to exist just because her body died.' Callie said, 'Maybe Ruby will give you a sign to let you know that she is all right.' He thought about Callie's words and before bed he said, 'Ruby, give me a sign that you are okay.' In the morning, Gerald awoke with a start. Someone seemed to be knocking at the living room window. He grabbed his robe and hurried through. When he got to the window he saw one of the most unusual things he had ever seen.

There was a brightly coloured blue jay tapping at the windowpane. He got close to the window and the blue jay stopped pecking at the window and just looked at him very intently. After a few seconds he flew off. Gerald's heart opened and the floodgate of grief that he had reserved since Ruby's funeral flowed through him. Blue jays were Ruby's favourite bird. She once had told Gerald about a blue jay that came to her family's vacation house one summer and pecked on the window for a few minutes every morning. Gerald said, 'As soon as I saw that blue jay pecking at the window I knew it was a sign from Ruby. I knew she was all right. After that I felt the heavy sadness that I had been carrying around with me just lift.'

It's not unusual to gain signs regarding those who have passed over. These signs usually offer comfort and solace to loved ones.

Physical Environment

One of the most obvious ways that signs appear is through objects and occurrences in your physical environment, whether natural or manmade.

Jonathan was thinking about leaving his mid-management job in a large corporation to start his own business. Though he was excited about the prospect of having his own small company, he was also nervous. He knew if his venture was a failure he would not have an easy time getting another corporate position because jobs were scarce. He took a walk while he was contemplating whether to follow his dream or stay at his uninspiring, yet safe, job. As he meandered down a wooded pathway he observed a large acorn in the middle of the path. He stooped down and picked it up. There were no oak trees in that area so he was very surprised to see it. Though finding an acorn on one's path is a seemingly insignificant event, to Jonathan it gave him just the message he needed at the time to help him with his decision. As he held the smooth, brown nut in his hand he thought about how small acorns become great and powerful oak trees. He knew the acorn was a sign for him that, even though he was starting small, his business would become strong like the oak tree. He gave in his notice that very day and embarked on his own business which became a strong and profitable one.

Sam's girlfriend lived in the country and Sam used to drive every Friday night, after work, from the city to visit her. It was a route that he often drove and though he was a cautious driver, he usually went over the speed limit. One Friday morning, on his way to work, he saw two police cars on separate occasions. Then while he was at work, a police car stopped outside his office window. Sam felt that seeing so many police cars was a sign to slow down and observe the speed limit on his way to the country. (Though Sam associated police with speeding, police cars can symbolize different things to different people. It's important to find what a particular sign symbolizes to you.) During Sam's drive to his girlfriend's, he paid particular attention to the posted speed limits. He wasn't surprised when he rounded a bend (that he normally drove through quickly) to see a police car had pulled someone over for speeding. Had he not listened to the signs he was sure that *he* would have got the ticket.

Home Systems

The systems within your home and its materials can be messengers of important signs. Water often represents emotions and feelings, so the state of plumbing in your home can be a sign of your emotional state. If your plumbing is clogged it can be a sign that your emotions are blocked. If a toilet overflows it can be a sign that your emotions are overflowing. Frozen pipes can symbolize that your emotions are frozen. A leaky tap can represent a constant drain on your emotions. Of course a leaking tap could just mean that you need new washers, but often there is a correlation between plumbing and one's emotional state.

Electricity in your home can represent your life force or be a sign of your personal energy field. If the circuits keep overloading, take a look and see if you need to downgrade your life a bit. Maybe you are taking on too much. If light bulbs keep blowing out maybe you are giving out too much energy and not taking in enough energy. An electrical outage can symbolize a complete energy burnout. An outage might be a sign that says you need to slow down and take life at a slower pace.

The floors in your home can represent or be a sign of your foundations in life. If your basement floor begins to crack or your floor begins to buckle, see if there is some area of your life where you feel on shaky ground. The walls in your home can symbolize your structure and support in life. If termites are eating away at your walls, notice if there is anything in your life that is eating away at your support systems. Every part of your home and your immediate environment can offer signs to you regarding your body and your life.

Illness and Disease

Every illness is a sign that reflects the inner workings of your subconscious mind. It is very, very important to listen to the signs that your body is giving you at the onset of an illness. If you don't listen to these gentle whispers, your body may intensify your symptoms until you can hear the message your body is trying to give you. Listen to the whispers so you don't have to hear the screams.

Disease can be your body's way of giving you signs about some area of your life that is imbalanced. There is always an accompanying message with any disease or illness. The message might be as simple as, 'Slow down, take some time off' or there might be a deeper message. Emily had a sore throat which eventually led to laryngitis. She realized that losing her voice was a sign that there was something in her life that she was afraid to say. (The particular disease you have, as well as the particular part of your body affected, are both indicative of the message being given.)

At Emily's job, she had been passed over for a promotion that was given to someone with less experience and credentials. She wanted to say, 'This isn't fair. I deserve the promotion,' but she was afraid to speak her truth so she said nothing. However, internally Emily was upset and her emotional quandary manifested itself as a physical illness. When she took time to listen to the message that her body was sending her, she plucked up courage and spoke to her boss about her true feelings. She didn't get the promotion but she felt that it was a big step for her in life to say what she was feeling. Also, after talking to her boss she better understood her situation at work.

It's difficult enough being sick without blaming yourself for being ill, so it's important to be loving and understanding to yourself and not reproach yourself for your illness. Every illness and disease allows you to gain a greater understanding of yourself and can offer you great lessons in life. However, it is valuable in the healing process to listen to the messages and signs your body is giving you. These signs can help you understand the source of the illness and can help you to heal it.

When you are ill, it's valuable to discover the emotion that you have regarding an illness for it is usually a sign of the emotion that initiated your disease in the first place. For example, Joan came to me with her concerns about uterine cysts. I asked her what emotion she had in regard to the cysts. Without hesitation, she said that they made her really angry. When I suggested to her that the emotions she had about the cysts could be a sign of the emotions that precipitated them in the first place, she was amazed. She said that prior to the onset of the cysts she had been in an emotionally and sexually abusive relationship that made her angry. She felt angry particularly regarding their sex life. She hypothesized that her anger concerning her sexual partner had contributed to the formation of the cysts.

Accidents

As much havoc as accidents create in our life, there is almost always an underlying sign present at the exact time of the accident. One of the quickest ways to ascertain what the message is, is to examine your thoughts just immediately prior to the accident. You will usually find that there is a connection between your thoughts at the moment of the accident and the incident itself.

Ravi was driving his late model Ford one rainy night. Suddenly he rounded a corner and a deer was standing frozen by the lights in the middle of the road. Ravi hit the brakes and his car careened out of control off the side of the road. He was a bit shaken up but not injured. When he examined his thoughts just prior to the point of impact, he realized that he had been mulling over a business proposition made to him by his brother. He felt that there was a connection between his thoughts just prior to the accident. He felt that his losing control of the car was a sign not to engage in the business, so he told his brother that he regretfully declined the offer. It's interesting to note that in the subsequent year Ravi's brother talked about his business venture, saying that he felt 'out of control'. Eventually Ravi's brother actually did lose control of the business. Ravi stated that he was glad that he had followed the signs.

Not only are your thoughts immediately prior to an accident a sign but the part of your body that is injured has a corresponding sign for you as well. Whenever you have an accident, take a moment to evaluate the part of your body that is injured. Though the body signs can vary person to person, some seem to span the planet. For example, if you hurt your foot ask yourself, 'Do you feel that you don't have a leg to stand on in life?' or 'Are you afraid to make a stand in life?' or 'Are you willing to stand up for yourself?' Each part of the body symbolizes a different part of your life. To gain more understanding about signs in relation to different parts of the body look up the specific body part in the Signposts Dictionary.

When discovering the sign contained in an accident, examine the kind of accident. For example, if the accident occurs because you are going too fast, it might be your higher self saying, 'Slow down.' If an accident happens because you were afraid to make a move, this could be a sign that you need to be more decisive in life.

Carter was washing the outside windows of his house and was standing on the very top of the ladder to reach a high window. He lost his balance and fell. Though nothing was broken, he was very bruised. He said that he felt that the message of his fall was that he should stop taking so many risks in life. He was at a point in his business where he had to make a decision either to take a safe, low-risk low-yield road or to take a financial risk. He felt that taking the risk of standing on the top rung of the ladder (and falling off) was a sign that he should take the safe route at work rather than follow the path that entailed a risk. He reported in hindsight he felt that he made the right decision.

Mistakes

Often the seemingly random mistakes that occur in life are actually signs in disguise. For example, when I was planning my garden I decided that I wanted it to convey peace and tranquillity so I planted only flowers in soft peaceful shades of blue, purple, pale pink and white. This seemed like a great idea to create a template for peace in the area surrounding our home. However, every year, despite my intensive planning, bright red, orange and yellow plants *that I never planted* kept appearing in my garden. I realized that this cacophony of floral colours was a sign that signified vitality and energy. Though I consciously wanted peace in my life (symbolized by the serene placid colours), my subconscious desired excitement and movement. Examining my life, I could see that I was settling into old comfortable patterns rather than fully experiencing life. The bright coloured flowers that kept popping up in my garden were a sign to say it's time to add some zest to life. Thus I decided to let the garden colours unfold naturally and I began to change my life and expand my inner horizons.

Incidentally, it is not an accident when a flower mistakenly appears in your garden. Each unplanned flower mistake has an individual message for you. For example, a sunflower spontaneously appearing in your garden can be a sign that it is time to open yourself to the light and to life. It can mean open your heart and your soul to the universe around you in the same way that the sunflower opens itself to the sun. Thyme appearing in your garden can mean to take more time for yourself (see section on homophones). Lavender popping up in your yard can be a sign to spend time nurturing a state of relaxing inner peace within yourself (lavender is used in aromatherapy for its calming, soothing qualities).

Thomas and his family were on a vacation during the school holidays. They were from the north-western part of the United States and they decided to drive to the south-east to explore a different part of the country. Usually they followed the maps and manoeuvred easily through each of the big cities that they passed en route. However, when they drove into Atlanta, Georgia, Thomas kept 'mistakenly' taking wrong turns as he was trying to get to his destination. It was a blistering hot day and Thomas and his family were anxious to cool off in their hotel as the car air conditioner was broken. Everyone was getting frustrated. They took so many wrong turns that Thomas finally pulled in to the side of the road to take a moment to be still and take stock of the situation. He realized that all the wrong turns were actually signs to take a different route to the hotel. As soon as Thomas decided on a new route, even though it was longer, they got to the hotel easily. When they checked in the clerk asked them if they had been caught in the big freeway traffic jam. Thomas said, 'No, What happened?' The clerk replied, 'A semi-truck overturned on the road and traffic has been backed up for three hours. You were lucky that you didn't come that way, or you would have been stuck in traffic for a long time.' Thomas' whole family sighed with relief. If they had taken the route they planned, they would have been caught in traffic for a long time in a very hot car.

Coincidences

Every day we are constantly bombarded by little coincidences and all coincidences are signs. They happen so often that, for the most part, they just seem like normal reality. The people you bump into on the street, or sit next to in a restaurant or plane, and the small events that surround you regularly in life are invariably filled with coincidence, though it is usually only the striking ones that catch our attention.

When I was twenty years old I moved from the midwest of the United States to Hawaii. As I didn't know anyone in Hawaii, a friend gave me a piece of paper with the name of a friend of hers who lived in Hawaii written on it. She said I could contact her friend if I needed help. I folded the piece of paper and stuck it in my purse without looking at it. The piece of paper stayed lodged in the side compartment of my purse while I subsequently moved to Hawaii and found a job as a waitress through the Help Wanted section in the local newspaper. At my job I became attracted to Tony, a fellow co-worker, whom I began to date. One day, after I had been living in Hawaii for a number of months, I cleaned my purse and came across the folded piece of paper that my friend had given me. I was astonished when I opened it up. On the piece of paper was *the name and address of Tony*. Though a sceptic might say it was just a coincidence, I felt that it was a sign that I was predestined to meet Tony. Though we didn't stay together for a long period of time, I gained valuable insights about myself during my relationship with him.

Synchronicity

Carl Jung, the renowned Swiss psychoanalyst, coined the term synchronicity to describe the coincidence of a concurring psychic and physical event, that defies the probability of chance and is meaningful. Most sceptics would deem these types of concurring events as coincidence; however Jung felt that there was a realm beyond time where mind, matter and spirit merged as one. He felt that meaningful coincidences (synchronicity) occurred through some mechanism outside the realm of cause and effect.

His most famous example of synchronicity occurred when one of his patients, who was having difficulty making headway in her therapy, came to a session describing her dream in which a golden scarab appeared. The golden scarab is the ancient Egyptian symbol of regeneration. Just as they were discussing the dream, a beetle flew in the window. The beetle was a rose chafer which is the nearest thing to a golden scarab that exists in Switzerland. At this point the patient went through a transformation and entered an entire new level of therapy. For Jung this was clearly a case of a significant connection or synchronicity. When you think of someone and they call, or you need something and it appears in your life, these are examples of synchronicity and there is always a corresponding sign that goes hand in hand with the synchronicity. Sometimes the sign is saying that you are expanding your horizons beyond the material physical plane. And sometimes the sign is giving you a profound look at your inner spiritual path. Pay particular attention to the signs that come to you through synchronicity.

Homonyms and Homophones

Homonyms are words having the same pronunciation and perhaps spelling as another word but different meanings and origins; an example is the *bark* (of a tree) and the *bark* (of a dog). Homophones are one of two or more words, such as *night* and *knight,* or *great* and *grate* that are pronounced the same but differ in meaning and spelling. Sometimes signs appear in life as either homonyms or homophones.

Jasper was disabled and without a job. He was in a particularly low period in his life where his self-esteem was plummeting. He was shopping in a grocery store when his wheelchair hit a display of cans and they all loudly cascaded down around him. He looked at what seemed like hundreds of cans of sliced peaches rolling in all directions around him and in an instant a thought occurred to him. 'Cans! *Can!* I *can* do it. I *can* make it. I *can* turn my life around.' When the dismayed store staff scurried to the scene they found Jasper, in the middle of an ocean of cans, smiling ear to ear. The cans were a homonymic sign that Jasper could rise up out of the despair that he had settled into in his life.

Pets

Your animals and pets often are purveyors of signs. They can warn you of coming danger and they can also give signs of your possible future symptoms or behaviour.

Frederick had a small terrier named Sammy. Every day they went for a long walk in the woods, which was the highlight of Sammy's day. He would sit at the door at the same time every afternoon waiting for his walk. As soon as they were out of the door, his little body would tug desperately on the leash as they neared the woods in anticipation of his free run.

However, one afternoon as Frederick prepared for their walk, Sammy wasn't waiting at the door. On this particular day Sammy didn't tug at the leash. In fact, when he was finally given free rein, he turned to go back home. Sammy had never done that before so Frederick was concerned. He took Sammy's reluctance as a sign that he needed to return home. It was fortunate that they went back, for shortly after they arrived Frederick had a heart attack. His wife Sara immediately called the ambulance and Frederick made an excellent recovery. The doctor said that if Frederick had had the heart attack in the woods, without the immediate attendance of medical staff, he might not have been so lucky.

Your pets can also give you signs about energy flows in your environment. I was attending a dinner party when a particularly good-looking young man arrived. The house cat immediately sought out his company. After dinner we were seated in a circle in the living room. The cat royally walked into the centre of the room and stretched herself out between two people sitting across the room from each other. Her head was in the direction of the hostess of the party and her feet stretched in the direction of the young man. This lent itself to the idea that energy was flowing between these two individuals. I didn't mention my observations to anyone; however it later became known that there was a tryst between the married hostess and the young man. Though their countenances did not betray their secret, the cat's activity was a sign of the energy flow between them that was generated by their clandestine activities.

Pets, in addition, will reflect their owner's energy and can often give signs indicating circumstances in a person's life. In my practice as a healer I consistently observed a connection between an animal's health and its owner's health. I often find that an animal will come down with a disease or physical or emotional ailment before the owner does. I believe that this occurs because animals often offer themselves in service to their owner, mitigating a difficult emotional or physical situation by acting as a buffering zone for their humans.

For example, Maureen came to me with severe back pain. Coincidentally her dog had back problems (which preceded Maureen's back problems). I believe that our pets will take on our ailments as a way to lessen them for us. As Maureen began to heal her back, *coincidentally* her dog's back problem cleared up.

Not every animal ailment is a sign of that impending condition for the pet's owner, but often the psychological associations with physical conditions can be reflected by the pet. For example, if a pet has cancer this can be a sign that some emotional problem is eating away at the owner. By observing the health and behaviour of your animal, you are often given signs that can reflect *your* state of being.

3 CALLING FOR A SIGN

Though we are constantly surrounded by signs, there are times when we can't feel the subtle currents of energy and we don't seem able to hear the whispers of the universe that give us understanding, insight and direction in life. During these times it can be valuable to call a sign. There are traditional time-honoured ways to do this as well as simple present-day techniques.

Yes/No

Perhaps the simplest technique to use to call a sign is the Yes/No method. This method can be as easy as making a decision as a result of tossing a coin. Any time you use this technique, it's suggested that you follow a three-step programme.

1. Relax
2. Focus
3. Designate

First, clear your mind and completely relax. This is a very important step. Take a few minutes to allow your mind to become still. You can do this by taking slow, deep breaths. While doing this type of breathing, fix your attention on one object such as a candle or a flower and allow your entire body to relax.

The second step is to focus on your question. Bringing your area of concern into your mind, be as neutral as you can. You have decided to call for an answer from the universe, so it's important to be open to receiving that answer when it arrives. Let go of your preconceived notions about what the answer should be while staying focused on the question.

The third step is to clearly allocate or designate what is a 'Yes' answer and what is a 'No' answer. If you are using a coin, begin by allocating one side of the coin for 'Yes' and the other side for 'No'. If you are using a pendulum, designate, for example, that when the pendulum swings clockwise this means 'Yes' and when it swings anti-clockwise this means 'No'. It is not so important what direction or side you designate. When you are given an answer (whether it is a coin toss or another Yes/No method), you do not always need to accept the answer, if it doesn't feel right. Sometimes Yes/No methods work because the answer we receive feels so objectionable that our opinion becomes polarized and we are catapulted into our own intuitive knowing.

Open a Book

Looking for a sign can be as easy as randomly opening a book. It is, of course, much easier to use a spiritual book with which you feel aligned rather than a dictionary, for example. But almost any book will do at a pinch. The first two steps are the same as in the Yes/No method. First relax your mind. Then focus your intention and be very clear to what purpose you are calling for a sign. Even if your purpose is somewhat nebulous such as, 'What is my message for the day?' make sure that you are clear about your focus. Then close your eyes and open the book randomly. You can choose the first page you open to, or you can thumb back and forth until your fingers find a page that just feels right. Once you have found the page, with your eyes closed, allow your fingers to move up and down the page until they seem to be drawn to one particular area. To some people this area feels warm, to others it feels rather sticky. Then open your eyes and read the area where your fingers stopped to gain your sign.

Jackson wasn't sure whether he should opt for early retirement at his job. The advantage was that he would have time to enjoy his life without the pressures of a 9-to-5 job. The disadvantage was that if he retired early, his pension would be much smaller than if he continued to work for an additional six years. He decided that he would call a sign using the 'Open a Book' method. Jackson had been studying a spiritual book called the *Course in Miracles* so he decided to use that book for his sign. He first relaxed his mind; then he focused on his concern about his retirement. He flipped back and forth through the book without looking at the pages until one particular page seemed to stick to his fingers. With closed eyes, he took one finger and scrolled up and down the text until his finger stopped in one place. He opened his eyes and read, 'My home awaits me. I will hasten there . . . what need have I to linger in a place of vain desires and shattered dreams.' Jackson knew that this was a very definite sign that he should go into early retirement. This was a very clear and very obvious sign. If you open a book and the meaning of the sign that you choose is not immediately obvious to you, use the methods described in Chapter 4 to understand what your sign means.

Creating Sign Conditions

Who hasn't plucked petals off a flower saying, 'He (she) loves me. He loves me not.' This is a very common way to call for a sign, which is to create conditions upon which the sign will appear. You can do this by saying, 'If I am meant to take the bus rather than walk [for example] then the bus will come in the next three minutes.' If the bus comes, it's a sign that you are meant to take the bus. If it doesn't come, it's a sign that you are meant to walk. In this way you are creating conditions that precipitate a sign.

For example, Carlos couldn't decide between two different schools that had accepted his college enrolment. They both had advantages and he just couldn't decide. He therefore decided to create conditions to elicit a sign as to which school to attend. Carlos said, 'If I am meant to go to one of these schools then their mascot will come into my life as a sign.' Carlos decided that if he was meant to go to the first college he would be given a tiger sign (which was the school's mascot) and if he was meant to go to the second college, he would see a wolf sign (which was the second school's mascot). The very next day, Carlos was walking his dog when he passed a man who had a dog held on his leash that looked exactly like a wolf. He stopped the man to ask him about his unusual dog. The man replied that his dog was actually half-wolf and half-dog. That was the sign that Carlos was waiting for. He chose the school with the wolf for its mascot.

You don't always have to make specific conditions for the sign. You can request an unspecified sign. Darla's son, John, was in the military and was sent off to the Gulf War. She was having a difficult time coming to terms with his leaving and was concerned with his safety. Darla said, 'If John will be okay, please send me a sign.' She didn't ask for a particular sign, rather she opened herself to receive a non-specific sign. (If you have a request such as Darla's you can address God, or your guardian angel or your higher self or personal spiritual source.) Two days later Darla opened her front door to find a perfectly formed bird nest in the centre of the walkway. Her logical mind asserted that the nest must have fallen from the overhanging tree branches. But in her heart she knew that it was the sign that her son would be all right. (Darla's son had a most unusual hobby of collecting bird nests. Her garage was full of bird nests that he had collected over the years.) She knew it was God's way of saying that John would be just fine.

Designating Signs

An effective method of working with signs is to designate signs. To do this you assign something to be a particular sign for you. In my childhood, I fell in love with red-winged black birds. I loved the brilliant red flourish on their shiny black wings. I'm not exactly sure why, but I decided that whenever I saw these birds I would have good luck. 'Whatever is expected tends to be realized,' so whenever I saw a red-winged black bird I always had good luck. I had designated these beautiful birds as my signs and because I expected good luck, whenever I saw one, I always had nice things happen to me. Conversely, if good luck was headed my way, the universe would conspire to present this sign to me.

Anything can be designated as a sign. I have some friends who have designated ants as their signs. Whenever they see an ant they stop to take time to listen to their inner voice because they believe that the ant is a messenger from spirit. Sometimes designated signs can come from other people. Feathers are a sign for me that came from my teacher, Dancing Feather, who was a Taos Pueblo Indian. I was with him as he lay dying in the Santa Fe Indian hospital. His last words to me, as he lay on his hospital bed were, 'Wherever you are, wherever you go, I will be there.' After his death, feathers began to appear to me spontaneously in the most unusual circumstances. I came to know that these feathers were designated signs or messages from Dancing Feather and from the realm of spirit. Feathers came when I needed assurance that I was on the right path. They came when I was unsure of my direction in life. And they came as joyous messengers from the realm beyond this one. Now whenever I see a feather I know that it is a personal sign for me.

Sometimes my feather signs come in ordinary ways such as during walks through a park; however sometimes they appear in mysterious and inexplicable ways. One morning I rose early because I had a very important meeting later in the day, for which I particularly wanted to be well prepared. I was nervous about the meeting. I sleepily stumbled into the bathroom, lit a small candle to avoid the trauma of a bright bathroom light, and began to run the bath.

With only the small candle for light, I slid into the warm bath. As I gradually woke up, I became aware of something large floating in the bath. Reaching out, I drew a large white feather out of the water. I stared at it. I was the last person to use the bathroom the night before and there hadn't been a feather in the bathtub then. The window was closed so it couldn't have blown in the window. There was no logical way to explain the feather. Yet I was holding a huge, long, slightly waterlogged white feather in my hand. Sometimes it's best just to accept the unexplainable without always searching for a rational explanation so I accepted the feather as a sign from Dancing Feather to not to worry about my meeting. I knew the message accompanying the feather was that the meeting would go well . . . and it did.

A curious phenomenon has begun to occur regarding feathers as signs. After people attend my lectures, they report that feathers also begin to appear for them as signs, sometimes in the most unusual circumstances. You also may find feathers appearing for you as signs. If so, whenever you see one take just a moment to be still and listen for the message that it brings.

Traditional Sign Systems

Astrology

Systems have been developed over the years that are used to gain access to signs. Perhaps the system that has gained the most popularity in the Western world in the last few years is astrology. Most major newspapers have astrology sections, and millions of people including heads of state and monarchs consult the stars on a daily basis to gain messages for their future. There is value in seeing a professional astrologer, for often they can offer you profound insights. (My paternal grandmother was an astrologer. She did my chart the day I was born. The things that she foresaw in my stars so long ago have come to pass.) However you don't necessarily need to go to an astrologer. You can designate a newspaper astrology section as your vehicle to gain your signs for the day. Though the daily horoscopes don't always agree with each other, once you designate a particular column as your source of signs then it will tend to be appropriate for you.

I Ching

Another ancient system for gaining signs is the *I Ching*, from the fabled Chinese *Book of Changes,* purportedly the oldest book in the world. It is a compendium of knowledge that seems deceptively simple, yet often offers powerful insights. To consult the *I Ching* you think of your question and then toss three coins six times. The sequence of the coin tosses is converted into a series of straight and broken lines which are called a hexagram. There are sixty-four hexagrams in the *I Ching.* Your answer comes from reading the essay associated with the hexagram that you have chosen. Carl Jung was an enthusiastic proponent of the *I Ching.* He believed that the hexagrams represented universal themes within the collective unconscious and that the relationships between the hexagrams and events in one's life could be attributed to synchronicity. Jung experimented with the *Book of Changes*, 'sitting for hours on the ground with the *I Ching* beside me', he wrote. He asked questions and received 'undeniably remarkable, meaningful connections'. To consult the *I Ching* for a sign you can either use the coins or even use the 'Open a Book' method. The *I Ching* is seen by some to be somewhat obscure, but often it is that very obscurity that allows one's intuition to assert itself in the interpretation.

Tarot

Jung was also intrigued by the Tarot which, though not as old as the *I Ching,* is just as abstract. The Tarot consists of seventy-eight illustrated cards. Each card has a specific meaning ranging from wealth and good fortune to death. As in other divination methods, the Tarot is a tool to bridge the symbolism within each card to the deep intuition within us all. If you decide to work with the Tarot, it's valuable to obtain a book with definitions for the various individual cards. Alternatively you can use your intuition and look at the individual card until you can get a feeling of what the message is. To use the Tarot to gain signs, you can follow a traditional method of laying out the cards in a particular alignment to observe the relationships between the cards or another way to gain a sign using a Tarot deck is to relax, focus and pull one card out randomly from the pack. Either way the Tarot is an excellent way to gain signs.

Numerology

It is not known exactly where the art of numerology began, but research can trace its source back thousands of years. Ancient Mayans were known to practise numerology as well as the Mesopotamians, who originated the idea that numbers can explain the structure of the universe. The Kabala, an ancient Jewish mystical system of understanding the universe, maintains that God created the universe using letters and numbers. Many believe that the pyramids in Egypt and Mexico contain numerological secrets in their architecture and structure.

Certainly it was the ancient Greek philosopher Pythagoras who developed this ancient art into a science. He not only venerated numbers for their mathematical qualities, he also believed that each number had a mystical significance. Pythagoras thought that numbers were an expression of the fundamental laws of the universe. He stated, 'Were it not for Number and its nature nothing that exists would be clear to anyone either in itself or in relation to other things. You can observe the power of Number . . . in all the acts and thoughts of man.'

Numbers can be thought to be the language of the universe. All that exists in the physical cosmos, every atom, molecule, dimension or form can be represented by numbers. The theory of numerology is that symbolically numbers are not merely expressions of quantities, but are symbols and each number has a spiritual essence and capacity. To use numerology for signs it is valuable to study the meanings of the different numbers, for in modern life we are constantly surrounded by them. A very basic overview of the meaning of some numbers is given in the Signposts Dictionary (under Numbers).

Darren was having trouble deciding whether to move into an apartment by himself or to move in with room-mates. He decided to use numbers for his signs to help him with his decision. As he began to notice the numbers that kept appearing in his life, he kept seeing the number seven everywhere. He saw it on licence plates and on billboards and on pamphlets. He knew that seven, in numerology, was a number signifying the individual path and the inner life. He felt that this was a sign that he needed to move into an apartment and live by himself for a while.

By looking for the numbers that spontaneously appear in your life you can gain personal signs to give you understanding and help you decide personal direction in life.

Vision Quest

One of the oldest tribal traditions for seeking signs is the Vision Quest, which is a ritualized retreat taking place in solitude within nature. In Native American culture the Vision Quest is used as a rite of passage to initiate young men (and sometimes women) into adulthood. The visions and signs received by the young man or woman on their quest would help determine what role he or she would play as an adult member of their tribe. The Vision Quest could also be used throughout life, whenever an individual wished to receive greater understanding or help from the spirit powers.

For Native American people, the Vision Quest was an extension of a religious experience that was based on the earth they walked on, the air above them, the animals around them, and the reality of life which permeated every waking moment. They saw life as one long, mystical adventure where spirit spoke to them through every blade of grass and bird song. They knew they were constantly surrounded with signs and the Vision Quest would allow them to be still so that they could really hear these signs.

The Vision Quest is a time to focus on personal questions and to wait in silence for answers to come in the form of signs from nature. Nature is perhaps the most powerful purveyor of signs, but modern people living in cities no longer feel that immediate connection with the earth and many have lost the ability to listen to the signs in nature. The Vision Quest is a powerful way in which modern, urban people can reclaim that sense of wonder and connection to the earth. It is an act of power that can change one's life forever.

'The thirst for a dream from above . . . without this you are nothing,' said the Sioux medicine man John Lame Deer.

If you decide to go on a Vision Quest, it is definitely best to work with someone who has led these experiences before. However, in modern life it is not always possible to have a shaman or a guide as you seek your signs and visions. You can therefore create a modified Vision Quest for yourself.

You may first want to create a personal medicine wheel (a circle of stones to sit in during your Vision Quest) somewhere in nature where you will not be disturbed and where you can observe the ebbing and flowing of nature. The medicine wheel is an outward representation of an inner Native philosophy that states that life is not linear but rather occurs in circles. The medicine wheel circle of stones represents the great circles in life. Just as a circle has no beginning and no end, life is seen by native peoples as a circle from birth to death to rebirth again. The medicine wheel also represents the seasons, the four elements and all the different stages of life.

The first stage in setting up a medicine wheel for your Vision Quest is to collect stones that feel significant to you. You will need to have four cardinal stones that represent the four directions and the four elements. Begin with the stone that is in the east and continue clockwise. These are laid out to form the perimeter of the circle. Allow sufficient space for you to step inside the circle, which should be approximately six to twelve feet wide, allowing equal space between each stone. The beginning of the wheel is the east stone. Always enter and leave the wheel through the east. In between each quadrant other stones may be positioned, which create the pathway from one direction to the other. Take time setting up your wheel. This is a sacred space so treat the circle with reverence.

When creating the medicine wheel use your own intuition to guide you in developing the appropriate ceremony. The most important point is that the rituals are carried out respectfully and with good intentions. Prior to entering the wheel to begin your Vision Quest you need to purify yourself. Cleanse yourself with water. Native Americans purify and consecrate themselves by 'smudging'. This means burning sage, sweet grass, or cedar (incense is equally good if the other herbs are not available). A prayer is then offered to the Creator to ask for a blessing.

You might want to start out by planning a twenty-four-hour Vision Quest for yourself. Start just before sunrise and complete after the sun has risen the next day. Though traditionally no food or water was taken on the Vision Quest, I suggest taking a water container with you into your circle of stones. And if you are hypoglycaemic or diabetic or pregnant then take appropriate food into the sacred circle with you. You can leave the circle when you need to void, but remember to be ecological with any used tissue and take it away with you when you leave.

You can just sit by yourself and tune in to all the information your senses present to you from within and without. Or take a journal with you to record the experience as it unfolds. Either way, you can call for signs by asking specific questions which you would like to have answered. Some questions which you might try are as follows:

Who am I?
What is my purpose?
What are my goals?
Is there anything in my life I must change?

As you sit in silence in the centre of your circle, listen and watch the movements of nature around you. Watch the activities of the birds, insects, and animals. Listen to the wind. Watch the movements of the clouds and the weather. When you really take the time to listen, you will be given remarkable signs that can change the course of your life. (See Chapter 4 on how to decipher the signs.)

When your quest is over you may dismantle your circle but do it ceremoniously, moving in an anti-clockwise direction. You may keep your sacred stones or return them back to the sea or land.

Sometimes signs come as a feeling during a Vision Quest, rather than in an exacting form. Bryce came on one of the Vision Quests that I lead every year in the United States. He was very successful and he was, for the most part, satisfied in life. However, he still felt that there was something missing. He couldn't quite put his finger on it, but he thought that if he went on a Vision Quest he could find out what it might be. The first day of the Vision Quest he carefully arranged his circle of stones and sat in the centre. He was restless. He thought about his business, making mental notes of things he needed to do. He thought of how he was going to remodel his home. He planned the details of a coming trip. His mind was occupied with mental chatter and he couldn't seem to relax.

At night Bryce watched the stars and he vowed to try to still his mind the next day. However when he woke up the next morning, instead of stilling his mind, it seemed to become more active. He thought of his ex-wife. He thought of childhood experiences. He thought of his parents and people he hadn't thought of in years.

Bryce just couldn't stop thinking and he certainly wasn't seeing any signs. Dejected, Bryce watched the sunset as the last rays of the sun sank beneath the horizon. Suddenly it was as if the entire world stopped. There was no wind, not even a tiny whisper of a breeze. The chatter of evening birds stopped. Even the constant hum of the insects stopped. Bryce took a deep breath and he felt a stillness fill him. Abruptly, the call of an owl pierced the rapidly approaching dusk. Bryce felt the sound resonate through his entire body. As he looked up to locate where the sound had come from, an opening appeared in the thin cloud cover. In the middle of the opening was a single star. He knew that this star was the sign that he had called for. It was the most radiant star that Bryce had ever seen. As he looked at the star he began to sob. He felt as if his life could be likened to the cloud cover. Yet behind the clouds was a deeper reality; a brilliant light. That star light was like his true self that had been hidden from him for so long. He realized that all he ever needed to do was quiet his thoughts and he could touch into his own radiant self.

Bryce stayed up all night watching the soft interplay of the night clouds and the stars. He said he experienced himself as an infinite being. He knew that he wasn't limited to just his body and his life. He felt a deep and underlying connection between himself and all of life. When the sun rose the next morning he felt as if he was seeing the world anew. The light was brighter. The colours were more intense. The air seemed fresher. He had called for a sign and the answer had reverberated in his soul.

Surrounding Yourself with Signs

Everything around you is a reflection of your inner being. The visible signs surrounding you are symbols of your invisible world. In every moment of your life you are walking in a 'forest of symbols' which are constantly reflecting your personal reality. However, if you want to change your personal reality, you can actually change the signs around you and this creates an energy template. (A template is a pattern or gauge, such as a thin metal plate with a cut pattern, used as a guide in making something accurately, as in woodworking. It is also a term used in biochemistry meaning a molecule of a nucleic acid, such as DNA, that serves as a pattern or mould for the synthesis of a macromolecule, as of RNA.)

Surrounding yourself with your personal signs can create a new pattern or a template that will penetrate deep into your subconscious. A template can help change deep, subconscious, negative programming. As your inner programming is altered by your new template, you begin to project a new energy field. Life and people around you will then respond to this new energy field. Literally the universe around you will coalesce to match the energy that you are projecting. For example, if you want to feel a deep inner peace, surround yourself with signs that symbolize deep inner peace to you. If your signs for peace are the white dove', the colour blue and the moon then put visible representations of these signs in your home and in your environment. This type of reverse symbolism works: for example, if you have bad habits in life that you want to weed out, weed your garden, or if you want more flow in your life, clean out your rain gutter. Encompassing yourself with signs of what you desire to create or project into the world will assist you in conceiving what you want in life.

Joan wanted to become more involved in healing. Her designated signs for healing were the ancient Egyptian symbol, the Ankh and the colour green. She therefore created a template for healing by putting green plants and the colour green in her home in abundant amounts. She also obtained several Ankh figurines to place in her home. This way her personal signs were not only reflecting her inner conscious state, but these signs were also acting as messages to her subconscious mind to programme these qualities into her life.

There are no wrong choices

There may be times in your life when all the signs are pointing you in one direction yet your desires (or intuition) are pointing you in another way. There are never any wrong choices; for every choice in life allows you to grow and expand as a human being. Choose the direction that is kindest to you, even if it means that it seems that you are not following the signs.

When my husband and I were planning to purchase our first home, we looked at a nice two-bedroom home. As we approached the house I saw a large feather in the grass near the front door. I reached down and picked up one of the most perfect owl feathers that I have ever seen. And as we went out of the back door, there was a perfect shining crow feather on the back porch. I thought, These are very, very good signs. (Owl and crow are two of my totem animals.) All the signs were excellent for that particular home. Yet my husband said, 'There is much remodelling to be done in this house. If we move into this home we will be living in a construction site for a year.' We eventually chose a house that didn't need as much remodelling, and even though the signs pointed to another house, I've never regretted my decision. When observing the signs in your life be as loving as possible to yourself. Don't use your signs as yet another way to view yourself in a negative light or to do something that you don't want to do. The signs are gentle nudges from the universe, from your higher self, from your guides and angels and from the Creator, but you are the creator of your destiny and there are no wrong choices.

There may be times in your life when you follow all the signs and the end result seems completely wrong. However, on looking back, one will usually find that though the immediate goal didn't seem agreeable, the long term result was valuable.

Hanna was asked to go on a blind date. All the signs were positive so she accepted. When her date arrived at her door she immediately realized that the evening was going to be a disaster because she felt an immediate and powerful dislike for the young man. However, as she could find no gracious way to excuse herself from the date, she accompanied him to the local dance hall. During one dance, as she silently swore to herself never to accept blind dates again (even if the signs were great) a tall handsome man cut in. She literally felt swept off her feet and the end result was a lasting and loving relationship.

4 HOW TO INTERPRET SIGNS

Signs are a distillation point through which the cosmos filters into our physical reality. They integrate spiritual abstractions and give them meaning within our life. They are not staid and lifeless; they are living, viable symbols that reflect the dynamic interplay of the forces in the universe. When a sign appears for you, the meaning may be immediately obvious. However, if you are not clear about the meaning of your sign, there are many methods that you can use for interpretation. Every method has its own value. Each may take you on a unique pathway in understanding yourself. How you interpret a sign is less important than the meaning that you derive from it. You may look at each sign as a separate and new revelation, or view your signs over time as a collective whole.

Here are some methods you can use to interpret your signs. You might work with several of them or use one at a time. Experiment until you find the method that works best for you. Remember, the best system is the system that works best for you.

Method 1: Intuition

Perhaps the most powerful tool for sign interpretation is your intuition. When a sign enters your life, you can ask yourself a very simple question that will help you tune in to your innate intuition. Ask yourself, 'If I knew, what would this sign mean?' If your conscious mind asserts that it doesn't have a clue what the sign means, this very simple question will allow you to step beneath the conscious mind to travel to the deeper subconscious mind. The question allows you to address your conscious mind, saying, 'I know that you don't know, but if you did know what would the meaning be?' This method almost seems too easy to be effective, yet it often produces remarkable results.

Ron saw a very dramatic event unfold in nature. As he was sitting on a rock by the sea enjoying the calm ebbing and flowing of the waves, he saw a bald eagle swoop down and grab its talons into the back of a large salmon. The salmon was heavy and the eagle couldn't quite bring the salmon fully out of the water. A life-and-death struggle ensued as the eagle furiously flapped its wings to stay aloft and the powerful salmon fought to dive to the depths of the sea. Suddenly, with one violent flip of his fin, the salmon dived into the sea with the eagle still clinging to its back. Almost immediately the surface of the sea returned to a calm stillness.

Ron knew that this was a powerful personal sign. However, he didn't know what it meant so he came to me to ask about it. I said, 'Ron, I know that you don't know what it means; but *if* you did know what would it mean?' Almost immediately Ron replied, 'Well, I don't really know, but *if* I did know, it would be that I need to let go of a particular relationship. Otherwise I will be pulled down into a depth of despair.' He went on to explain that he had always had a hard time letting go of relationships and situations, even when they weren't nurturing or supporting him. The particular relationship he was in was no longer supportive and, in fact, was very negative but he was holding onto it. He took the drowning of the eagle as a sign that it was really time to let go.

Symbology is often different for different people, so when working with your intuition it's important to trust whatever first comes into your mind. Someone else seeing the same scenario might have identified with the salmon instead of identifying with the eagle, and felt that the sign was, 'No matter how overwhelming the odds are, *never* give up!' Another person, after observing the calm sea after the struggle, might interpret this event as, 'No matter how dramatic the struggle seems in life, it's only a small event in the great vastness of life.'

Method 2: Watch the Feeling

Finding the feeling or emotion that you associate with a sign can often offer a valuable clue to its meaning. To locate the emotion, think of the sign, close your eyes, still your mind, and notice what emotion you would most likely link with the sign. Once you have located that emotion, look back over your life and remember the last time you had that exact feeling. Recall a situation which evoked that same emotion. Notice any memories associated with those feelings. What is the message from the memories? Most often your sign is either associated with that particular situation or with the issues underlying that situation. Observing the emotions connected to a sign can be a real clue to assist you to find the significance of your sign.

Chellie was taking a walk through the park when she heard a loud crash behind her. She turned to see what it was. Less than fifty feet away a large tree had fallen down. She knew it was a sign but didn't know what it meant. When I asked her to find the feeling that she associated with the tree, she said that it made her feel sad. I asked her to locate that last time she remembered feeling that exact same kind of sadness. Spontaneously, a memory of herself as a child in the forest with her grandfather came into her mind.

Chellie used to go out with her grandfather into the forest every year to cut firewood. Sometimes her grandfather would cut down an entire tree and it would come crashing down to the ground. She loved her grandfather and was very sad when one year, shortly after their tree cutting excursion, he went on a vacation and died in an automobile accident. When she examined the circumstances of her present life she realized that her oldest son who reminded her of her grandfather, was going away on vacation and she had a subconscious fear that something would happen to him. The tree falling in the park was a reflection sign meaning that it was reflecting her own subconscious fears for her son. She was able to use the sign to discover what was occurring in her subconscious mind. This allowed her to realize that her current anxiety was actually a fear based in the past and not grounded in present reality. When she realized this her anxiety disappeared.

Method 3: Become the Sign

This method entails imagining that *you* are the sign. To use this method you would say, 'I am the .... sign and I represent _____ .' (Here you would say whatever first comes into your mind.) If there is more than one sign that occurred at the same time, (for example, the previous event with the eagle, salmon and sea) imagine that one by one you become each sign. Continue to do this for each of the different signs until each one is clearly defined.

After you have defined the different signs in this way, imagine that they are talking to each other. For example, Geraldine had just dropped off her daughter at a dance class when she saw a cat chasing a dog down the pavement. At one point the dog tentatively turned to face his attacker and the cat became a furious ball of fur and claws. The dog pivoted and ran off. Geraldine intuitively recognized that this was a sign but didn't know what it meant, so she used the 'Become the Sign' method. She first imagined that she was the cat. As she imagined herself as the cat, she said to herself, 'I am the cat and I am indomitable and courageous.' Then she imagined herself as the dog and she felt, 'I am the dog and everyone expects me to be brave but really I don't feel brave at all and I don't like fighting.' She then had the two signs imagine that they were speaking to each other. The cat said, 'You are so cowardly that even a cat can scare you.' The dog replied, 'I don't want to fight and I don't even want to be a dog.' As Geraldine continued the inner dialogue between the two signs, she realized that the cat and dog were reflective signs signifying the internal struggle that was occurring within her.

Geraldine was in the midst of a very difficult divorce. She had always been a pleasant, sometimes acquiescent, person and her natural inclination during the divorce proceedings was not to ask for anything because she 'didn't like to fight'. As she interpreted her signs she realized that they were telling her to stand up for herself because she was much in a stronger position than she thought. For, just as most dogs are stronger than cats, *she* was actually stronger than she felt. She knew the sign was saying that she should stick up for herself. Geraldine had a second interpretation as well, but the message was essentially the same. She saw that, even though the cat was smaller, its strength and courage had turned away adversity. She realized that even though she was seemingly smaller than her ex-husband, if she had courage and she stuck up for herself instead of acquiescing, the situation would go in her favour. She was later happy to report that she followed the advice of the signs and it did go well for her.

Method 4: Make a Sign Journal

Record your personal signs. Watch for recurring themes, feelings or symbols. Important messages from the unconscious can be uncovered through this method. Whenever a sign appears in your life, write it down and then list the meanings that you associate with that sign. Include signs that have come from your heritage, your family, your culture and your past lives (see Introduction). As you begin to assemble a collection of your personal signs, put them in dictionary form. Refer to this dictionary each time a sign appears in your life. You will find the more you use your personal sign dictionary the more insight you will gain into the symbols that you have listed. This is a powerful way to gain self-awareness.

Method 5: Ask your Guide

Everyone has guides, whether they know it or not, and those who consciously communicate with their guides have an enormous wealth of resources to tap into. Guides come to us from the world of spirit. They hold a unique perspective of the universe, creation, and spirit. They are non-physical beings or entities that give guidance, assistance and love. They can be teachers and protectors and they can assist in directing our path as well as helping us gain access to our inner life.

When I began doing past life regressions with my clients, I was first intrigued with a phenomenon that spontaneously occurred again and again during the regression. While my client was in a deep meditation, a guardian figure would appear in their inner explorations. Sometimes this guardian or guide would appear in period clothes or dressed as if in another time in history. Sometimes the guide would come as a light or sound or a symbol or even an animal. But always there was a wondrous, loving feeling that accompanied these guides.

There seems to be something inherent in our inner journeys that allow guardian beings to surface. Not only do they spontaneously appear for people who are being regressed but they also appear in other inner voyages. Individuals who have had near-death experiences often report that they were guided by very protective, loving spiritual entities. Meditators and even individuals who spend time in isolation tanks report seeing guides and guardians. It may be that when we take the time to be still and turn our awareness inwards their presence can be felt.

I believe that guides are actual spiritual beings who exist on higher planes of consciousness and are working to help us in our evolution. Another way to view guides is as a part of ourselves. Psychologists usually share this view, explaining that guides are actually aspects of ourselves that we haven't yet owned or integrated into our personalities. No matter what you believe about the origin of guides, they can be of enormous assistance in finding the meaning of a sign.

To access your guide, spend a few minutes relaxing, then visualize or imagine your guide. If you don't have a visual image for your guide, then say to yourself, 'If I had a guide what might that guide look like?' and imagine a visual image for your guide. Another method is to imagine or sense a large glowing sphere of golden, white or silvery light. Feel yourself surrounded in a bubble of light and love and protection. After you have done this you might say to yourself, either out loud or quietly: *'Dear Guardian, I ask for your assistance and understanding regarding this sign. Help me understand the meaning of the sign in my life. I send peace and give thanks for your loving blessings.'*

After you have done this, imagine your guide telling you what your sign means. As simple as this exercise sounds, it can often garner remarkable insights.

Method 6: Free Association

This method consists of writing associations (the first idea that comes to mind) for each sign. This may give you a clue to the meaning of the sign. For example, imagine that you see a sign of a tulip. A free association might be: tulip – two lips – too much lip – 'Hey, my kids are giving me too much lip! I'm feeling taken advantage of in my life.' Another example might be that you see a sign of a bell. A free association might be: bell – ring – wedding ring – 'Oh my gosh, I left my wedding ring in the restaurant ladies room.'

Method 7: Pretend you Meet a Martian

Pretend that you are telling your sign to an alien from another planet. Imagine the alien doesn't know anything about earth. For example, if your sign is a ram, how would you describe a ram to your friend from Mars? You might say, 'A ram is an animal with masculine, thrusting strength. It charges forward with great power and certainty no matter what gets in its way.' After you have described the ram to your imaginary alien friend, you might examine your life and notice if there is anything in your life that equates with the qualities of a ram. For example, you might be involved in a project where you really need to ram your way through it to get it done. As you begin to describe literally your definition of the sign to the alien in the most basic language, often the meaning of your sign becomes clear.

Method 8: Research your Heritage

Within each person's heritage are signs that were used by their ancestors or their culture. Even if you aren't consciously aware of what those signs are for you, they are still in the genetic encoding in your cellular memory. For example, in one eastern European culture it is felt that a dream of water means someone is going to pass away. In another culture if you hear an owl it means that it is going to rain. As you research your own heritage's use of signs, you can find meanings that might be valuable in your life today (see Chapter 2).

Method 9: Use A Dictionary.

A very simple method to decipher your sign is to look it up in a standard dictionary. Very often just reading the exact definition of a sign can be of assistance in your interpretation.

Method 10: Sign Dictionary

Use the following Sign Dictionary to look up your sign. Although all the definitions might not be exactly accurate for you personally, this method can get you off to a good start.

When interpreting your signs find the meaning that is the kindest to you. For example, if you have a heart attack, you could think, This is a sign that I'm not giving enough love, or you could interpret it in a much kinder way such as, This is a sign to rest and spend more time pursuing joy. Or if you experience a horrific disaster, this doesn't necessarily mean that you are a disaster. Maybe your presence was needed to mitigate the difficulty. Perhaps you were meant to be a compassionate light, amidst darkness. If you have poor self-esteem don't use signs as yet another way to condemn yourself. Always look for the kindest interpretation for your signs.

This dictionary is in no way complete, yet it attempts to give you a starting point for understanding your signs. Remember, only you can know the true meaning of a sign. Use the suggestions you find in this book as a starting place when you are interpreting your signs. After a sign appears for you, read over the meanings in the dictionary to see if any seem to fit. Sometimes the recognition that the definition in the Sign Dictionary isn't the right one for you is as beneficial as the feeling that the definition is correct. When you know that something isn't accurate, this means that on some level, you know what is right. Many signs will have seemingly opposite meanings listed. Pick the meaning that feels right for you. You will be drawn to the definition that you need at the time. The meanings listed are to stimulate your own inner knowingness. Some of the meanings presented are literal, some are common symbolic interpretations, some are metaphors or puns, and some are just plain intuition. With many of the sign meanings I have included questions for you to answer as a way for you to gain further insight.

SIGNPOSTS DICTIONARY

Abandoned/Abandonment

• Are you feeling left out or not included in some area of your life? Are you feeling abandoned? Have you given some group, person or social convention authority over your life, and are you now feeling separate from this? If so, this is the time to take authority for your own life. Find your own inner truth.

• Is there anything that you have abandoned that you shouldn't?

• Is there something that you need to abandon or release? Is it time to leave behind people, circumstances or characteristics that aren't necessary any more?

• Abandonment might represent subconscious issues from your childhood or even past life issues of feeling not cared for. If this is the case then it's important to deal with these issues now. Self-pity is destructive.

• Abandonment symbols can also appear as a result of the death of someone close to you who provided you with your sense of purpose or self-worth. This is the time to look within for a sense of your own worthiness.

• Abandonment can denote a need for self-acceptance. Is there some part of yourself that you have abandoned? It might be a potential talent or ability or an instinctive drive. Take the time to identify what it might be and find a place for it in your life.

• Abandonment signs can also indicate that it's time to throw off inhibitions . . . enter into a state of abandonment. It might mean that it is a time for greater freedom, time to abandon the chains of convention that have shackled you.

• Portents of abandonment can occur just before you become more independent and on your own.

Abbey   (See also *Church, Home, Monastery, Temple*)

• An abbey is usually an old and holy place that can be a powerful symbol of the ancient holy and divine place within yourself. It can represent your spiritual essence.

Abdomen

• This often represents the second chakra which is called the hara or tanden. This energy centre which is located in the area beneath the navel, is associated with emotions. The lower area of the abdomen can also represent sexual feelings.

• Perhaps there is some health issue that needs addressing in the area of your abdomen.

• The abdomen might relate to feelings of vulnerability. Are you feeling vulnerable?
• This symbol can pertain to digestion issues. Are you digesting life's lessons, absorbing what you need and releasing the rest?

Abduction
• Are you feeling that you have no control in a situation and that you are a victim of circumstances? Is there a circumstance in your life where you feel out of control? Assess your inner strengths and never underestimate the inner power within yourself.

Aborigine
• An aborigine can symbolize the very primordial part of you – your instinctive self. Do you need to connect with your primordial nature?
• It can also represent a part of your basic nature that perhaps is still foreign to you. Get back to your roots. Spend time near the earth and listen to the wisdom of Mother Earth.

Abort/Abortion
• This can symbolize the loss of some new potential in your life. Perhaps there was some project or idea you were working on which did not come to completion, either through a conscious decision you made or due to factors outside your control.
• Sometimes abortions occur spontaneously. Are you prepared for sudden changes in your life or sudden changes in plans? Know that you can choose the direction of your destiny.
• An abortion can be a miscarriage of justice.
• Notice the feelings that you have about the word abortion. This sign may represent the surfacing of old, unresolved issues in your life.

Above
• This can denote inspiration or the higher self.
• This might represent things looming above you. Sometimes things seem bigger than you are. View the situation from a higher perspective.

Abyss
• An abyss might symbolize an impassable chasm in your life. Is there something which seems impassable to you?
• It can also symbolize impending danger, either internal or external. If the abyss appears dark or foreboding it might represent something from the depths of your subconscious, perhaps a painful past experience. To release fears and past experiences you must face them.
• An abyss can also be a sign of an ego death. There are times in life when you must allow your old ego to dissolve so you can evolve into

the next level of your awareness. Following death there is always rebirth.

Accident

• An accident can result from not paying attention. Do you need to pay more attention to the details in your life?
• Do you feel like the victim of sudden change? Remember that there are no victims, only volunteers. If you are feeling victimized, try to find an area of your experience where you have responsibility and can take control. This will increase your sense of power and enhance your energy field. Victims have weaker energy fields than people who take responsibility for their actions.
• If the accident resulted from speed, is there an area of your life where you are going too fast? Slow down, pay attention and integrate.
• This sign might be a premonition of an accident. Remember that nothing is set in stone. Take time to relax. Be careful and conscientious to avert a possible catastrophe. Accidents are really less accidental than we usually think. If you accept the notion that subconscious beliefs determine many of the external circumstances of your life, then it logically follows that many so-called 'accidents' are actually the direct result of subconscious decisions. Avoid whatever actions might expose you to an accident-prone situation.

Ace

• An ace can indicate hidden talents; an ace up your sleeve.
• It can also mean that you are truly excelling at something.

Achilles Tendon

• This traditionally represents a place of vulnerability. Is there an area of your life where you are feeling very vulnerable?

Acorn

• From a small beginning can come great power. This is a good sign for self-potential. Is there something in your life you can nurture that has the potential for bringing you strength, power and stability?

Actor/Actress

• The roles we play in life are only illusions. Is there an area of your life where you feel that you need to put up false pretences or where you are escaping from reality?
• This can symbolize deception or false appearance. Is someone in your life acting a role and not being real with you? Or do you feel that you are a phony?
• Are you satisfied with the way you are acting in life?

• Acting signs can represent glamour, excitement, larger-than-life, centre-stage attention while basking in the admiration of others. Do you need to step out of tedium and become the star of your own life?
• Is professional or amateur acting an area you would like to explore in your life?
• This sign can also mean act now. Do it!

Addict

• This sign can mean that you are giving your power away to someone or something. Is there someone or something that you are addicted to in your life? Seek outside help, either from other people or from spiritual guidance.

Adolescent

• Adolescence is a time of great change and sometimes turmoil. It is a time when one is seeking to define self and direction in life. What are your values? What is really important to you?

Adrenals

• Adrenal glands are utilized during excitement or times of anxiety when you get an adrenal rush. Are you depleting your adrenals because of being anxious or stressed?
• This can also be a sign of the gathering of power for a new beginning.

Adultery

• Adultery can symbolize the conflict between your duties and your desires. Is there an area of your life where you feel a conflict between what you want to do and what you feel you must do?
• This can also represent being drawn to a quality in another that you don't experience within yourself.
• Are you thinking of adultery? Is someone important to you involved in adultery? Are you overly jealous and unsure of your position with your mate?

Aeroplane

• An aeroplane can be a sign of high ideals and a striving towards higher consciousness or spiritual aspirations.
• It might also represent soaring to new heights, liberation, release, freedom and expansion.
• An aeroplane can be a sign of a consuming drive for success; a thrusting upwards at the greatest possible speed.
• When you are aboard an aeroplane, others are in control during the

time that you are travelling. Are you willing to trust that you are being guided to your destination?
• Aeroplane crashes can be a sign of falling from great heights. Or sometimes this can be a sign to stay off aeroplanes for a while.

Aggression

• If you are surrounded by aggressive people or if you are seeing signs of aggression all around you, there is probably hidden aggression within yourself that you are denying. Hidden aggression is very self destructive, so it's important to recognize it, accept it, and then release it.
• It may also be that there is someone who is being aggressive towards you, even if you are not consciously aware of it. Take a moment to check through your life and see if anyone fits this description, and then take appropriate actions.

Airport

• An airport is a point of departure for other places and foreign lands. Is it time to take a journey or risk a new venture? Do you desire adventure?

Aladdin

• Life can be magical. You can have your wishes fulfilled.

Alarm

• This can be a warning. Be cautious, danger may be afoot. Are you on the correct path for yourself right now?

Alcohol

• Alcohol can be a sign of a dulling of the senses; not feeling. This can represent denial of self and escape from the reality of life.
• This can symbolize camaraderie and celebration; 'wine, women [men] and song'.
• It can also symbolize transformation. Jesus said, 'This is my blood,' in regard to the water he turned into wine at the Last Supper.

Alien

• An alien can be a sign of the part of ourselves we aren't acknowledging. Alien usually means unfamiliar and can carry a connotation of the enemy. It can represent the alien part of ourselves. Is there something within yourself that feels foreign or alien to you? It's important to love all parts of yourself including the parts that seem alien to you.
• Alternatively alien can symbolize higher wisdom such as UFOs being ships of higher-conscious beings. Or it might symbolize fear, such as alien abductions.

Allergy

• An allergy is a sensitivity to the external environment, not being able to resist or assimilate external stimuli. Is there something that you are having trouble resisting or assimilating, or are overly sensitive to? Is there something you should be immune to that you aren't?

Alley

• Though alleys can be cute and cobblestoned, most connotations of alleys are of garbage-strewn, dark, closed-in, and grimy places. They are the backside behind the facade we show to the world. Is there an area of your life you need to clean up and integrate? Do you feel cut off from the image you are projecting to others? Are there areas of shame you need to resolve in your life?

Alligator   (See Crocodile)

Altar

• An altar is a focus for worship and honouring the spiritual aspects of life, a place dedicated to remembering what is truly important. Do you need to create an altar within your home, or within yourself?

• This can be associated with sacrifice. Are you spiritually sacrificing yourself for a higher ideal? Are you happy about this?

Ammunition

• This might symbolize gathering ammunition for one's own causes. Are you gathering your inner resources for negative or positive action? Are you clear about the ultimate result you wish to attain and how it will affect you and others in the future?

Amputation

• This could symbolize giving up a part of yourself associated with the body part that was amputated in the dream. For example, an amputated leg may mean you feel like you don't have a leg to stand on. Or perhaps you feel you have a lack of mobility in your life. An amputated hand might signify an inability to grasp a situation.

• Are you in the process of releasing part of yourself that you previously identified with, but that actually isn't an integral part of your true being?

• Are you cutting off people, situations, or parts of yourself which should be integrated instead of released?

Anaesthesia

• Anaesthesia can mean being numb to your senses. It is an inability to perceive what's going on around you. It can even be an avoidance of life. Are you avoiding your emotions? Even if it is painful, let yourself feel and express your emotions. This can be very healing.

Anchor

• An anchor offers strength and security. Are you feeling the need for security, for an anchor in your life? Or conversely, is there someone or something that is a constraint to your freedom? Is there someone to whom you feel anchored, or who is holding you back?

Angel

• An angel is a messenger from God. It represents our most spiritual ideals and is a special symbol of pure love.
• To see angel signs is to be blessed.

Anger

• If you are constantly seeing angry people or situations, this is usually a sign that you are subconsciously angry about something. Take time to review the people and situations in your life to check and see if you are repressing your own anger, even if you consciously feel emotionally balanced. Anger is not necessarily a bad emotion. It only becomes destructive when it is internalized or inappropriately dumped on someone else.
• Is there a situation in your life where you need the vital fire provided by anger to make the changes you want to make? Righteous indignation can be a life-transforming force you can make good use of in the right context.

Animals   (See also entries for individual animals)

• Animals can be a sign of a primal, instinctive part of your being. If the animals are wild and ferocious, they can represent the primitive, aggressive part of your nature. If the animals are tame, they can represent the controlled expression of your instinctual nature. And if they are wild and free, they can be connecting you to nature.

Ankh

• The ankh is an ancient Egyptian symbol of spiritual wisdom and healing. This perhaps can be a sign from a past life.

Ankle

• Your ankle allows you mobility in life. Are you feeling mobile or immobile in your life?

Anorexia

• This represents a lack of self-acceptance. Are you depriving yourself

of nourishment, either physically, spiritually, or emotionally? Are you starving for an unattainable, deluded idea of perfection? Are you asking too much of yourself? Relax. Enjoy. You are perfect exactly as you are.
• This might symbolize a desire for total control. Do you need to let go, go with the flow and trust more? Or do you need to make changes so that you have more of a sense of controlling your own life? Find ways that are more fulfilling and effective than starving yourself.

Ant

• Ants are universally considered industrious, productive, and busy. They carry more than their own weight. Do you need to become more industrious in your life?
• They can also symbolize working for the community and social cooperation, sometimes to the detriment of individuality. Do you feel like you are losing your individuality for the good of the greater community?
• The word ant can also be a homophone for aunt and would then perhaps be a reference to your own aunts.

Antenna

• An antenna transmits and receives ideas and energy. It expands an awareness of the world around you. Take time to be still and tune in.

Antique

• An antique is a connection or a relic from the past. Do you have an old pattern or belief system that is no longer useful? It is now time to let it go.
• Antique can also signify revering the past. Is there something from your past you need to honour, care for or cherish?

Antlers

• Antlers can portray a protection of the divine masculine part of yourself as well as strength, power and protection.

Anxiety

• Anxiety can come from not trusting that everything will turn out according to a greater plan for your life. Trust in yourself. Trust in the process of life. Trust that there is a higher being who is looking out for you.

Ape

• An ape can represent a copying or mimicking others rather than finding your own truth. Are you afraid to express your individuality and live your truth?

• Apes can mean primal power. Do you need to assert your strength in a powerful way?

Applause

• Applause is self-acknowledgment or needing acknowledgment. Do you need to applaud yourself or gain approval from others?

Apple

• An apple is a sign of healing potential, wholesomeness, health and vitality. 'An apple a day keeps the doctor away.'
• An apple can also mean temptation such as Eve faced in the Garden of Eden.

Archer/Archery

• An archer is focused on a specific direction; clarity; single-mindedness. Do you need to hone your focus in life?

Architect

• An architect creates blueprints for new buildings. Do you need to make plans in your life or create a blueprint for your future?

Arctic   (See also *Water*)

• The Arctic can be a sign of frozen feelings and emotions. Sometimes it's necessary to isolate oneself and our emotions. Is this necessary for you now, or do you need to thaw and open up to your feelings?

Arguments

• There are parts of yourself that are in conflict. Find an inner resolution, whereby all parts are heard, acknowledged, and integrated.
• Sometimes arguments clear the air. Is there some grievance you need to give voice to?

Ark

• An ark can provide safety and protection in the midst of the deep waters of emotion. Do you feel the need for safety and security now? What makes you feel secure emotionally? Take steps to move in this direction.

Armour

• Armour is protection. Is there something or someone you are trying to protect yourself from? Are you in a situation where you don't have personal boundaries and you need to armour yourself?
• Wearing armour is being sealed off. Can you find a way of alleviat-

ing your fear, taking care of yourself, or eliminating the threat without closing yourself off from sources of support and love?

Arms
• Open arms symbolize being open and reaching out to life; closed arms are closed to life.
• Arms can be symbolic of weapons. Are you being defensive about something?

Army
• An army is a sign of major obstacles or opposition to be overcome. Do you need to amass your inner resources to overcome obstacles?

Arrow
• An arrow is a sign of a clear direction; a straight course ahead in life.

Art/Artist
• Art offers a creative expression in life. An artist represents your potential and ability. Is it time to unleash your creative potential?

Ascent   (See also *Climbing, Ladder, Mountain*)
• Ascending or climbing may symbolize that you are ascending in life. Your energy level is rising and life is on the up and up.
• It may also signify that you need to come down to earth, that you are too lofty or idealistic.
• In special instances it may symbolize that life is an uphill struggle. Know that life is not meant to be a struggle. You can relax and enjoy yourself.

Ashes
• Ashes can be a sign of spiritual purification.
• They can also be a sign of death or absence of life or vitality.
• When something has completely burned all that is left are the ashes and so ashes can be a symbol of the very essence of something.

Ass
• Are you being an ass in your life? Is there an area of your life where you are acting stupidly? Is someone being an ass to you?
• An ass can be a symbol of plodding, patience, or long-suffering.

Asthma
• Asthma is not being able to get enough oxygen. This can symbolize suppressed grief. Or it could mean that you feel that someone is constricting you so much that you feel as if you can't breathe.

• Asthma can be a sign of stress and not feeling connected with life. Relax, meditate, breathe. Are you going too fast, so that you feel that you are not able to catch your breath? Do you need to slow down?

Astronomer

• Is this the time to reach for the stars and strive to reach your ambition?

Atomic Energy

• Atomic energy has incredible potential. It is great power that can be used negatively or positively. There is a need to harness that power for constructive ends. Harness that great potential within yourself towards constructive purposes.
• Signs of atomic energy might mean you are tuning in to the collective consciousness of fear for planetary and personal safety. There is real power in your intentions. As you focus your intention on inner peace, you can make a difference in our planetary evolution by projecting peace into the world.

Attic

• A house can symbolize different levels of consciousness. The basement is your base self and the attic can mean high ideals or the upper levels of consciousness.
• An attic could represent old issues from your personal or familial past which you have put away without really going through. Is it time to sort through some of this material to see what is still of value to you, and what you might want to let go of?

Audience

• An audience can be a sign that congratulations are in order. If the audience is responding positively, this is an acknowledgment of self-acceptance. If they are not responding positively, you need to work on self-acceptance.

Aunt

• Can represent the industrious part of self. (See also **Ant** for homophone word association)
• Feminine aspects of the self. The qualities you associate with a particular aunt may be projected aspects of yourself. This sign may also pertain to an actual aunt of yours.

Aura

• An aura is the energy field surrounding a person or thing. It is invisible to most people, yet very real. A bright, clear aura indicates clarity and good health. An aura that is dim and close to the body indicates a lack of clarity and health disturbances. Is your aura radiant and clear or do you need to purify and simplify your life?

Automobile   (See *Car*)

Avalanche   (See also *Water*)
• Can signify a completely overwhelming experience of previously frozen emotions.
• Is there any area of your life where there is the potential of utter overwhelm? To avoid feelings of being overwhelmed, separate difficult areas into smaller portions and tackle one part at a time. Take the most important aspect first and then prioritize the other parts.

Axe
• An axe is a sign of wielding power with certainty. Is it time to take control of a situation?
• An axe could be a sign of fear of loss. Could it be that your job is going to be axed? Are you in danger of losing something important to you? Take steps now to prevent this, or make preparations for dealing with it.
• An axe can be cutting away that which is not needed. Old trees are axed down to make way for new growth (potential). Is there something you need to axe from your life?
• Sometimes an axe can represent the executioner's axe – a powerful symbol of judgment. Is there something you feel guilty or anxious about?

Baboon
• A baboon lives by instincts and is community-minded and social, while living close to nature. Do you need to be more in touch with your natural instincts in regard to your community life?
• People who are considered oafish are sometimes called baboons. Does this apply to you?

Baby   (See also *Birth*)
• A baby is a sign of new birth within yourself; new beginnings; new spiritual awareness.
• It is a sign for potential for growth.
• Are you wanting to get pregnant? If not, take the appropriate measures. Seeing babies everywhere is often a subconscious yearning for a child. Many women notice babies everywhere (both human and animal) right before they get pregnant. (This includes unplanned pregnancies.)

- Can also indicate a yearning to be babied and pampered and the centre of attention. Are you feeling the need for love? Does the inner baby inside you cry out for love?
- Birth of a new idea.

Back

- This can be a sign to retreat, to back up, back off, or back out of a situation. It can be turning one's back on something or someone. In life there are times to advance and times to retreat. There is no dishonour in retreating. Access the situation and see if it is time to back away.
- This can also be a sign to pay attention to the health of your physical back, which is the support of your body.
- It may be a sign referring to your support systems in life. Do you need more support in life?

Badger

- Badgering someone is baiting or teasing them. Is someone badgering you, or are you badgering someone else?

Baggage   (See also *Luggage*)

- Baggage can be a sign of things, thoughts or attitudes that you carry around that aren't necessary. Is there old conditioning you need to release?
- Do you have a desire to pack your bags and get out of some present situation?

Ball

- The spherical shape of a ball suggests completion, wholeness or unity.
- A ball can represent a social occasion such as going to the ball. 'Having a ball', and 'playing ball', suggest joy. Have fun. Enjoy yourself.
- The 'ball's in your court' means that it is now your turn to take action.
- It can have sexual connotations. Do you have the 'balls' to get the job done?

Balloon

- A balloon is a sign of unrestrained joy and soaring to new personal heights.
- If the balloon breaks, an illusion is shattered.
- A balloon afloat can mean you are at the mercy of the winds of change.

Bank

• A bank is a reservoir of financial resources. Invest in yourself. Draw upon your inner resources.

• May mean you need to reconsider your banking habits. Perhaps you need to bank more of your income, change banks, or pay attention to the details of your finances.

Basement / Cellar

• Very often houses will symbolize your body with the attic associated with higher aspirations and the basement representing the lower or base energy centres. Because basements are often dark and below ground, they can represent the deepest part of your subconscious. There is great value in exploring the repressed levels of your subconscious mind. The very things you have repressed or forgotten, such as guilt, shame or fear, when brought to the light of day are often seen to be quite appropriate expressions of human behaviour. You can then integrate them into your understanding and release them. Perhaps now is the time to do it.

• A basement can represent the base or root of a problem that you are struggling with. Notice the other associated signs.

Bat

• Bats are creatures of the night and sometimes reside in dark caves. They can represent fear of the unknown, yet they also know how to navigate in the darkness. If you are in a time of uncertainty in your life and the bat appears as a sign, remember that you can steer your course amidst uncertainty and not knowing. Trust your intuition. You do know what to do. Look deep inside yourself for the answer.

• A bat can be an old scolding woman. Are you acting like an old bat? Alternatively someone who is batty is a little crazy or unconventional.

• Batting around an idea can mean that you are considering several alternatives. Sometimes this is the best way to come to a feeling of certainty.

• To the Chinese the bat was symbolic of long life and happiness. To the tribal people of the Americas the bat was emblematic of shamanistic initiation and rebirth. The bat goes into the womb-like darkness of the cave only to emerge again. This sign can appear when you are about to enter into the deep unknown and hidden fears which dwell inside you. After symbolic death, you will experience rebirth and renewal.

Bath / Bathing

• Bathing can be a symbol of purification, ablution and cleansing. Is there something you need to cleanse or purify within yourself?

- Is it time to wash your hands of a situation, or of old habits or attitudes?
- It can also signify baptism or rebirth.

Battle/Battlefield

- Do you have a deep inner conflict? Do you have any antagonism directed towards an external situation or person? Or perhaps you are experiencing an internal conflict within yourself. This can point to a need for resolution and integration.

Beach

- The beach is the border between the subconscious, emotional part of you that is represented by water, and the earthly physical side of you. This is an excellent sign for balance in life.
- Beaches can be purifying and rejuvenating. Go to the beach, either physically or in meditation.

Bear

- The bear represents the power of Mother Earth. Every winter the bear retreats into the womb-like comfort of the caves of the Eternal Mother. If you are given bear as a sign this could mean that you need to enter into a time of introspection and subsequent renewal.
- A bear sign can represent the protective, mothering, female aspect of force and power. Very few animals represent such aggressive power as a mother bear when her cubs are threatened. Is there a part of yourself, or is there someone in your life that you need to defend passionately and aggressively?
- Many Native American people consider the bear to be a totem (or sign) of the healer. We all have the inner ability to be a healer. This could be a sign to step into your inner healing abilities.
- In Western culture the bear is associated with the teddy bear which is cuddly and lovable. This could be a sign to take time to be soft, cuddly and return to the simple joys of life.

Beaver

- The beaver is busy and industrious. This is a sign of action and building and accomplishment. This can be a good sign of prosperity through your own efforts. Are you working hard enough towards the goals in your life? Are you working too hard? Take time to rest and review before forging ahead.

Bed

- The bed is an obvious symbol which may refer to sexuality and intimacy.

• The bed can also signify rejuvenation, relaxation, nurturing, comfort, security, safety and the eternal womb. Do you need to rest, withdraw and relax more in your life?

• A bed can be a sign of the connecting point between conscious and subconscious and your dreams. Listen to your dreams. They contain important messages for you.

• A bed could indicate coming illness and the need to rest more.

• A bed can occasionally refer to repressed memories about things that have happened in bed in your past. If you have negative feelings about bed then consider getting therapy to discover why you are having these feelings.

Bedbug

• A bedbug is something unpleasant that is covered up; it is a small nuisance.

Bee

• In ancient Egyptian hieroglyphics the bee was associated with the royal social order, probably because it represented industry, production and cooperation. In Greece bees symbolized work and productivity. In the Oracle of Delphi souls were symbolized by bees because they swarmed together and it was thought that souls travelled together in a swarm-like manner. In the Romanesque period in Europe bees were symbols of diligence. This might be a sign to be more industrious in your life.

• Perhaps you are feeling stung by some circumstance or remark?

• Just BE!

Beetles

• Beetles can be a sign of good luck. They represented eternal life to the ancient Egyptians.

Bell

• A bell can be a sign of personal attunement. If the sound is clear, then this can reflect a resonance within the wellspring of your life. If the sound is muffled or unclear then perhaps you need to take some time for personal attunement.

• A bell can offer a warning. Be alert.

• Bells are played during celebrations. Joyous developments are in store for you.

Bill

• This might relate to karmic payment. Are there bills that you are overlooking that you owe someone or something? Make plans for reparation. Are there bills that are owed to you? Sometimes the bills of birds can be a homonym which is symbolic for bills that you owe.

Bird (See also listings for individual Birds)

- A bird can be a sign of soaring to new heights; soaring above your problems. It can mean flight into spiritual realms.
- Birds represent freedom. Do you want to take wing in your life?
- Birds are universally considered to be messengers to and from spirit. The shaman turns himself into a bird to connect with spirits and the Creator. Do you need to connect more with the divine source present in everything that surrounds you?
- Birds have the ability to see things from afar. Do you need to distance yourself from a situation to gain perspective?
- A bird can mean a flight of fancy, flight of the imagination. Let your creative imagination take wing.
- Birds have long been emblematic of unpretentiousness and simplicity. Do you long to return to the sweet purity of nature?
- If the bird is singing, it may be the harbinger of good news.
- A bird in a cage may symbolize feeling a loss of freedom.

Bird's Eggs

- Bird's eggs in a nest can signify new beginnings.

Birth

- This is usually a powerful sign of renewal or rebirth. It can symbolize a new phase in your life, either inner or outer. Birth may represent the spiritual awakening or unleashing of powerful creative forces within you.
- Is it time to give birth to a new project, ideal or path in your life? Is this the time to start in a new fresh way on an old commitment?
- With the birth of something new comes the corresponding and necessary death or release of something old – perhaps an old negative attitude or limiting pattern. Be willing to forge ahead, even if it means letting go of some things.
- Signs of birth are signs of new beginnings, but they can also represent feelings of vulnerability or dependence.

Birthday

- A birthday is a celebration of life. It is also an anniversary of accomplishments. Take time to look back and see how far you've come. Celebrate yourself. Celebrate your life.
- A birthday is a sign of new beginnings. It's never too late to start again.

Black

• Black may symbolize the unknown, your shadow or the mysteries of your unconscious mind. Are there inner issues that you need to explore?
• The expression 'in the dark' means feeling confused. Do you feel uncertainty as to which way to go in life?
• Black can also represent the comforting cover of night. Perhaps this is a time for you to rest and make time for dreams in your life.
• Black has also been associated with depression and despair. Are you suppressing sadness or anger? It's okay to feel every emotion. There are no bad emotions, but when you suppress them, they can turn into depression. If you feel depressed, you need to process and release the underlying emotions and find some way of taking action. If this process is too overwhelming, find someone to help you.
• In Western cultures black is connected with mourning. Is there some area of your life that you are mourning?
• For some people, black symbolizes strength. The Chinese see black as a symbol of good.

Bladder

• Bladder can mean a fear of letting go; holding on to old beliefs. Find a place where you feel safe enough to trust and let go.
• Being pissed off means being angry. Is there a situation right now in your life that is making you mad? Know that you can comfortably release anger by communicating and trusting your inner knowing.

Blind

• This can be a sign that you are being blind to something or turning a blind eye. Are you unsure of your way? Don't know where you are going? Is there an issue or person in your life that you are avoiding or don't want to see? Are you refusing to see some internal conflict within yourself? Stop avoiding it. Take time to face and trace whatever you are repressing. You may want to enlist the help of a trained therapist to guide you.

Blizzard   (See also *Water*)

• A blizzard can signal extreme emotional upheaval.
• A blizzard sign can mean a snow job on someone, or on you. Are you being deceived by someone, or are you trying to deceive someone?

Blood

• Blood symbolizes many things that are seemingly opposed to each other. Choose the definition that most closely corresponds to your feelings. Look at your own emotional response to the signs.

• Blood can be a sign of life force, dynamic strength, power and energy. It can also indicate a free flow within the body and within life.

• Blood can represent powerful emotions and passion, especially rage or love.

• Blood can represent a young girl's defoliation or a girl maturing into womanhood. It might also be activating memories of an early childhood sexual experience that is buried in the subconscious mind.

• Blood is a powerful sign of the renewal of life. In a woman's monthly cycles her inner cycles are sometimes symbolized by her bleeding.

• Bleeding can symbolize the draining away of vital life force or energy. Is your life force being drained away?

• Blood can mean pain, suffering and injury. Is there some area of your life where you are in deep pain? Or is there something that is bringing you suffering? Or have you inflicted injury upon yourself or another?

• Blood sucking can mean that someone is taking advantage of you.

• Blood Brothers indicates unity and commune.

• The blood of Christ is holy sacrifice.

Blue

• The most powerful symbols of blue in our world are the sea and the sky. The blue sea can represent the subconscious, the feminine, the great mother, and your deep secrets. The blue sky can represent the conscious mind, the masculine, the great father, and the open, expansive part of yourself.

• Blue as a colour is soothing, emotionally healing, peaceful, and relaxing. It also can represent mystical perceptions in life. If you find blue continually appearing in your life, ask yourself if you need to relax more and tune in to the inner spiritual realm.

• Depression is often called the blues. Is there something in your life that is making you feel unhappy, sad, or disappointed? Notice your emotional response to the colour to gain insight to the meaning.

• When someone is turning blue it means that they are growing cold. Do you need to 'cool it' or relax and slow down for a while or are you 'growing cold' towards somebody or a situation? Turning blue can also indicate a symbolic lack of oxygen. What do you need in order to breathe more freely in your life? Take action, since breathing is obviously of vital importance to your survival.

• When someone becomes bruised their body becomes black and blue. Are you feeling bruised from a recent situation?

Boar

- This can be a sign of the ferocious, primitive aggressive power of the wild boar.
- Someone who has a swinish personality is often called a boar.
- Someone or something is boring. (Boar is a homophone for bore.) Are you bored in your life, or are you boring to others?

Boat

- A boat can be symbolic of your emotional journey through life. As a house can represent your physical body, a boat can represent your emotional body.
- A boat can be a sign of travelling through emotional times. Water usually represents your emotions, and the boat can represent how you are manoeuvring through your emotions. Does the boat have a destination? Is it on course or is it just drifting? Are you in control of your emotional life or do you need to take the helm? Are there too many people on board? Is the person steering the boat too controlling? Is the boat in good shape or is it rusty? The ways you perceive the boat and its journey can be powerful indicators about your relationship to your emotions.
- A boat can also be a sign of leaving for distant shores, leaving the stability of the land and trying new waters in your life.

Body   (See also definitions for specific body parts, as all parts of the body have particular symbolic associations)

- The right side of the body can signify the projecting, masculine, moral (right) side of yourself and your outer strength. (If you are left-handed, reverse meanings.)
- The left side of the body can represent the receptive, feminine, inner part of you.
- The lower part of the body can represent the primordial instinctual part of yourself, and also can represent your lower chakras, groundedness and sexuality.
- A naked body can represent vulnerability, while an overly clothed body can represent hiding yourself.

Bog

- Are you feeling bogged down by a project or situation?
- Are you feeling in an emotional bog?

Boil

- A boil can either be an acute infection, or it can refer to a liquid reaching boiling point. In either case the message is similar: a situation

about to erupt. Is there something in your life that is about to come to a head? Is there a situation in your life that is about to reach boiling point? Evaluate it and meet it head on.
• Water (emotions) boiling can indicate emotions purifying, moving and changing.
• This can be a sign of suppressed anger that is beginning to surface.

Bomb
• This can represent an explosive situation in your life.
• A bomb has emotional potential power. Do you feel that you are in imminent peril of your emotions exploding?
• This can also represent an emotional failure, as in 'the concert was a complete bomb.'

Books
• Books as a sign can represent wisdom and knowledge as well as lessons in life.
• Seeing a book can also be a symbolic representation of booking an appointment or an event. Is there anything that you need to book yourself in for, or have you forgotten a booking?

Boss
• This can represent taking authority in your life or mastering a situation.
• Are you feeling bossed around, submitting to another's will? Do you need to take more control over your existence? Do you need to set boundaries about the role others are playing in your life?

Bottle
• Are you feeling bottled up?
• A message in a bottle can be an answer from an unexpected source.
• A bottle with the cap off is more open than one with the top securely fastened down. A full bottle can represent feeling emotionally full while an empty bottle can indicate feeling emotionally exhausted or depleted.
• If you find yourself in a bottleneck, is there something impeding the flow of your energy?

Box
• A box can represent self-imposed limitations. Do you feel boxed in? Break out of your box, expand your limitations.
• Pandora's box can represent all that you fear. Fear is an illusion. Face your fears and let them out of the box. Pandora, in mythology, originally meant 'all-gifts' or 'all-giving'. It was later when male deities arose

and female deities were denigrated that Pandora and her box became symbols of ill-will and fear.

• Freudians would say that a box represents the vagina or the womb. This can be the inner feminine aspect of either a man or woman.

Boy

• A boy can represent the masculine child within us all. In a man it can represent his own childhood.

Bread

• When Jesus met with his twelve disciples they shared bread. Bread can represent communion with others and unity of spirit.

• Bread is often a powerful symbol for life; hence the 'bread of life'.

• When someone is talking about needing some 'bread' or some 'dough,' both these nouns can connote money or abundance. If you use the word bread for money notice the quality of the bread and your feelings towards it.

Break

• A break can be a sign of sudden and unexpected change coming in your life. An old situation may be about to break up.

• It can also be a sign to slow down and be more careful than usual if you are continually aware of things breaking around you and especially if you are the person breaking things.

• Is it time to break out of a situation? Is there a relationship that is about to break off? Examine what you have gained from the relationship. Evaluate whether or not you are ready for completion with this individual.

• Are you in a time in your life where there is a breaking of illusions or broken faith? Remember when one illusion is broken you can then see the world around you more clearly and honestly. And seasons of despair make way for times of renewal and lush growth, just as spring and summer follow winter every year.

Breast/Bosom

• A woman's breast can symbolize unconditional love and nurturing, as well as the Universal Mother.

Brick

• Bricks can represent strength, endurance and strong foundations. Are you building solid foundations for yourself? Are you building for the future?

Bride/Bridegroom

• Both brides and bridegrooms can represent the communion of the masculine and feminine forces within us. A wedding is a time for celebrating these forces within ourselves. Marriage is a time of new beginnings through union. This is the time for integrating the male and female forces within yourself.

Bridge

• A bridge can be a powerful symbol for change and transition. You are going from one experience to another. This can indicate a new job, new relationship, new home, career change, or any change taking you from one stage in life to another. Or it could represent a change in your personal experience of reality.
• A bridge can symbolize an emotional transition in life if the bridge is crossing over water.

Brother

• This sign can signify something about you and your actual brother(s), or it can be symbolic of universal brotherhood. If you were an only child before a brother (or sister) arrived, you may subconsciously associate the idea of 'brother' with being usurped in the family. You may have jealous feelings associated with the word 'brother' as a carryover from childhood. If you had an older brother, was he your protector or did he try to dominate or ignore you? Did you always yearn for a brother that you never had? Whatever perceptions and associations you have about the concept of brother are intertwined with this sign.
• In a monastery the monks are called brothers, so brother might represent the religious male aspect of the self, or a common tie between men – a brotherhood.

Brown

• Brown has long been associated with the earth and the ground. Are you needing to be more grounded right now?
• The leaves turn brown in the autumn. Do you need to pull your resources inwards?

Brush

• Brush might be related to phrases such as 'brush with fate', 'brush with disaster' or 'brush with death' - all signifying a close call.
• Thick underbrush can mean are you feeling stymied or that you can't move ahead in life.
• Brushes used for cleaning, from scrubbing brushes to toothbrushes, can mean that you need to pay more attention to cleaning the spaces

around you, either the physical spaces surrounding you or your inner spaces. Or perhaps you are overly concerned with cleaning. If so do you have guilt feelings that you are trying to hide or clean away? Or do you have a feeling of lack of inner control so you compensate for it by obsessively cleaning to gain outer control? Learn to accept yourself just the way you are.

Bubble

• Bubbles can symbolize childlike joy and exuberance. Lighten up. Embrace the childlike joy within yourself.
• Are you isolating yourself, as if in a bubble? Get out and see the world!
• Burst bubbles can signify a disappointment in your life. Disappointments usually come from having expectations. As you begin to accept life in every moment for what it is you will have fewer disappointments in your life.

Bud

• A bud occurs on a plant in springtime. It is a new beginning. This sign can represent new life and a new beginning for you.
• A bud can also be a homonym for a buddy or a friend.

Buffalo

• The buffalo is sacred to the American Indian. It represented sustenance for the Plains Indians. It gave them clothing and food. A sign of a buffalo can represent abundance, harvest and plenty, and great power.

Bug

• Is something bugging you? Take a greater perspective of life. You are bigger than the small annoyances or inconveniences in life.

Build/Building   (See also Home)

• Creating new foundations in life. Specific kinds of buildings will have individual meanings. For example a church might suggest religion or spirituality or rigid adherence to a belief system. A government building might symbolize authority and organization or politics. A fortress could suggest that you are fortifying yourself against outside influences.

Bulb

• A flower bulb has new potential for beauty.
• A light bulb brings light where there was darkness. Is there an area of your life that you need to illuminate? It can also signify the coming of a great idea.

Bull

• A bull sign may indicate great strength, force, power. Step into your strength. Take control. Get the job done. You have all the inner strength that you need to forge ahead.

• This is an optimistic sign for your finances. When it is a bullish market finances are on an upswing.

• In mythology a bull was a sign of fertility, of the masculine principle penetrating the feminine principle.

• In astrology the bull is equated with the sign Taurus which is tenacious, sensuous, earthy and practical. Are these qualities that you need to develop more in your life? Is there a Taurus in your life now that is important to you? Check other signs to determine the significance of this individual to you.

Bulldog

• A bulldog has tenacity and holding power. Seize the opportunity and don't let go. Hang in there.

• A bulldog can also mean defiance. Is someone defying you, or do you need to stand up for yourself and defy authority?

Bulldozer

• A bulldozer can signify clearing the way by pushing through obstacles. Go for it. Just do it.

• Are you trying to bulldoze someone, or is someone trying to bulldoze or force you into doing something that you don't want to do? Take time to assess your options.

Burglar

• Is someone robbing you of energy or of something that is rightfully yours? This can also be a sign to safeguard your valuables against being robbed in the future.

Burial/Bury

• Burial signs can mean the death of old patterns and thought forms. Very rarely will a burial sign indicate the imminent death of someone. It almost always means a completion of an area in your life.

• Is something buried in your subconscious that you need to retrieve? It can mean denial of a situation or something that is hidden from you. Check other signs to see what's buried in your subconscious.

• Bury the hatchet. Release old grudges. If the sign is in connection with a specific person, clear any emotional blockages that you may have with that person.

Butter

• This can connote flattery as when you butter someone up. Is someone flattering you? Is it sincere? Should you use flattery instead of aggression in a situation to gain an end result?

Butterfly

• This is a powerful sign of a new beginning on a higher plane. Just as the butterfly emerges from its cocoon, it can mean emerging in beauty and new awareness, signifying a time of rebirth and transformation. Among the ancients the butterfly represented the soul and even life itself. Are you in a time of rebirth?

• A 'social butterfly' is someone who flits here and there without ever making a real commitment to a relationship. Does this apply to any aspect of your life?

• A butterfly can also signify joy and bliss.

Buzzard

• Feeling picked on or preyed upon; preying on others. Does this apply to any aspect of your life?

• Though buzzards are an important part of the web of life they are often thought to be contemptible and rapacious. Is there someone in your life who is acting buzzard-like?

Cabin   (See also **Home, Boat**)

• If the cabin is in the woods, it can connote peace and contentment.

Cactus

• Cactus can mean a prickly situation is coming your way. Take time to evaluate your life and ease any areas of sharp dissension in your life.

• A cactus is something or someone that can't be touched. Is there someone in your life whom you are afraid to touch, or someone who is afraid to be touched by you? Take time to create a safe environment for both of you to relate within.

Cage

• When one is in a cage there is often a feeling of being trapped. Remember there is always a way out. Go through your options and look at them from different perspectives. Loosen your current way of viewing your reality. Let go. You are free.

• Do you feel restrained from doing what you really want to do? Or do you need to restrain yourself in some area of your life?

• A cage can also signal self-imprisonment through fear. Examine your fears. Ferret out which ones have validity and which ones you can discard.

Cake
• Celebrate the sweetness of life! When you've accomplished or completed something it's important to celebrate.

Calf
• A calf is a contented, youthful image in pastoral, healthy surroundings.
• Notice the details of the symbolism. It could also refer to the calf of the leg.

Camel
• A camel can travel for long periods of time on its own inner reserves. It represents endurance and perseverance, especially during dry spells in your life.
• The camel has been called the ship of the desert. It can symbolize finding a way through a very difficult or inhospitable impasse.

Camera
• A camera might represent keeping a distance between yourself and life, always viewing things through the filtering lens of perception, instead of directly, face-to-face and straight on.
• A camera also might relate to a desire to preserve the past. Perhaps you want to make a record of fond memories as a way of honouring them.

Camp
• A camp can be a kind of temporary home. It may be a retreat out in the woods where you go to get away from it all and connect to nature. Or it could be formed out of necessity, as when you are between permanent living situations, and feel like you are just camping out in the meantime.
• Camp can also refer to making fun of something through exaggeration.

Can   (See also *Box*)
• You can do it. You can achieve it. Yes, you can!

Canal
• A canal is a long, narrow passage, and often is related to childbirth and delivery. This symbol might refer to feelings about an actual birth, or it might relate to the emergence of new aspects of yourself on an emotional or spiritual level.
• A canal might also symbolize a directed and narrow emotional path, since water often represents the emotions, and a canal is a very

restricted, contained path for water to flow through.

Canary

• A canary represents music, harmony, joy, and the lightness of a small bird.
• This symbol could also refer to the saying, 'He looked like the cat that swallowed the canary.' In this case, it may indicate guilt about tattling or the telling of secrets.

Cancer

• Is something eating away at you emotionally? Express yourself. Say what is in your mind and in your heart. Be honest with yourself.

Candle

• This is a universal symbol of light and connection to Great Spirit. You are touching the Great Light within all things.
• The spiritual life force within you; your true inner light.

Cane

• Do you feel as though you need some support in life? Accept help from whatever source it comes. You don't have to do it all alone.
• A cane can also be used as a cruel form of punishment. Do you feel like you are being harshly judged or punished by someone or something? Are you judging or punishing yourself?
• A cane might also be sugar cane, a natural source of sweetness. Extract the joy from your life. Enjoy!

Cannibalism

• Do you feel like you are being eaten up by a situation?
• This symbol can refer to taking the energy of another instead of using one's own energy. For example, a person might be using the creative ideas, money or psychic energy belonging to someone else. Are you taking the life force from someone, or is someone taking yours? Are you living off someone, or do you feel as though someone is living off you?
• He's so cute I could just eat him! Cannibalism could also symbolize extreme possessiveness. Are you wanting to devour someone, or do you feel someone wants to consume you?

Canyon

• A canyon is a vast opening of unconsciousness.
• It can be a seemingly impassable chasm. There is always a way to cross any canyon in life. Go around it, fly above it, climb down into it.

Capsize

- Capsizing could symbolize falling off your course, being dumped into emotions (water). Get back into your vessel. Get back on course.

Captain

- A captain is a person in control. You are at the helm in the emotional waters of your life. Take control.

Car

- A car most often represents your physical body or self. If the car is having problems, notice what the mechanics of these are, as they can be significant. Here are a few examples:
- A failed brake may mean that you need to put the brakes on in your life. Is there a situation that you need to stop? If the brakes in your car are not working ask yourself if you need to put the brakes on and slow down in life.
- If your radiator keeps overheating ask yourself if you need to stop and relax. Overheating can mean that you need to cool down. You are reaching your boiling point too fast. Try some more constructive ways to deal with your anger and the overheating of your emotions.
- Bald tyres can mean that you are not getting the traction you need in life. Take time to ground and connect with people and situations in your life.
- If the tyres are slick and you keep skidding out of control, ask yourself if you are feeling out of control in your life.
- Constant window fogging might be pointing to something you are not willing to see.

Cards

- Do you feel as if some situation in your life is like a house of cards? This project might be built on a shaky foundation. Rethink it.
- Life is a game and can even be a gamble. Put your attention on the process rather than the end result.
- If the cards are Tarot cards or any other cards being used for fortune telling, then this symbol relates to a sense of fate. The cards hold your future. Whatever specific feelings you have about the cards can be indicative of future trends in your life.

Carpenter

- This might represent building or rebuilding in your life. Is there a situation or relationship that needs rebuilding?
- Are you making repairs in your life? Is this a time of rebuilding physically, emotionally and spiritually?
- This could also be a symbol for Jesus as he was a carpenter.

Castle   (See also *Home*)

- A castle can be a kind of fortress. It can also refer to a magical realm.

Cat

- A cat can represent your deep, intuitive self.
- This might relate to feelings of independence or luxury, grace and power.
- A cat could also represent your feminine essence or the female part of yourself – the goddess within.
- This symbol might also relate to being catty.
- Black cats can be considered very good luck or very bad luck, depending on where you live.

Caterpillar

- The caterpillar represents unharnessed potential of which you are unaware. You can become a butterfly.

Cathedral   (See *Church*)

Cave

- A powerful symbol for the unconscious. A cave can be thought of as an entrance into the subconscious, inner, primordial realms of self. It contains the mysterious depths of humans. Ancient wisdom is stored in the caves of the subconscious.
- Spiritual hermits and renunciants go into ascetic isolation in the cave. It is a place of spiritual retreat, renewal and rebirth. Is this sign telling you to retreat within yourself to gain wisdom and insight?
- In mythology dragons guarded the treasure deep in the cave. A cave can represent your great spiritual wealth.
- Legends are replete with tales of the power within caves. The cave was the residing place of the oracles, the wise woman or man. A crystal cave often represented a powerful level of enlightenment in the depths of the unconscious mind. Retreat into your inner magic.
- A cave may represent the security of the womb as it is literally a cavity in the Mother Earth. It can represent a place of conception and rebirth. This is the time to incubate your direction in life.
- A cave may also represent a refuge from life's difficulties. Sometimes a cave can be a symbol of repressed traumatic memories that are emerging. However you must become like a dragon-slayer and bring these hidden fears to light. Trust yourself. Trust the process that you are guided to take.

Cellar   (See *Basement*)

Cemetery

• Cemeteries usually represent rest, peace and completion, though they might rarely signify a fear of death. They can also represent emerging feelings about someone who is dead. Are there any past issues you need to resolve with someone who has passed on?

Centre

• A centre is a place of community activity where people come together to achieve a common purpose. Do you need to go to the centre of yourself to connect with your purpose? Evaluate what is really important in your life. Go to the centre of the situation.

• In almost every tradition throughout the world, the centre is considered to be the residence of the Creator. Hindu tradition says that God resides in the centre of the cosmos. Some ancient Chinese portray God as being a point at the centre of concentric circles spreading outwards. In Native American tradition the centre of the medicine wheel is always Great Spirit.

• When you go to the centre you are integrating all the parts of yourself and bringing them together within the centre of your being. Leaving the centre is the same as travelling from the inner to the outer, from space to form, from the realm of the timeless to the realm of time. Take time to notice your relationship and feelings towards this sign as it appears in your life. It is an important sign.

Chain

• A chain has many links joined together to create strength. All links must be of equal strength or there will be a point of weakness that creates difficulty for the entire chain. Is there a situation in your life that requires linking together for a common goal?

• Are you feeling chained to a situation or a person? You can change this. The first step is realizing that you do feel chained or restrained. The next step is to take positive action to release yourself from this condition, either by conscious effort on your own, or through therapy.

Chair

• Where you sit in regard to a matter is your position or attitude.

• Often prior to an out-of-body experience one perceives an inner rocking. A rocking chair can indicate an out-of-body experience or a building of psychic energy.

• A rocking chair can also be a subconscious connection to your early childhood if you were rocked in a rocking chair.

Chalice
• The chalice is a powerful sign that points towards that which is sacred and holy. It can represent the holy Grail and the Christ.

Chameleon
• The chameleon represents adaptability, flexibility.
• This symbol might also relate to whimsy. The chameleon is capricious and ever changing.
• The chameleon could represent not showing one's true colours. Do you change like a chameleon to match every person and situation you encounter, rather than acting out your own truth?

Chaos
• If everything around you is in chaos, you may be in a process of renewing your life. In some ancient traditions it was said that the cosmos was created by chaos. A stagnant pond can be made clear again by adding clean spring water, but there will be a period where the water seems more murky and in great chaos. Eventually, however, the old putrid waters are flushed completely out, leaving a crystal-clear spring. Madame Blavatsky, a mystic and philosopher in the late 1800s stated: 'What is primordial chaos but the ether containing within itself all forms and all beings, all seeds of universal creation?'

Chase/Chasing/Being Chased
• What are you running from? What are you afraid to face in your life?
• What are you pursuing? Is it what you really want? Are you taking the steps necessary to overtake and achieve what you truly desire?

Chest
• A chest symbolizes inner treasures, the potential that exists within you. Perhaps they are undiscovered as yet.
• This also might relate to your heart chakra (the emotional centre of love). Is there an area of your life you need to open to love?

Chicken
• When we say someone is 'chicken' we are referring to fear, cowardice, lack of self-esteem or timidity. Are you in a fearful place in your life? Gather your inner resources and ask for assistance from your inner helpers. You are not alone, there are always those in the spirit realm ready and available to help you.
• Counting your chickens before they are hatched means counting on something prematurely. Do you have high expectations for something that may not come to fruition? Take stock and have realistic goals

and expectations.
• When the expression 'hen-pecked' is used it means one is feeling dominated by another person. Are you being bossed around or are you bossing someone else?

Child/Children
• The child can symbolize the child within you that houses those inner aspects of yourself such as playfulness, joy, spontaneity and openness. Very often it is the child part that isn't being acknowledged. Let the inner child within play and have fun in life. If not now, when? This is the time now.
• This sign can also mean that old unresolved issues from childhood are rising to the surface to be resolved. If childhood memories are coming into your mind, even if they are unpleasant, it is an indication that there is an emotional cleansing and re-evaluating of the past occurring within you.
• Are you subconsciously wishing to have children? Very often before a woman becomes pregnant she will begin to see children everywhere, even if consciously she doesn't want children. If you aren't in a place in your life where you want children and begin to see children and especially babies everywhere take extra precautions against pregnancy.

Christ
• Christ can be a powerful sign of the God force within you, unconditional love, forgiveness, healing, or spiritual attunement to higher energies.
• This can also be a sign of sacrifice and martyrdom. Are you sacrificing yourself for others? Do you feel like a martyr in your life? Giving of yourself freely and lovingly benefits all. However, sacrificing yourself usually benefits no one in the long run.

Christmas
• If this sign appears out of season it can mean a celebration of friends and family. It can also mean a spiritual birth. Examine your Christmas associations from the past. Old memories may be surfacing.

Church
• A church can signify faith, hope and love, a sanctuary, spiritual haven, safety, or the temple of the soul.
• It can represent the dogma and restriction of religion.

Cigar/Cigarette
• Examine your emotional response to the cigar or cigarette. If your

associated feeling is relaxation, then take more time in life to relax. If it is anxiety ask yourself what you are substituting for gratifying the basic needs in life. If guilty, is this a sign or an inner admonition to give up smoking?

Circle

• This is a very powerful symbol. It signifies harmony, beauty, balance. It can also mean completeness and wholeness.
• The Native American Sacred Circle of Life is called the great medicine wheel which represents all the never-ending cycles of life. It encompasses death and rebirth, beginnings and endings, the four directions, the four elements of life (air, water, fire and earth) as well as every circle within the world around us.
• Do you feel that you are running in circles without achieving anything? Stop and evaluate what your true priorities are and eliminate anything that isn't essential in your life.
• Are you in a vicious circle? Look at the situation in an entirely new way.

Circus

• Step into your own childlike joy. Laugh. Enjoy yourself in life.
• Is there too much going on in your life? Is your life a real circus?

City

• The perception that you have of the city is usually a reflection of what is occurring within you. What thoughts or feelings do you have of the city? Excitement? Entertainment? Chaos? Business? Commerce? Crime? Pollution? Examine your judgment about the city to see if it relates to something in your life.

Clam

• Clamming up means someone is not talking or can indicate a lack of communication. If you are not communicating your truth, create situations in your life where you feel safe enough to let people know how you feel.
• Are you concerned over something that must be kept secret?

Clay

• Are you ready to mould your life as you want it? Is someone trying to mould you in a way that you are not happy about?

Cliff

• A sign of a cliff can indicate a big change in life. It means taking a risk and going where there aren't any guarantees or certainties. Get

ready to take a leap of faith. Trust that your life is guided.
•   A cliff can indicate a critical time in your life. The cliff is the end of the road. It's time to make a decision.

Climbing

•   Climbing upwards can be a personal ascension in regard to business or a personal goal. It can mean that you are reaching the top of the ladder in your profession.
•   Climbing can be entering into a higher level of consciousness. In Jacob's dream, he climbed upwards to heaven.
•   Climbing upwards can also mean that everything is an uphill battle. Relax and stop every once in a while to enjoy the view.
•   Are you climbing out of a difficult situation?
•   Climbing may have sexual connotations in terms of sexual excitement.
•   Climbing down can be the opposite of ascending. It can also be the exploration of your subconscious.

Clocks

•   Are you tied to time? Do you need to be on time more often? Are you running out of time? Is time passing you by? What is your relationship to time? The mystic has an entirely different perception of time than an ordinary person. The more you reach into your centre and touch the divine within the less you will be bound to the constraints of time.

Closet

•   Are you closeting yourself from self or from others?
•   Are you coming 'out of the closet'? Or are there any skeletons in your closet? Deal with them, so that you can live more honestly and without fear.

Clothes

•   Your clothes are your outer persona and they are your protection from the elements. What is your emotional response to clothes? 'The clothes make the man.' Do your clothes express how you feel about yourself and what you want to present to the world? If not, change them. It's better to have several perfect outfits than an entire closet of clothes that don't honour the way that you perceive yourself.
•   Clothes can also represent the roles that you play in life.

Clouds

•   Clouds are a very powerful signpost. They are one of the easiest and fastest ways to gain signs for your life. Clouds can be powerful purveyors of messages and can provide a beautiful transmission of signs. Watching the clouds can bring direct and clear messages from spirit. As you watch the ever-changing movements of the clouds, symbols and shapes within the clouds will begin to take meaning. Native Americans call the spirits in the clouds the Cloud People. These beings presented messages through their movements in the sky.

• Clear clouds can denote spiritual uplifting. This is a positive, healthy sign associated with inner peace.

• Storm clouds may indicate spiritual questioning. A personal storm is brewing. This can also represent a time of clearing the air and personal purification.

• Do you have your head in the clouds?

Clown

• Laugh at yourself. Be happy, don't worry. Enjoy life.

• Are you clowning around when you should get serious in life?

Cobra

• The cobra can be a powerful symbol of the kundalini energy, which is the life force energy that dwells at the base of the spine. It can indicate transformation and power.

• The cobra can also represent wariness and fear.

Cobwebs

• Cobwebs can mean memories that are hidden away or talents that are unused, 'hidden in the cobwebs of your mind'. Do you feel that a valuable part of you is being unused or lying dormant?

• Are you caught in a web of intrigue? Do you feel that you are caught in someone's web?

Cock

• If someone is 'cocky' they are considered strutting, proud and egotistical. Are you being too cocky? Perhaps it's time to develop a little humility.

• The cock is often used to refer to a male's genitalia, so it is a common symbol of masculine energy or virility.

• Is there a situation in your life that is about to erupt or go off as when a gun is 'cocked?'

• A cock crowing means it's time to wake up. Wake up spiritually. Wake up to life.

• During the Middle Ages cocks were put on weathervanes on church towers representing alertness; waiting to meet the morning sun-Christ even before sunrise.

Cocoon

• A cocoon represents incredible potential awaiting transformation.
• Are you cocooning or separating yourself from others and even from reality? There are times in life when it is important to isolate yourself for renewal and rejuvenation, however sometimes it can be a way of isolating yourself from others or from what you are really feeling.

Coffee

• Coffee can represent stimulation or relaxation. It depends on your personal associations. It can be an adrenal rush to get up and go, or it can be a sign to relax and have a coffee break with friends and family.

Coffin

• A coffin can symbolize completion, the end of a situation, or perhaps death of a relationship.

Coin   (See *Money*)

Cold

• Cold can mean shutting down your feelings and withdrawing inwards. If this is true for you do things that make you feel warm, safe and loving.

Collision

• If you find yourself in a collision or there are collisions around you this can indicate severe inner conflicts or deep unresolved issues in your life. Slow down. Take time to evaluate your life.

Colon

• Is it time for elimination of things from the past?
• Could also be a sign that you need to pay attention to the health of your colon. Maybe this is the time for a colonic cleansing.

Colours   (See also definitions for individual colours in this dictionary)

• Each colour will be a specific signpost for you. In general, red equates with dynamic energy and sexuality, orange is social and fun, yellow is uplifting and communicative, green is healing and abundant, blue relates to peace and spirituality, purple is linked to spiritual wisdom and psychic perceptions, pink is love, black is the unknown and darkness, white is purity and light, gold is illumination and wealth, and silver is related to moonlight and the magical and mystical.

Comet

• A comet is a powerful symbol which heralds tremendous personal and spiritual expansion.

Compass

• What direction do you want to go in life? Are you feeling lost or disorientated? Take time to evaluate where you are by tuning in to your inner knowing.

Conflict

• If you see conflict all around you most likely you have some area of unresolved inner conflict within you, even if you feel calm and balanced on the surface.

Confusion

• Though there can be many reasons for confusion (e.g., eating foods that you are allergic to), it often occurs when there is something in your life that you don't want to look at or confront. If there seems to be confusion all around you, take time to enter into the depths of your soul to see what your truth is.

Constipation

• Are you holding onto things, situations or people in your life that you no longer need? It could also be that a change in diet is indicated.

Convent   (See also *Monastery*)

• A convent can represent going within to touch the divine feminine within yourself.
• It is a sanctuary from worldly life. Take time to be still and simple in your life.
• It can also be a symbol for hiding from yourself by withdrawing. Discover that you can be within your inner place of serenity and yet still be in the world, too.

Cook/Cooking

• A cook can signify nourishment and material comfort.
• This might be a time to synthesize the different elements in your life into something digestible and nourishing for your soul.
• When life is exciting it is said that 'Things are really cooking.'

Corner

• Are you feeling cornered in your life? Check your options. There is always a way out.

Court

• Is there some part of yourself or some situation for which you are judging yourself or another? Every experience that you have ever had (even if you judge it as bad) was valuable because it helped you to evolve and grow as a human being.

Cow

• A cow is universally thought of as a peaceful animal. Are you feeling peaceful or do you need to cultivate more peace in your life?
• Cows can mean patience and passive endurance. Is there something that you are putting up with or patiently enduring?
• In some cultures the cow is identified with the earth, the moon and mothering. Many lunar goddesses wear the horns of a cow on their head. In Hindu belief the cow and the bull represent the regenerating forces of the universe.

Coward

• What are you afraid of not confronting? Face your fears. Even if you are afraid, do it anyway. It takes more energy to avoid that which you fear than to face it head on.

Crab

• Are you scuttling around issues in your life instead of facing them straight on? Are you going sideways around a situation?
• Are you being crabby or in a bad mood?
• The crab is the sign of Cancer in the horoscope. As the crab is one of the symbols of the sea, which is the cradle of all life, Cancer in the horoscope is a life-giving, nurturing sign. Are there any people who have the sign of Cancer astrologically who are important to you? Notice your feelings about the crab to discover the meaning of the Cancer people in your life.

Crack

• A crack can indicate a situation that is about to break through. A chick has to crack the egg in order to hatch.
• A crack can signify a situation that seems sturdy on the surface but actually has some cracks in it. Examine all the circumstances of your life. Is there some area that seems sturdy but actually isn't as strong as it seems?
• This expression can be used when someone is cracking up mentally. Do you feel like you are cracking up?
• This can be an idiomatic expression, 'It really cracks me up,' meaning that it gives you great amusement.

Cradle

• A cradle can signify caring and nurturing. Are you feeling the need to be cradled and cared for?

Crash

• A crash is a powerful symbol that says slow down. Assess your present situation. What do you want out of life? Go forward deliberately and slowly. A car crash can represent your physical body; a boat crash your emotional body, and an aeroplane crash your spiritual body.

Cricket

• The chorus of crickets in the early evening often generates a feeling of domestic joy and a general sense of peace. It can be a very soothing sign.
• In some cultures the cricket symbolizes long life and happiness.
• A cricket can be a homonym for the field game of cricket.

Crisis

• Usually it is in times of crisis that human beings search for meaning in life and turn to their spiritual connections. A crisis can be a crossroads in life. It is a time to say, Who am I? Where am I going in life? What is my spiritual source? It can be a turning point in life.

Critic

• Are you being overly critical of yourself or others? Do you need to be more discerning of situations that you are involved in?

Crocodile

• In ancient Egypt there were two basic meanings for the crocodile. In one interpretation, the crocodile was thought to represent viciousness and fury. However, they also appeared in hieroglyphics showing the dead transformed into crocodiles of knowledge and thus representing power and wisdom.
• Crocodiles can mean trouble or danger beneath the surface. This danger can either be coming from within yourself or from someone else in your life. Look beneath the surface and see what the truth of the situation is.
• A show of false feeling, such as when someone cries crocodile tears can indicate dishonesty or falseness. The expression 'it's a crock' indicates hypocrisy.

Cross

• A cross was a mystic symbol even before the time of Christ. In ancient times it represented a holy balance of opposites, the celestial and the earthly. It was likened to a ladder through which one could reach God.

• In Christianity it is equated with infinite love. It can also symbolize sacrifice and suffering on the cross. The expressions the 'burden of the cross' and 'I have a cross to bear' refer to sacrifice. Are you sacrificing yourself for someone or something? Giving of yourself and your possessions freely increases your energy; sacrificing yourself will lower your energy and will benefit no one ultimately. Are you giving freely or sacrificing?

• The cross was also used to ward off evil. Do you feel the need to protect yourself? Call the angels and call the divine energy within yourself and you will be safe.

Crossroads

• A crossroads signifies a time of decision is ahead. Take time and tune in to your intuition before choosing your future path.

• Jung stated that crossroads were a symbol of mother. He said, 'Where the roads cross and enter into one another, thereby symbolizing the union of opposites, there is "mother," the object and epitome of all union.'

Crow   (See also **Raven**)

• In many cultures the crow is considered a powerful sign. Ancient Chinese thought that the crow signified the isolation of the individual who lives on a superior realm. For some Native Americans the crow had mystic powers and was the creator of the visible world. There was a similar meaning for the Celts, the Germanic tribes and the Siberians. The eye of the crow was thought to be the entrance to the supernatural realms and the inner mysteries of life. The crow was also the bringer of messages from the spirit realm.

Native people consider the crow to be a shape-shifter with the ability to expand into other realms of consciousness. The shape-shifter can be in two places at once and take on other physical forms. The crow dwells beyond the realm of time and space. The crow can merge into the past, present and future and travel in and out of darkness and light. Early alchemists had a similar symbolism associating the crow with the 'initial' state which embodies both matter and spirit.

If this sign appears to you take heed, for the crow is a portent of change in your life. This is a sign to step beyond the usual way that you view reality and look into the inner realms. To do this your integrity must be impeccable. If there are some areas in your life where you are being unethical, change them. Keep your word, speak your truth. Get ready to shape-shift and release your old reality, to embrace a new way of viewing yourself and the world around you. Listen to the messages all around you from the mysterious inner realms.

• In some traditions crows were feared because they were associated with death. This association was because they were black and represented the void and the unknown inner realms. Do you fear your own death and inner darkness? If the crow appears to you as a sign, take time to explore your inner darkness and listen to the ancient wisdom within yourself.

• The crow and raven are of the same genus and in some respects have similar meanings.

• The idiom 'as the crow flies' means travelling in a straight line. Walk your talk. Travel straight forward with clarity and decisiveness in your life.

• To crow can be to exult loudly, as over another's defeat, to boast. It can also mean to articulate sound expressive of pleasure or delight. Do you have something to crow about in your life?

Crowd

• When one is in a crowd there is a sense of anonymity and even secrecy. Is there a part of yourself that you want to keep anonymous?

• Crowds are usually perceived to be filled with strangers. Are you feeling like a stranger in your life?

• Take time to isolate how you might perceive the opinion that the crowd might have of you. This is usually a good indication of the sub-conscious opinion that you have of yourself.

• Sometimes a crowd can indicate feeling a part of something or a cause larger than yourself.

Crown

• A crowning achievement can be a pinnacle of accomplishment. A crown can also indicate inner royalty.

Crucifixion

• This is the ultimate sacrifice. Do you feel that someone is trying to crucify you emotionally? Are you allowing yourself to be crucified? You do not need to suffer in order to grow. Transcend the situation and see it from a higher perspective.

Crutch

• Do you feel unable to support yourself? Do you need support at this time in your life? There is great power in being willing to ask for help, especially if you are the kind of person who has always felt that you have to do everything yourself. Be willing to accept assistance when it is offered.

Crying
- If you are aware of crying all around you, yet you do not feel sad, this may be an indicator that you are subconsciously grieving about something.
- Tears of joy can indicate a resolution of a difficulty or release of an attitude that was not serving you.

Crystal
- A crystal is a transmitter and magnifier. Spiritually it is a powerful symbol signifying clarity, spiritual energy. It is the sign of the mystic. Listen carefully to this symbol.

Cutting
- Depending on the context, this can mean the cutting away of undesired opinions, habits, attitudes and beliefs.
- Cutting can also be a desire to cut away from a person or a situation. It can mean cutting the ties that bind.
- If you are cut and bleeding, you are losing your vital force.
- Cutting can also signify initiation. In tribal tradition often cutting of the body is done to signify initiation into a new rank or into manhood or womanhood.
- When someone is cut down to size they have been reduced in esteem. Are you afraid of being cut down or ridiculed?

Daffodil
- The daffodil is the purveyor of spring which is the time of new beginnings. It can be a sign of new potential, renewal and new life.

Dam
- A dam can be a sign of pent-up emotions about to be released. Is there a situation that is long overdue to be unblocked? Attend to this situation with care soon, or the dam may burst.

Dancing
- This sign depends on the type of dance. If it is a free-form dance or a trance dance the message is to allow spontaneous movement and flow into your life. If it is a very structured dance, such as ballet, be willing to move forward in life but take care to keep form, structure and discipline in place as you go.
- Dancing can also signify extreme joy. It is the dance of life.
- Dancing is often thought to connote sexual enthusiasm and sensuality.

Danger
- If you sense danger around you or find yourself consistently in

dangerous situations, there most likely is a very deep-seated internal conflict that needs attention.

Dark

• The dark can represent the unknown and your subconscious mind.
• The dark is often equated with your fears. It takes more energy to be afraid than it does actually to face your fears.
• Do you have the feeling that you need to shed some light on a situation?
• The womb-like power of the deepest parts of your being. The dark is the Dark Goddess. It is your ancient inner wisdom.
• The dark may represent death or the dark night of the soul. This sign can also be emblematic of depression or gloom. Are you feeling depressed? Get out. Move. Dance. Physically express yourself. Almost always any kind of movement will begin to unsettle depression.

Daughter

• The daughter can be a sign of the feminine-child part of us.
• This sign may refer to your own daughter. Notice the other accompanying signs.

Dawn

• Dawn is a new awakening. It is illumination and seeing the light. Is it time to make a fresh start?

Deaf

• What is that you don't want to hear in life? Is there anything that you are closing your ears to? Open your ears. Open your heart.

Death/Dying

• This is not usually a bad omen. Very rarely does this sign indicate the death of someone you know or your own death. Usually it symbolizes transformation, the death of old patterns and programmes, and making way for rebirth. Make way for new growth in life.
• This sign can also relate to anxiety about your death or the death of another. Remember that your spirit and your essence are eternal. Also, you cannot truly live until you confront and accept your own physical mortality.

Debt

• Is there something you owe or which is owed to you? Take care of all debts whether you owe or are owed. Either way, it blocks your energy flow.

Deep/Depths

• Any kind of depth whether it is a deep well, deep hole in the earth, depth of the sea, or basement can represent your unconscious mind. Notice what you associate with the depths. Is it wisdom, fear or inner power?

Deer

• A deer can represent the gentle aspects of yourself.
• This can also be a sign of feeling victimized and defenceless. Remember there are no victims, only volunteers. Try to find areas in your life where you can take control and make changes. If you identify with the innocent deer, remember too the power of the stag . . . magnificent and forceful.

Defecation   (See *Excrement*)

Delay

• Your timing is off. Change your strategy. It's not the right time. Rethink your plans, or perhaps try again later.

Demon   (See *Devil*)

Desert

• Jesus went to the desert for spiritual rejuvenation. It can be a place of purification, and emotional clarity.
• The desert can also be a sign of desolation. A desert can seem forsaken, barren, a place of no growth. Do you feel that your resources have dried up? Are you feeling isolated and barren? Do you feel deserted in your life? If the desert is a sign of lack for you, then surrounding yourself with water, either by swimming or soaking in bath waters, can begin symbolically to address this inner feeling. Take actions to fill your life with love and abundance once again. Cultivate your garden.

Devil/Demons

• This sign can signal the internal struggle between the part of you that you have labelled as 'good' and that part you have labelled 'bad'. It is important not to reject those things that you judge in yourself, because what you resist persists. Face those parts of yourself that you label as 'bad' or your 'inner demons' as a way to become more integrated.

Diamond

• When coal is under great pressure it creates diamonds. Those areas of your life that seem like pressure in fact may be helping you to achieve the crystal clarity of a diamond.

• A diamond can signify the many facets of your pure being.

Diarrhoea

• Animals (and people) get diarrhoea when frightened. Are there any unresolved areas of fear in your life? Repeat the affirmation to yourself, 'I am at complete peace with all of my life.'

• Diarrhoea can be not assimilating what you need to assimilate in life. Affirm to yourself that you absorb all that you need in life and release the rest.

Dirt/Dirty

• Dirt is connection with the Mother Earth, which is grounding.

• Dirt can also signal that there is something in your life that needs to be cleaned up. If you feel dirty even when you are not this is often an indication that there is something that you feel guilty about. Examine your shame and find ways to heal and accept it.

Disease

• Disease is often a sign of dis–ease or disharmony. However, disease has the healing effect of bringing to the surface deep internal issues. It is important to notice how the disease manifests itself in your body to gain understanding of the messages which the disease has for you. It's also valuable to note your emotions regarding the disease. Often the emotions that you have in regards to the disease are what brought it on in the first place.

• If you are seeing disease all around you, this could be a sign to be careful of your health and take extra precautions. Your subconscious is aware of the onslaught of disease before it actually affects your physical body.

Diving

• Diving is delving into the subconscious, especially regarding emotional issues, as water usually represents emotions.

• This can be a sign of getting in touch with subconscious motivations or fears, or the deep wisdom that dwells within you.

• Diving can also be a sexual symbol, as water can represent the feminine principle and diving is a penetration into this.

Divorce

• Is there a situation or person that you wish to divorce yourself from? Do you have a hidden desire to end a relationship? Are you afraid that your relationship may end in divorce? Do you subconsciously fear that

your partner is considering divorce? Evaluate the situation and decide what actions you want to take to achieve what you most desire.
• Divorce can represent a split within your inner psyche, e.g., between head and heart, or your male and female parts of self.

Doctor

• Perhaps it's time to see a doctor for a check-up.
• A doctor can symbolize your inner healer.

Dog

• A dog is a sign of faithfulness, loyalty, protection and friendship. It is a sign of service and making a contribution to others. Have you been a loyal friend or have you taken for granted someone who was being a loyal friend to you? Have you been loyal to your true mission in life?

Dolphin

• This is a significant symbol. Dolphins are a sign of unharnessed joy, playfulness, spontaneity and even of spiritual enlightenment. They are super-conscious, intelligent beings who have learned to live together in harmony and joy. Do you need to play more and be more joyful in your life?

Donkey

• A donkey is a sign of long forbearing patience. Are you being patient enough with yourself and others? Are you being too patient instead of taking productive action?
• This can also be a sign of stubbornness. Are you being stubborn and not being willing to see the situation from different points of view?

Door

• This is a significant symbol. A door can mean a great opportunity for new adventure and self-discovery. An open door means that you are ready and a closed door that it is not quite time.
• A door can mean that you are entering a new phase of your life.

Dove

• A dove is a sign of peace and love. It is associated with the goddesses of love, Aphrodite and Venus, and thus appears on Valentines.
• Is there someone or something with which you wish to make peace?

Dragon

• This is a powerful symbol. The dragon represents life force and great potency. This is the time to step into your power. Become the power of the dragon.

• Lift up out of the struggle, conquer your fears and become the dragon-slayer. Slaying the dragon can be garnering your inner strength to achieve self-liberation.

• Dragons guard treasure. Is there some fear or power that stands between you and what you most desire?

• The winged dragon is a powerful symbol for transcendence. This sign means ascending to spiritual and mystical heights.

Drowning   (See also *Water*)

• This sign can mean that you are feeling overwhelmed by emotions or subconscious forces, as water usually represents emotions. Is there a situation where you feel that you are unable to keep your head above water?

• Drowning can also be a symbol of death and rebirth, such as baptism.

Drum

• This is a powerful sign of connecting to your inner rhythms. Ancient tribal people felt that drums were holy and alive. The drum carried the powerful pulse of life. To the Native American, the medicine man could travel to the inner spiritual realms on the vibration of the beat, and thus enter into a state of ecstasy.

• Is it time to march to the rhythm of your own drum?

Dust

• Whatever is covered by dust hasn't been used or has been forgotten. Is there something inside you that hasn't been touched or is a forgotten part of yourself?

Duty

• Are you forgetting your duties? Your first duty is to yourself – when you are fulfilled, then you can assist others. Are you fulfilling your duty to yourself?

• Are you feeling guilty about not conforming to external conventional notions of right and wrong?

Dwarf

• Are you feeling dwarfed by a situation? Are you limiting your potential?

• The symbolism for dwarves might come from the classic fairy tale *Snow White*, where the dwarves were her guardians and true friends.

Dynamite

• Dynamite is a sign of an explosive situation that is about to erupt. Take time to defuse any potential disruptive situations.

Eagle

• This is a sign of great significance. To native people around the world the eagle was a symbol of the Creator. The eagle connects you to the Great Sprit above. In ancient Egypt the eagle was the symbol of the day and the full light of the sun, and was therefore considered to be emblematic of illumination. In ancient northern Europe the eagle was associated with the gods of strength, power and war. In many ancient cultures the eagle was a messenger from the heavens. On Roman coins it was the emblem of imperial power. Listen carefully when this sign appears for you; it can signal a time of power and strength in your life.
• An eagle can be a sign of soaring freedom, seeing life from new heights. If you find yourself mired in a situation look at it from a new height.

Ears

• Listen. Take time to 'hear' the signs around you. Be willing to pay attention and hear the truth. Is there something that you are afraid to hear?

Earth

• The Mother Earth is the female, receptive, rejuvenating principle of the universe. The earth can represent the earthy and sensual part of you. Do you need to be more earthy? Do you need to be more grounded? Spend time in your garden. Walk barefoot on the land. Honour the living spirit of the earth.
• The earth can be equated with the physical part of yourself. The earth gives form to spirit.

Earthquake

• This is a sign that great change is approaching. It can be that your very foundations are in the process of being shaken. Are you afraid of the change you are undergoing? Even though sometimes change is uncomfortable it will always bring new experiences and new growth.
• This can also be a sign that a physical earthquake is imminent, especially if you live in earthquake country. Assess your supplies. Are you prepared if an earthquake hits? If not, take appropriate measures.

East

• The east is the place of the rising sun and new beginnings. It can mark a spiritual reawakening.

Echo

• Really listen to what you are saying and what you are projecting out into the universe, because what you put out will come back to you.

Egg

• The egg is a very powerful sign that signals new life and new potential. In numerous ancient traditions the egg represented immortality. In Egyptian hieroglyphs the egg represented great potential and even the container for the mystery of all life. In one Egyptian papyrus illustration an egg was shown floating above a mummy and was thought to signify life forever in the hereafter. If this sign appears to you, you are truly about to step into your potential. It is a time of new beginnings.

Eight   (See also *Numbers*)

• By virtue of its shape this number has been associated with the caduceus, the two intertwined serpents that are the sign of the healer. Also because of its shape, it symbolizes the DNA helix and the spiralling nature of the heavens. In Pythagorean numerology the number eight is the number of the material realm and can signify infinity, self-power, abundance, cosmic consciousness, reward, authority and leadership. In China the number eight is associated with wealth because it rhymes with the word for money in Chinese. This number can signify that through organization, discipline and work you can achieve success in the material world.

Elastic

• Stretch yourself into new areas of life. Be willing to be flexible.

Electricity

• You have bio-electrical systems that surge through you. Electricity can represent the life force. Pay attention to the electrical fields around you, for they will respond to your personal electrical fields. Blown fuses might symbolize that you are blowing your own inner fuses. If this occurs, then take time to rest and renew your self. Weak currents can mean that your life force is weak.

• Often when a person begins a spiritual quest, their personal electrical field will go through a change. This can affect the electrical fields around them. For example light bulbs might blow out, street lights might go off or on, televisions might come on spontaneously and magnetic strips on credit cards might erase. These may all be indications that one's personal bio-electrical field is changing. Once the bio-electrical field has stabilized to the new circuitry then the effect on electrical fields will subside.

Elephant

• The elephant is a sign for power. This can either be gentle, loving power or angry, destructive power. The powerful Hindu elephant god Ganesha was the remover of obstacles. You have all the inner strength and power that you need to remove obstacles from your life.

• It is said that an elephant never forgets. Is there something in your life that needs to be remembered? Or is the elephant a gentle reminder not to forget?

• When someone is thick-skinned it means that they are slow to take offence at the small irritations in life. The thick-skinned elephant is a reminder to let things roll off your back. Life is too short to be concerned with petty matters. Or perhaps you need to be more sensitive, to your own feelings and those of the people you care about.

Elevator   (See *Climbing*)

Elf

• The elf is a sign to be more mischievous in life. Take time to be madcap and impish and childlike. Have fun. Enjoy yourself and your own inner magic.

Elk

• The elk is a sign of power, beauty, stamina and dignity. Elk have the power of pushing through obstacles. When a deer goes through the forest it will delicately go around things in its path, whereas an elk will crash through them. If you have an obstacle in your life that is creating a difficulty, the elk sign is saying just power through it.

Emerald

• Emerald can be a sign of the magnificent healing power within you. Emerald was used for its healing properties in many cultures. It was used by the ancient Egyptians and has also been called the jewel of Venus and of love. It can also represent the magic within you. Just as Dorothy entered the Emerald City looking for the Wizard of Oz, it can be a sign for you to enter into your own inner magic.

Emotions

• Whatever emotions you perceive in the people around you are usually a reflection of your own inner emotional state. If you are aware of an array of sad people in your life (even if you are not consciously feeling sad), this is a good indication that you are repressing inner sadness. If everyone around you seems angry, even if you think you feel calm, look within to see if perhaps you have some unresolved anger. Conversely if everyone around you seems happy and balanced, even if your surface emotions are a bit wobbly, most likely your inner emotional state is healthy and happy.

Empty

• Simplify your life. Empty yourself of your concepts, patterns, and ideals. Often one has to become empty to become fulfilled. Being empty is potential waiting to be filled.

• Are you feeling empty and alone as if there is nothing left inside you? Take time to replenish yourself. Be caring and nurturing towards yourself. Do those things that give you the greatest joy.

Enemy

• This can be a sign that there is an interior war going on inside you. Reconcile with those parts of yourself that you have denied or disowned.

Eruption

• This can be a sign of a situation or person that is about to erupt or explode. This eruption can be healing as it lets the pressure off the situation. Give your emotions free rein as otherwise they will build up and create great difficulty for you.

Escalator   (See also *Climbing*)

• This can be a sign of changing levels of consciousness.

Escape

• This sign can have two seemingly opposite meanings. Notice your emotional response to the sign to understand which is accurate for you:

• Quit trying to escape the situation facing you. Face it head on and confront the problem.

• Alternatively, sometimes escaping can be liberating. If you have tried every avenue to resolve the problem, then escape is sometimes the best plan. Quit trying to no avail and just walk away from the difficulty. However, instead of escaping (which is running away from something) change the context in which you see the situation so that you feel that you are going towards something instead of escaping from something you fear.

Exam/Examination

• Self-examination. It is valuable periodically to examine your life, noticing recurring problems and patterns, and examining the direction you choose for your future. Is this sign telling you that this is the time for self-examination?

• Are you being tested in life?

• Do you feel that you need to prove yourself to others? Do you have a fear of failure? Do you feel that you are being evaluated by an outside source? Trust yourself. Set your own standards, and know the peace of mind that comes from living by them.

Excrement

• This can be a sign of needing to release or expel the waste products of your life such as quilt, resentment, and shame.
• Is there something poisoning you from within?
• Is someone treating you poorly?
• This can also be a sign of something (within yourself or reflected in others) that you disapprove of or despise.

Exile

• This can be a sign that you feel cut off from people or situations or even yourself.

Explosion   (See also *Eruption*)

• Personal crisis, particularly in regard to a relationship.

Eyes

• Being willing to see with clarity and truth. Is there something in your life that you do not want to see?
• Eyes are called the 'window to the soul'. The third eye is thought to be your connection to the spiritual realms.
• Is someone the 'apple of your eye'?
• 'Eye' can refer to the ego 'I'. It can symbolize the subjective way you view the world around you.

Face/Faces

• What do you need to face in your life? Is it time to face up to a situation?
• Are you 'two-faced', or is someone being dishonest with you? Take actions to clear up the duplicity, so that you can live with clarity and honesty.

Failure

• Constantly being aware of failures, such as power failures, bank failures, etc. can signify that perhaps you are feeling like a failure. Reassess your life. Something viewed as a failure from one point of view can be viewed as a success from another vantage point. Failures can also be turning points in our lives, where we abandon a strategy or course of action which was not right for us in favour of something much better.

Fairy

• A fairy can be a sign of the inner magic inside you. Fairies are also spirits of nature and can be a sign to access your inner mysteries through the realm of nature.

Fall/Falling

• In the process of learning to walk, we often fall. If you are on unsure ground in a situation or you are in a personal growth spurt and unsure of yourself, there will be signs of falling. Being willing to risk trying something new or walking on new ground can help you succeed. Often we have to risk and fail before we can succeed. Be willing to take some risks in your life.

• Falling can be a sign of feeling a loss of control, or feeling out of control in your life. If this is so for you then find, and own, at least one area of your life where you do feel in control. This can help you begin to gain control of other parts of your life.

• 'Falling in love', 'falling on your face', a 'fallen woman', are all expressions we have in our language. Do any of these expressions seem to relate to the sign that you were given?

• Fall is also the autumn time of year. In this regard, fall can be a sign of completion.

Fast

• Are you going too fast and feeling out of control? Slow down, smell the daisies.

• Being in the 'fast lane' means living life at an accelerated pace. Are you happy with the current pace of your life, or is it time to shift gears and go at a slower pace.

• Fast can be a sign that it is time to fast for purification and cleansing.

Fat

• This sign can mean abundance; for example 'living on the fat of the land', or the 'fatted calf', or he had a 'fat' wallet.

• Fat can also be a sign of inactivity, of overeating or suppression of emotions and feelings. To find the significance for you, observe your emotional response to the various meanings. The meaning that you have the strongest response to is very likely what the sign means for you.

Father

• This sign can mean God; the Divine Father.

• It can be a sign of a protector or provider. Do you need to father or protect yourself?

• This can be a sign that pertains to your own fathering skills or your biological father, or even a father image. Check the other surrounding signs.

Fear/Foreboding

• If there are many people around you feeling or expressing fear, there is a high likelihood that there is repressed fear within you ready to be released, even if you are not consciously feeling afraid. If anything is fearful in your life, face it. It is most likely a representation of an un-acknowledged part of yourself.

• If you feel foreboding, maybe your intuition is trying to tell you something. Listen, and act accordingly!

Feather

• In many native traditions feathers are thought to be the connection between man and the supreme being. They symbolize the flight to spirit and to the heavens above. The feathers on the headdress worn by a Native American connected the wearer with Great Spirit. To the ancient Egyptians feathers represented the winds and the creator gods, Ptah, Hathor, Osiris and Amon. In Christianity, St Gregory states that feathers symbolize faith and contemplation and a quill signifies the Word. Finding a feather can signify an important message from the Creator.

• This can be a sign of something soft or light as a feather. Enter into the receptive state of softness.

• When you have a 'feather in your cap' this means a job well done. You can congratulate yourself. You have done well.

Feet/Foot

• Feet are your connection with the earth, your grounding connection. Jung says that feet are man's direct association with the reality of the earth. If you are not feeling grounded and centred, spend time walking barefoot on the earth. Very often this will help you become more grounded.

• Are you afraid of stepping forward in life? Perhaps it is time to put your best foot forward and take a stand in life.

• Feet can symbolize your under-standing in life.

• Are you feeling awkward? Have you put your foot in your mouth?

• Feet can represent a new direction in life.

• Washing feet can connote worship and healing, such as sitting at the feet of the master.

Female

• The female energy is the feminine principle within us all. It symbolizes the inner states of receptivity and nurturing that dwell in both men and women.

Fence

• Do you feel fenced in? Know that most situations where you feel fenced in are self-created. View the situation from a higher perspective and know that you can change it, or at least the way you experience the circumstances that you are presently in.
• Do you need boundaries in life? Be clear on what you will do and will not do and stick to it.
• Wild animals are placed behind fences. Do you feel that the primal energy inside you is being fenced or contained?
• Have you been 'sitting on a fence' in your life? It's time to make up your mind and take a stand. Do it now!

Fight/Fighting

• This is usually a sign of inner conflict. If fights are occurring around you, examine your inner emotional life to see if there are conflicting, unresolved issues within you.
• This can also be a sign of suppressed emotions. Be willing to have and enjoy all your emotions, including your anger. They are a part of life. Repressed anger can cause physical problems.
• Are you willing to fight for what you believe in? There are times in life to be patient and understanding and there are times when it is appropriate to fight. Is this the time for you to fight?
• This can be a sign that there is an inner conflict between what you want to do and what you think you should do, or a conflict between societal morals and your individual needs, or what your inner child wants to do and what your inner adult knows is best. It's time for you to discover which is the right path for you and to follow it with your entire heart and soul.

Fingers

• Individual fingers have definite meanings, especially depending upon your culture, as different cultures assign different meanings to the fingers. In Western cultures, the ring finger often represents marriage and relationships. The middle finger can signify anger or can be a phallic symbol. The thumb can mean everything is okay.
• Pointing a finger at something can be a pointing of blame. Is someone pointing their finger at you? Are you pointing the blame at someone?

Fire

• Fire is a sign of the incredible life force within you. It can signal

potency, power and psychic energy. 'All fired up' means being filled with energy and ready to go forward.
• Since the beginning of time fire has been associated with initiation and opening to spiritual communication and energy. In many traditions initiates went through a symbolic purification by fire, because fire represented the transcendent state between man and spirit. The alchemists in Europe talked about fire as being an 'agent of transmutation' since they felt all things sprang forth and returned to fire.
• Fire can be a sign of your sexual passion such as when one is 'ablaze with passion', or 'burning with desire'.
• 'Hot with anger', and 'fiery words', signify extreme anger.

Fish

• Fish have traditionally been a spiritual symbol of Christianity. Christ was the 'fisher of men'. Fish, in a spiritual sense, can represent spiritual food, renewal, and rebirth.
• As fish travel within watery realms which usually represent emotions or consciousness, they have been associated with psychic realizations from the deepest level of subconscious emotions.
• To the ancient Babylonians, Phoenicians, Assyrians and Chinese, fish were associated with spiritual fecundity because of the large number of eggs that they produced. Fish were a fertility symbol.
• Are you feeling passionless or as cold as a fish?
• A fish may be a desire for acknowledgment or compliments; e.g. 'fishing for compliments'.
• Are you acting like a 'big fish in a small pool'?
• Does something seem 'fishy' to you or is it a 'red herring'?
• The fish is also associated with the horoscope sign of Pisces which is a sensitive, receptive and intuitive sign. Pisceans swim in the mystical realm of dreams and spirituality. Is there an important Piscean in your life now or in the past? This sign may be giving you information about that relationship.

Flame   (See also Fire)

• This can be a sign of your own eternal bright flame and the light of spirit.

Floating

• Floating can have many seemingly opposing meanings. Monitor your emotions to see which meaning applies to you:
• Floating can be a sign of liberation and letting go of problems and restrictions.
• Emotionally floating above a situation can be a way of removing yourself from a traumatic experience. Sometimes people report that

during times of trauma they feel like they are floating above it all.
• Floating can mean that you are in harmony with your intuition and your emotions. There is spiritual alignment within you and you are moving towards feeling at one with all things.
• Floating in water can mean allowing emotions to surface. Floating in air may mean you are above it all.
• Floating can mean that you are feeling directionless in life, like you are just floating. Ground yourself. Assess personal goals and take action.

Flood   (See also *Water*)
• A flood can be a sign that you have overwhelming emotions. Take time to 'dry out'. Divide your feelings of overwhelm into smaller parts, and prioritize. Tackle each task one at a time.

Floor
• The floor is your foundation or your support. Notice the particularities of the floor to discover the meaning of this sign for you. For example, is the floor so slippery that you don't feel safe to move quickly on it. This could signify that you don't feel like you can strive forward in life without substantial caution.
• Being 'floored' is be stunned or overwhelmed.

Flowers
• Flowers are usually a happy omen of beauty and unfoldment. Individual flowers have individual meanings. For example, roses can symbolize love and romance, daisies can be a sign of freshness and innocence.
• Sometimes flowers can signify a funeral.

Flying
• Usually a very good sign. Flying can be a sign of liberty and freedom and moving beyond the bounds of physical limitation. It can also be flying above a situation. Get ready to soar in your life.
• Are you up in the air about a decision?

Fog   (See also *Water* and *Air*)
• Fog can be a sign of emotional or mental confusion, either emotions or thoughts getting in the way of seeing clearly.
• Fog can be a sign that there is an area of your life or an obstacle that you can't quite see.
• Fog may also represent your unconscious mind.
• In many mystical traditions magic occurs in the fog and the mists. The fog is the realm of the fairies, the magicians, and mystics. This can be a sign to unite you with the deep magic that dwells inside you.

Food

• In general, food represents nourishment; this can be spiritual, mental, physical or emotional. Different foods have different meanings. For example, a rare steak has a much different meaning than a red, shiny apple. In addition food often has powerful memories associated with it. If your mother forced you to eat liver as a child, liver may represent revulsion to you. But if you wanted to become a football player when you were in school, and you ate liver thinking that it would make you stronger, then liver would represent strength to you. When regarding a particular food, notice the emotions and memories associated with it to find the meaning for you.

Foot (See *Feet*)

Forest

• The forest holds an important position in myths, legends and fairy tales. It is often connected with the female principle and the Great Mother.
• The forest can be a sign of abundance, growth and strength, for it is where vegetation thrives in bounty without cultivation.
• The forest can be seen as a place of protection, refuge and safety. Do you feel the need for refuge in your life? Take time to withdraw into yourself to re-evaluate who and where you are in life.
• Are you feeling overwhelmed as if you can't see the forest for the trees? Step back from the situation, or get another's perspective. Sometimes this helps put some distance between you and the matter so you can see more clearly.

Forgetting/Forgotten

• Forgetting usually means you are preoccupied with something else. Be still to locate what's really going on beneath your surface.
• This can be a sign of feeling forgotten and/or left out. If you often feel forgotten, affirm to yourself, 'I'm where the party is!' thus signifying that wherever you are is exciting and wonderful. Form often follows intention. Intend to be at the centre of everything and so it can be!

Fork

• If signs keep indicating cutlery forks to you, it could mean that you have reached a fork in the road of your life and are confronting a choice. You will have to make a decision.

Fountain

• This is an absolutely excellent symbol of intuition, free-flowing

emotions and spiritual rejuvenation if the fountain water is crystal clear. It is your spiritual wellspring.
• A fountain can be a sign of the fountain of youth.

Four   (See also *Numbers*)
• In many ancient cultures the number four represents the entire universe. Four is a number of wholeness. The Native American medicine wheel is based on the four elements (air, water, fire and earth) and the four cardinal directions. A cross with four directions is a pre-Christian symbol of totality.
• Four can be a sign of the four quadrants of your being: mental, emotional, physical and spiritual. If four continues to appear to you it is a sign that you are balancing all aspects of yourself.
• Are you for something or against it?

Fox
• In nature the fox has the ability to be unseen, to travel undetected. Foxes are known for their slyness, cunning and swift decisiveness. Are you outfoxing a situation? Is someone outfoxing you?
• This sign can concern physical attraction, as when someone attractive (usually a woman) is called a fox.

Frog
• A frog can be a sign of stillness, patience and focus. The frog sits seemingly completely still, waiting in patience for the fly. When one comes into sight, it has absolute, direct focus in attaining it.
• Many ancient rites associate the frog with the moon and also with rites to invoke rain. In Egypt the frogs that lined the Nile a few days before it flowed over its banks were regarded as symbols of fertility. Frog gods were placed on mummies. Madame Blavatsky, a mystic and philosopher, said the frog symbolized creation and resurrection because it lived in both water and on land, and because it would disappear in the autumn and reappear again in the spring.
• This may be a sign of inconsistency; hopping from one thing to another.
• In some cultures the frog is a sign of purification and cleansing. The Mayan and Aztec shamans sprayed water out of their mouths over those who were sick while thinking about frog energy.
• The frog sign may reflect a desire to find your shining prince, as the princess kisses the frog and it is transformed into a prince. This can be a sign of transformation and finding the beauty behind surface ugliness.

Frozen   (See also *Water*)
• This can be a sign of emotionally closing yourself off, or of frozen

emotions. Take a risk; share with others how you are really feeling.

Fruit
• This can be a sign of reaping the rewards of your labour, or of a fruitful harvest. If the fruit is healthy, your projects will bear fruit.

Galaxy (See also *Stars*)
• This is a sign of the expansive part of yourself. Reach for the stars. Unlimited possibilities are available to you now!

Gallbladder
• Gall can be a sign of anger or a sign of gumption; hence, the expression, 'He had a lot of gall.'

Garbage
• This can be a sign of those things you no longer need in your life or of something you need to release.

Garden
• A garden can be a sign of beauty and peace as well as creative activity. Various aspects of yourself are represented by the different plants in the garden.
• This can be a sign of aspects of your personality that are being cultivated.
• If the garden is well tended, this is a sign of harvesting the results of your labour.
• If the garden has weeds, there are things in your life you need to weed out.

Gas
• Are you running out of fuel in your life and feeling tired? Take time to recharge.
• Do you need to change your eating habits so that you digest your food and don't get gas?

Gate/Gateway
• A gate is an entrance between one realm and another. It can symbolize new opportunities.
• This sign can also symbolize the gates of heaven.

Genitals
• Are you feeling potent, powerful and sexual or are you feeling impotent in your life?
• This sign can also have negative connotations: for example, 'He was

a real dick,' or 'He was acting like a prick.'

Germ

- A germ is the earliest form of an organism whether it is a seed, bud or spore. It is also something that may serve as the basis of an idea, or of further growth or development. Is a germ of an idea beginning to form within you?
- This can be a sign that it's time to boost your immune system.

Geyser   (See also *Water*)

- This is a sign of a great release of emotional energy.

Ghost

- Is there some part of your feelings about a particular person which has not solidified?
- Do you have a hazy or unclear perception of yourself or others?
- This may be a sign of an undelivered communication with someone who has died. Take time to communicate with that individual; even if they are dead, they can hear you.
- This may be a sign that there is a ghost in your vicinity. Remember, it's important to have compassion for rather than fear of ghosts. Be matter-of-fact, but loving with ghosts, and kindly direct them to the Light.

Gift

- Accept the gifts that life has to offer. A gift is given to acknowledge you and the growth you have made. It is just as holy truly to receive as to give, for when you receive gifts with a completely open heart you are allowing another to experience the joy of giving.

Giraffe

- This can be a sign of stretching for what you want.
- Do you want to stand out from the crowd? Or do you feel like you stick out when you would rather fit in? Accept yourself and your own unique qualities.

Glacier   (See also *Water*)

- This can be a sign of frozen emotions.

Glass / Glasses

- Glass can be a sign of seeing from one realm to another. If the glass is broken, this can be a sign of a shattered illusion.
- The meaning for this sign can also be that you need to check with an optician if you need glasses.

Glider

- A glider can be a sign of gliding on the winds of change in life and going with the flow.

Glove

- Gloves protect you from the elements, as well as shielding you from contact with others. Are you isolating yourself too much from others? Or do you need to protect yourself more for health and safety reasons?
- This can be a sign that you really need to get down to work. Take off the gloves and go for it!

Glue

- This can be a sign of your stick-to-it-ness. Stick to your guns. You can do it!
- Glue is the connector between separate ideas or objects.
- 'Coming unglued' is losing your composure. Does your life feel like it is coming unglued? Do you come unglued easily? Affirm to yourself, 'I stick to my goals and dreams in life.'

Gnaw

- What is gnawing away at you? It might be easily dismissed as something small, but it is nevertheless bothering you. If you take care of the small things, the big things will be much easier.

Goat

- In Western culture a goat can refer to a lecherous, old, cranky man. Are you or someone you know acting like a goat?
- Are you feeling blamed or made the scapegoat for something you haven't done?
- The goat is the animal associated with the horoscope sign Capricorn. Those born under the sign of Capricorn are often single-minded, determined and sometimes solitary in their pursuits. Are there any Capricorns in your current or past life that need your attention?

God / Goddess

- This sign is obviously an omen of incredible unity and oneness, universal love, and total self-acceptance in that moment.
- For some who have been raised in a strict religious upbringing this can be a sign of admonishment from the heavens, particularly if you are involved in something about which you feel guilty.

Gold

- This is a very good sign. Gold is a symbol of the sun, representing spirit and life. In Hindu doctrine, gold is called 'mineral light'. The

Latin word for gold is the same as the Hebrew word for light. Gold is often associated with the golden light of inner peace.
• Gold can also be a sign of elusive treasure such as the gold at the end of the rainbow.
• When someone has a heart of gold, they truly embody goodness.

Goose

• Similar to the duck and the swan, the goose is associated with the Great Mother and the goose is often found in fairy tales in this regard.
• A goose can be a prod in the rear. Do you want someone or something to get going?
• A goose can also represent acting foolishly, as in a 'silly goose'.

Grain/Grains

• A grain has the potential for life, as it is a one-seeded fruit of a cereal grass having the potential for the entire plant within its walls.
• This can also be a sign of abundance. Cereal grasses, after having been harvested, are called grains. These grains are considered the staff of life as they are turned into bread and sustenance.
• A grain can also be a relatively small particulate or crystalline mass, a small amount or the smallest amount possible. Are you getting to the inner grain of an idea or concept? Is this the time in your life to reduce the form in your life to its smallest base components?
• Grain is also direction, or pattern, as in the fibrous tissue of wood. Are you going with the grain in your life? Are you involved in a situation that goes against the grain?
• Is there something in your life that you should have reservations about or take with a grain of salt?

Grandfather

• Grandfather is a sign of the wise old man. It is that mature aspect of yourself.
• To the American Indian, Grandfather was an honorific name for the sun and the Above Beings.
• This sign can refer to your own grandfather or your own grandfathering skills.

Grandmother

• Grandmother is a sign of the wise old woman. It is that wise, mature aspect of yourself.
• To Native Americans Grandmother Earth was the loving name given to the conscious, living earth.
• This sign can refer to your own grandmother or your own grandmothering skills.

Grasshopper

• In the parable of the grasshopper and the ant, the grasshopper symbolizes living for the moment and having fun at the expense of not preparing for the future. Does this have a parallel in your life?

Grave

• This sign may represent death and rebirth. Remember whenever something dies it makes way for new growth. This can also be a sign of self-imposed limitations. For example, the expression 'digging your own grave' means you have created your own demise.

• Grave can also mean being serious. Are you being too serious in life? Do you need to become more serious?

Green

• Green universally represents the fertility and abundance of nature. In the spring, new growth sprouts are green and this colour signifies new growth in your personal development. It is also the colour of healing.

Grey

• Grey is usually a sign that you are feeling lifeless and tired and have an unclear state of mind. Perhaps it's time to participate in activities that are rejuvenating.

• Grey is also the colour of neutrality. Do you need to be more neutral in your observations of life? Have you been lingering too long in the grey area? Is it time to take a stand and be decisive?

Greyhound

• This is a sign for speed and swiftness. Is there a situation in your life where you need to act with great speed?

Guilt

• If you find yourself surrounded by people who are always feeling guilty, you might want to ask yourself, 'What am I not taking responsibility for in my life?' Guilt can be a way to deny responsibility. If you have wronged someone, make reparations to them. After you accept responsibility for your actions, and have done what you could to repair the past, remember to go lightly on yourself, and to say 'So what!' If your guilt comes from a feeling of unworthiness, remember that every situation that you have been through allowed you to learn and to grow, and isn't good or bad except that you deem it so.

Gun

• This can symbolize feeling a need for protection or self-defence.

• Traditional therapists equate the gun as a sexual symbol representing the penis.

Guru

• The guru is giving you guidance. It can be your inner teacher.

Hair

• Hair can symbolize our identity and the meaning of this sign will depend on the form the hair takes. For example, brushing your hair can symbolize getting the tangles out of a situation. Cutting your hair can signify new beginnings. Putting gel or brilliantine on your hair can indicate smoothing a situation.

• Hair traditionally can symbolize strength or losing your strength, e.g., Samson and his hair. A full head of hair can represent potency, energy and strength. Hair falling out can indicate that you are worried or losing strength.

• Hair, because it grows out of the top of the head (which is the energy centre that connects us to spirit) can symbolize spiritual power flowing out and connecting you to the cosmos. The Hindus said that hairs symbolized the lines of force of the universe.

Halo

• A halo is a visual manifestation of the energy field around angels and holy people. This sign signifies a blessing and connects you to your inner, divine self.

Ham

• 'Ham it up.' Enjoy life fully.

• Are you being a 'ham'? If so, are you doing it out of discomfort with yourself or a situation?

Hand

• Your hands express your state of being. A raised hand can indicate attention. A hand on the chest can indicate love, two hands together can connote union, a hand in a fist can mean anger or strength, an open hand can be a sign of being open-handed, open to life, and honest, with nothing to hide. Closed-handed can mean closing yourself off to opportunities and to life.

• Negative connotations of a hand are: 'I can't get a handle on it,' 'I can't handle it,' or 'I can't grasp it.' Are you having a hard time getting a handle on life? Remember that you have the inner resources to handle the situation whatever it is.

• In Egyptian hieroglyphs the hand represented action and manifestation. In Colombian America the hand was a symbol of a magnetic

radiant force. In the Islamic religion an image of a hand was used as an amulet. In some cultures an eye in the middle of a hand is the sign of the clairvoyant. The sign of a hand can be telling you to harness your intuitive energy for manifestation and creation.
• A right hand will usually represent the logical, rational, projecting side of your being, while the left hand represents the subjective, receptive, intuitive part of your being.
• Are you willing to reach out to others?
• Do you need to wash your hands of a situation?

Hare

• In the fable 'The Rabbit and the Hare', the hare lost the race because of overconfidence. Are you being overconfident? This can lead to trouble, so don't forget to attend to the details, take precautionary measures and look before you leap.

Hatred

• If you experience hatred all around you, examine what it is about yourself that you hate. Almost always, hatred is self-loathing projected onto something or someone else. The person or thing that you think you hate represents that part of yourself with which you are angry. Often it is difficult to own up to one's own hatred, so it is projected outwards and reflected back by others. If hatred surrounds you, it is essential to do intensive self-examination.

Hawk

• In ancient Egypt, the hawk was the symbol of the soul. The hawk was a symbol of victory to the Egyptians, as well as in other ancient traditions, because the hawk swoops down on its prey with ferocity and power. Is this sign telling you to be swift and powerful in your pursuit of your goals?
• The hawk can also be telling you to view your life from a higher perspective. From your expanded vantage point you may be able to see possibilities that you are normally unaware of.

Head

• The head can be a symbol of getting ahead.
• The head is also associated with the intellect. Are you making headway in your life? Are you taking the time that is needed really to think and analyze the situation?

Heal/Healer

• You are being healed. Access the healing energy within yourself.
• Is this the time to see a healer?

Heart

• The heart is a sign of love and bliss. It is called the centre of true love and is thought to represent our emotions. The only organ left in the mummy of the ancient Egyptians was the heart because it was considered indispensable to the person for their journey into infinity. The expressions, 'He stole my heart,' 'My heart wasn't in it,' and 'She broke my heart,' all signify the symbolic significance of the heart to our emotions. Do you need to open your heart to life and to love? Your willingness to love deeply and fully is directly proportionate to your ability to be loved deeply.

Heat

• Heat is a sign of passion and intensity, as in the expression, 'She was in heat.' Is it time in your life to give full range to your passion?

• Heat can also be a sign of anger, such as when someone is in a heated argument. Are you responding to difficulties with anger instead of searching for the inner causes of the difficulties? Go to the source of the blockage to dissolve it instead of wasting valuable energy being angry.

Heaven

• This is a wonderful sign of enlightenment, bliss, oneness, and peace.

Heavy

• What is weighing you down? Are you feeling burdened in your life?

Heel

• A heel can symbolize a cad. 'He was a real heel.' Is someone 'being a heel' to you?

• To heel can be to come to attention, pay attention, or to submit to another's authority. Are you being commanded to walk or to be a certain way?

• Heel can also be a homophone for heal. Is there something in your life that you need to heal?

Hell

• This can be a sign of personal difficulties you are going through. There is always a way out. Try looking at the situation from a different perspective.

Hen

• This is a sign of the domestic, nesting instinct. This could be a good time to make your home a comfortable, warm sanctuary.

•   This can also signify feeling plump and satisfied.

Hide/Hiding

•   What are you hiding from in life? What don't you want anyone to know about you? Things that you have secreted away inside yourself can dramatically diminish your energy. Usually the things that we want to hide about ourselves when brought out into the light aren't as bad as we thought.

•   An animal's hide can be a homonym for hiding in your life.

Hills

•   Rounded hills can signify female sensuality and the breast like mounds of Mother Earth. This could be a sign to step into your sensuality.

•   This could also be a sign of some small issue that seems big. Are you making a mountain out of a molehill?

Hippopotamus

•   In ancient Egypt the hippopotamus represents the mother principle in the form of the goddess Taueret who attends all births. In nature the mother hippo gives birth in the water. She is careful to choose a safe place so that dangerous currents won't carry the newborn hippo away. The hippo can be a sign to understand and embrace your own birth. Sometimes current problems come from difficult births. If the hippo is a continual sign for you, consider taking time to re-examine the circumstances of your birth to heal and forgive any residual memories or traumas.

•   The hippo can be a sign of something weighty and ponderous in your life.

Hips

•   This can be a sign of support and power. Is there a project that you really need to throw your hip into?

•   This can also be a sign of celebration. 'Hip, hip hooray!'

•   If the hip is immobilized or damaged ask yourself if you have a fear of moving forward.

Hog

•   The hog can be a sign of over-indulgence.

•   This can be a sign of selfishness. Do you feel that you are not getting your share or not giving your share? 'He was hogging the toy.'

•   This can be a sign of being unclean or impure.

•   In nature hogs are intelligent and powerful, yet humans have given hogs a negative connotation. Is there something in your life that is positive and valuable that other people have defined as undesirable?

Hole

• This is an important sign. A hole might be pointing to a dark hole within yourself that you are not acknowledging or facing. However, a hole can also signify the opening between one realm and another. Hence the worldwide worship of perforated stones or stones with holes in them. A hole can signify the passageway from form to spirit. Many initiation ceremonies are held in holes. Examine other signs to decipher the meaning of this sign.
• Is there a hole in your argument?
• Is there something in your life that needs repair?
• Hole is a homophone signifying being whole or wholeness or holy.

Holy

• This is a sign of that which is holy, sacred or divine within you and life. This is a sign of the God Force within you.

Home/House

• The most common symbolism for a house is one's physical self, spiritual self, or both. Whatever you perceive is happening to the house is often a reflection of your life. For example, if the plumbing is clogged, it may be that your emotions (symbolized by the obstructed water in the pipes) are blocked.
• The different rooms in the house can symbolize different aspects of yourself. For example, the kitchen might represent nourishment, sustenance, or creativity, as in 'cooking' up ideas. The hallway is a transition area. A bathroom might be elimination of the old and purification. The basement might represent your subconscious, and the attic your superconscious. Clutter in a house can represent areas of your life that you need to clean up or things that need to be discarded.

Honey

• In mythology honey was the food of the gods and thus came to symbolize the life force in all things. 'The land of milk and honey.'
• This can be a sign pertaining to the sweetness in life or someone or something that you love.

Hook

• This can be a sign of getting hooked by someone or something. Take time to evaluate. Is this really what you want?
• A sign for someone who is feared or dishonest, e.g., Captain Hook. Is there someone who is being dishonest with you? Be careful.
• A hook for hanging things can indicate organization. Hang it up. Get organized.

Horn/Horns

• Jung stated that the horn was a symbol with two meanings. Though horned animals and horns are often associated with virility and male sexuality, the horn itself is shaped like a receptacle and therefore can also be feminine in nature.

• In ancient times the horn was carved into a cup and thus in China was one of the common emblems for abundance in all things such as the cornucopia, the horn of plenty. Ancient Gnostics said the horn represented the 'principle which bestows maturity and beauty on all things.'

• In some cultures horned animals psychologically represented evil, i.e. 'the horned one'. Horns can represent the destructive forces within one's psyche.

• Horns can symbolize the power of music and the celestial horns of heaven.

• In some cultures horns were used as a warning. They were also used to call the forces for the Holy War. This sign might be cautioning you to take care. Be alert.

Horse

• A stallion can symbolize power and male sexuality.

• A galloping horse can represent ecstasy, wild freedom and movement. You can go where you want to go. You are free. Express yourself freely.

• If the horse is tethered, are you feeling that something is tying you down, restricting your freedom?

• A horse can be a sign of gentle grace and beauty.

• Accept the gifts that come your way. 'Don't look a gift-horse in the mouth.'

• The Native American shamans said the spirit of the horse enabled them to travel to the inner realms. Before the horse reached the Americas travel was burdensome. However, with the advent of the horse they became free and could travel easily. You too are free to travel to the inner realms to find and express your power and wisdom.

Hospital

• Consider getting a check-up and evaluating your health. Are you taking care of your body? Is there anything that you can do to give strength and health to your body?

Hummingbird

• Are you being too busy and frantic in life? Is it time to slow down and relax?

• Hummingbirds represent the absolute energy and joy in delving into the nectar in life. They can fly upwards, downwards, and even backwards. Expand your joyous energy in all directions.

Hunt

• To hunt is to look for unknown parts of yourself. What are you looking for in life? Do you feel hunted? What are you pursuing? Is there something that you desire to kill in yourself?

Hyena

• This is a sign of noise and merriment out of proportion or perhaps not appropriate to the situation. Are you or someone you know acting like a hyena?
• In nature hyenas are ferocious and have a very powerful jaw. Is this the time to activate your power and ferocity?

Ice   (See also Water)

• Ice can be a sign of frozen emotions. Express yourself and all your emotions. Communicate from your heart openly and freely.
• On thin ice means a dubious circumstance. See if there is some area in your life that seems solid but perhaps is precarious.
• Slipping on ice is being in a circumstance where you don't feel on stable ground or where you are unsure of yourself.

Iceberg   (See also Water)

• The tip of the iceberg can signify that your blocked emotions are beginning to surface.
• This sign can mean drifting without emotional direction, perhaps in a dangerous situation.

Icicles   (See also Water)

• Whatever emotions have been blocked are beginning to release. There will be much more flow in your life.

Ignition

• This is your power switch, If you are having problems with the ignition in your car, ask yourself if you are having trouble getting started in life?

Illness

• Every illness has a corresponding symbolic meaning. For example heart problems are often symbolic of affairs of the heart. If you are aware of a particular physical difficulty in the signs around you, get a medical check-up in case the signs are reflecting the onset of that particular infirmity in your health.

• The circumstances, motives and beliefs surrounding any illness vary from person to person. Early childhood experiences, past life traumas and individual associations with certain illnesses and injuries are very powerful signposts in life. For example, someone who has difficulty speaking their truth might develop a throat problem. An individual who was sexually abused might develop physical difficulties with their sexual and reproductive organs. Illness is not bad. In fact, your illnesses keep you emotionally balanced by bringing to the surface deep psychological disturbances, so it is important to thank, not blame your body when you are ill. Sometimes illness can be a sign to slow down, to take time to be still and quiet within yourself, to re-evaluate your life.

Impotence

• This can be a sign of insecurity and fear. Affirm to yourself, 'I am strong, positive and healthy within myself. I like and accept myself exactly as I am.'

• Is there an area of your life where you feel impotent? (This can apply to either a man or woman.) Is someone making you feel impotent? Relax and accept yourself. Life was meant to be enjoyed. Go inside yourself to find and connect with a sense of your own personal power.

Incest

• This can be a sign of needing to integrate parts of yourself; i.e. integrating the adult part of you with the child part of you, or the male part of you with the female part of you.

• Is there hidden incest occurring in your environment?

• This can also be a sign of a forgotten childhood abuse beginning to surface. If this sign continues to show up in your life, consider exploring your childhood in therapy.

Indian

• The American Indians had a deep, primordial connection to nature. Do you need to spend more time in nature? Is there a part of your basic nature that is still foreign to you?

• This can also refer to Hindu Indians. Is there someone in your life who is from India? This sign could be referring to that person.

Indigestion

• Is there something that you can't stomach or assimilate in your life?

Initiation

• Initiation is a symbolic death and rebirth. It is being born into a new spiritual consciousness and awakening to a new level of consciousness. This is a sign of spiritual growth.

Injury   (See also *Illness*)

• There are no accidents. Notice and replay the exact thoughts that were going through your head when the injury occurred. You will usually discover clues as to what precipitated the injury. Also notice what part of the body is injured. Each part has its own symbolism. For example, if you injured your head you might ask yourself if you are being too headstrong in life? Another question that you might ask yourself is have you been listening to your head and forgetting your heart and feelings? If you injured your leg, are you afraid to step forward in life? Are you willing to take a stand in life?

Insect

• Is something bugging you?
• This sign can depend on the insect. Maggots can represent decay. Butterflies are transformational. Flies are small annoyances. Ants are industrious.

Invalid

• Is there some part of you that feels immobilized, unproductive or locked away?
• No matter what state your body is in, you are valuable and important. Your value doesn't come from what you have or do, but comes instead from who you are within yourself.

Iron

• Are there some problems in your life which need to be straightened out?
• Do you have too many irons in the fire?
• Is this the time in your life to tap into your iron will?
• Is someone in your life being inflexible with power, perhaps ruling with a rod of iron or an iron hand?

Island

• This can be a sign of isolating yourself from others or of being self-contained. 'No man is an island unto himself.' Do you need to reach out more to others for guidance and assistance?
• An island can be a refuge or sanctuary. Is this the time to pull in and isolate yourself for evaluation and discernment of your life?

Jack

• When someone is a 'jack of all trades' they are skilled in many dif-

ferent areas. Do you need to add some diversification in your life?
• An automobile jack can relieve you from having to lift a heavy burden all by yourself. This sign can mean that you don't have to accept the burden yourself, relief is on the way.
• This can be a sign of enthusiasm: 'jacking up one's spirits' or feeling 'jacked-up'. Are you feeling excited about something in your life?
• This can also be a sign of anger. Is someone 'jacking you around'?
• 'Jacking off' is a derogatory term referring to masturbation.

Jackal

• A jackal is a wild dog that lives chiefly as a scavenger. In some Asian and African cities at night, jackals act as street cleaners, eating animals they find dead on the streets. Is there a part of you that feels like a scavenger?
• The jackal has a mournful cry and yap that some associate with a warning. Is this sign telling you to be watchful and aware?
• In Egypt Anubis was the jackal god. He was the guardian of the underworld. He was also the one who prepared the way after death. This was perhaps because no matter how well the Egyptians sealed their tombs the jackals always found them, because of their finely tuned senses. Thus the jackal became the guardian of the dead. If the jackal appears to you as a sign, know that your senses can be trusted as you manoeuvre through the dark inner realms.

Jail

• Are you feeling confined in your life? Are you feeling controlled in your life, rather than in charge of your own destiny? Affirm to yourself, 'I am free and expansive in all areas of my life.'

Jam

• Jam is the sweetness in your life. Are you taking time to experience the sweetness in life?
• Traffic jams or logjams signify delays, confusion, and frustration, feeling stuck with no way to turn. Are you feeling like you are in a jam? Take time to be still. Reassess your life's situations.

Jar   (See also *Bottle*)
• Have you had a jarring experience?

Jaw

• To 'jaw' is to talk with friends comfortably. This can be a sign of communication. Are you comfortable talking informally and easily with others?
• If the jaw is tightly closed, there is a need for more open

communication.
- Giving someone some jaw can connote scolding.
- Someone who is 'jawing' is usually considered boring and long-winded. Are your communications concise and to the point, or are they sometimes too longwinded?
- A square jaw can mean strength and toughness. Do you need to 'take life on the jaw', meaning to be stronger in life?

Jealousy
- This is a sign of feeling not included and left out. Work on knowing that you are complete and whole exactly the way you are now. There is nothing more that you need to be, do, or have in order to be whole.
Your presence is enough right now.

Jelly   (See Jam)

Jellyfish
- Do you feel like you are just floating and drifting along?
- A jellyfish has no supporting inner structure. Are you acting spineless in some area of your life?

Jesus   (See also Christ)
- This is a powerful sign of the Christ light within yourself.
- This can also be a sign of sacrificing yourself for the good of others.

Jewel
- Every jewel has its own symbolism, but in general jewels are a sign of that which is precious, as well as abundance and brilliance. This can be a sign of coming riches.
- Look for the real jewels in life to find true happiness.

Jog
- Jogging connotes movement and self-betterment. Do you need to go jogging for exercise? Do you feel like you are jogging in place without getting anywhere?
- Do you need a reminder of something, or a jogging of your memory?

Journey
- A journey is usually a time of self-exploration and growth. This can be a sign that you need to prepare for an unexpected journey in the near future.

Judas

• This can be a sign of a betrayal, usually a self-betrayal. Are you not being true to yourself? Is someone in your life betraying you?

Judge

• Usually this is a sign of self-judgment. All judgment has its roots in self-judgment. Even if judgment is directed at another, look to see if it is something you have judged within yourself or if it is a reflection of your own inner morality. Are you judging yourself too harshly?

It's important to remember that even those experiences that you judged as bad were necessary for you to get to where you are now. They were important for your growth and evolution as a soul. Holding this viewpoint helps you release judgment and guilt.

• This can also be a sign of guidance from your higher self (your inner judge) giving you information.

Juggler

• Are you trying to juggle many things at once? If the juggler is doing a good job, so are you. If the juggler is a little out of control, consider eliminating some things from your life or taking some time to assess what is really important in your life.

Juice

• Juice is the essence of the fruit. Do you need to 'juice up' to give energy to your life?
• This can mean piquant or racy. Do you need to get 'juicier 'in your life?
• Sometimes being 'juiced' means being drunk. Are you drinking too much alcohol for your own good?

Jump

• Are you getting ahead or leaping into a new venture? Check other signs to see if this is a good idea. In other words, look before you leap.

Jungle

• This is the wild instinctual part of you. Access your wild man or wild woman within!

Junk

• Junk is that which is no longer needed by you, such as outdated ideas, feelings, habits, and relationships. To get rid of 'junk' in your emotional life, get rid of physical junk in your life. The symbolic act of cleaning closets and drawers and getting rid of things that you don't use or don't love will contribute to getting rid of those emotional states that aren't contributing to who you really are. It works!

Jury

• Usually this is a sign of self-criticism. Note the judgments that you feel the jury is making. Most often, these will be judgments you have made about yourself. Know that what you have done and who you have been was necessary for you to be who you are today. It was necessary for you to get where you are going. Your life is unfolding perfectly for your evolution.

Kangaroo

• This is a sign for great leaps forward in your life. Are you ready to leap ahead?
• Kangaroo represents mobility.

Key

• This is a very powerful sign connoting opening doors for yourself, both on the spiritual and the physical plane. Listen carefully when this sign appears for you. You now have the potential to go through a new door of perception.
• This sign can mean that the keys to the solution are at hand.

Keyhole

• This can represent being close to a solution or close to a new direction in life, but not quite there. Are you checking out future possibilities or observing a situation or person from a distance?

Kidnapping

• This sign can refer to feeling out of control in a situation, or feeling the victim of a situation. Are you feeling like a victim? Are you sabotaging yourself? Remember there are no victims, only volunteers. Affirm to yourself, 'I am in control of my life, and I am choosing my path in life.'
• If a child is kidnapped, it can symbolize the taking away of the childlike qualities within yourself.

Kidneys

• Kidneys can be a symbol of fear, disappointment, or criticism. Affirm to yourself, 'I have courage, confidence and strength in every moment.'
• In Chinese medicine kidneys hold chi (energy). Are you losing your energy? Do you need to have your kidneys checked medically?

Killing

• Notice the emotions associated with this sign. Are you feeling disgust, grief, shame, fear, sadness or abhorrence? The emotion that you feel is a clue as to the meaning of this sign. Delve into the associated emotions to gain an understanding of what this sign means to you. If this sign appears for you it usually means that you are releasing parts of yourself that aren't necessary in your present evolution. You are killing off beliefs or behaviours that you no longer need.

• This sign can mean that you are feeling a great loss of energy. Are you destroying part of yourself that you dislike? Affirm to yourself, 'All the different parts of me are valuable and important and I honour all aspects of myself.'

King

• A king often signifies power and majesty. It is now time to step into your own majesty. This may refer to the God, the Kings of Kings.

• In some regards the king represents the archetypal man. It is the male expression of the ruling or governing principle. The coronation of the king is the pinnacle of achievement, hence king may represent the pinnacle of the essential male within us all.

• This can also be a sign of authority, self-responsibility and taking charge of your own life. It is now time to claim your own strength.

• Is someone trying to lord over you?

Kiss

• A kiss can be a sign of warmth, affection or love.

• It can also represent a deep communion with self and an alignment of the masculine and feminine aspects within yourself.

• This symbol could refer to a kiss of death or betrayal. Is someone acting kindly towards you but their intent is less than pure?

Kite

• A kite can be seen as a symbol of incredible spiritual soaring, yet it is also grounded and anchored.

• This can be a sign of childlike freedom.

Knee

• A knee can represent fear, since when one is afraid the knees may shake or buckle. Affirm to yourself, 'I have courage to step forward in life with grace and ease.'

• This can also be a symbol of inflexibility, of not wanting to give in. Affirm, 'I am adaptable and flexible.'

• This symbol might represent being in awe of something, or kneeling in worship. Is this the time for you to honour and worship the divine being?

Knife

• This can be a powerful symbol of either creative forces or destructive ones. It can symbolize the cutting away of that which isn't needed, as in cutting away old patterns of thinking and being. Or it might be like cutting the thorns from a rose, or cutting away excess clay to make a beautiful piece of pottery. What do you need to cut out of your life? Make a clean cut of it and go on.

• Knives can symbolize a fear of being penetrated emotionally, physically or sexually. Are you feeling knifed in the back by someone?

Knitting

• Knitting is tying ideas and life themes together. Are you unifying different aspects of your life? If the knitting is coming apart, do you feel as if some situation in your life is unravelling?

• Knitting can be a wonderful sign of domestic peace. Your home will be blessed with comfort and peace.

• This can also be a sign of mending and repairing. A broken bone knits together.

Knock

• A knock can be a new awareness trying to make itself known to you. Opportunity is knocking at your door. Be prepared for new ventures.

• Getting knocked up is a term that refers to becoming pregnant. If you are not planning on becoming pregnant, then extra caution is advised.

Knot

• Are you experiencing tension? Is your stomach in knots? The most powerful way to deal with fear is to confront it head on. It is better to go through the short-lived discomfort of confrontation than the prolonged, extensive discomfort of being tied up in knots.

• It is time to make a commitment to the one you love and tie the knot.

• Untying a knot signifies creating relaxation in a certain area of your life. Are there any 'ties that bind' you which you wish you could just untie?

Label

• This can be a symbol for separating and organizing. Is it time to be discerning and to separate what you need from what you don't, to label things for easy reference?

• It can also signify stereotyping someone or something, placing them in a convenient pigeonhole. Expand your horizons. Release your old habit of seeing the world through the illusion of separation. Move towards perceptions of unity, oneness, wholeness.

• Do you feel like someone is labelling you? Affirm to yourself, 'I am a unique, magnificent individual.'

Laboratory

• This is a sign that you can find solutions through experimentation.

Labyrinth

• Winding through intricate passageways can signify feeling that there is no way out. The solution to being in a labyrinth is to stop and quiet your mind. Tune in to your intuition, and the way out of your difficulty will become clear.

Ladder

• A ladder can be a representation of attaining a higher awareness or reaching new heights in life.

• This can symbolize Jacob's ladder to heaven and ascending to the realm of the angels.

• If the ladder is going up you are climbing the ladder of success. Descending a ladder might symbolize going down into the subconscious mind, or it might be that your fortunes are diminishing.

Ladybird

• A ladybird is a great symbol of good luck.

• This can also be a sign that you need to tend to your personal home affairs, as in the old rhyme, 'Lady bird, lady bird fly away home, your house is on fire . . .'

Lake

• Notice the nature of the lake as water represents emotions. A still, clear lake connotes intuition, deep inner wisdom and emotional balance. Choppy water can indicate emotional turmoil. A cloudy lake can signify stagnant emotions.

• To the ancient Egyptians a lake symbolized the occult and mysterious inner realms. At certain times during the year priests would cross the lake in ceremonial procession. Celtic symbolism held that the Land of the Dead was at the bottom of the lake. Water can symbolize your subconscious and your deep unknown places. The inner mysterious realms are within you. Take time to be still and explore them.

Lamb

• Historically, the lamb has symbolized purity, innocence, and even meekness. There are times in life to be dynamic and aggressive and times to be meek and humble. Is this the time to be unassuming?

• Are you being made a sacrificial lamb? Let the lion inside you roar!

Lameness

• Are there self-imposed limitations that are keeping you from stepping forward in life? Affirm to yourself, 'I have the strength to step forward in my life. So be it.'

• Are you feeling ineffective, like a lame duck? Change the situation or the way you view it, so that you feel effective and strong.

Lamp/Lantern   (See also *Light*)

• The lamp is a sign of your inner light. Let your inner light shine brightly!

Land   (See also *Air*)

• This symbol represents your grounding, your solid foundation. Do you feel as if you are on solid ground in your life? If not, begin to create supportive structures and invite supportive people into your life.

• The landing of a plane is a coming to firm ground. This can represent the need to ground your thinking. Landing (going ashore in a boat) can represent a grounding of your emotions. There is a need for grounding and connecting to the earth in your life.

Large Intestine

• The large intestines allow the release of toxic matter. This is the time to release that which you do not need or use. Do it now!

• This may be a sign that you need to attend to your colon health.

• Are you assimilating food and information in your life effectively?

• You have the courage and the guts to go forward.

Laser

• Now is the time to pinpoint your consciousness and to use intense focus and concentration. Doing this at this time will generate rewards in later years for you.

Laughter

• Genuine laughter is a great healer. Don't take life so seriously. Laugh at yourself. Life was not meant to be a struggle.

Launching

• This is a sign for beginning a new venture. Observe other signs to see if the venture will succeed or fail.

Laundry

• It's time to clean up your act. Do some personal cleansing of your life.
• Are you inappropriately letting people know of your personal imbalances and 'airing your dirty laundry'?

Lava

• This is a powerful sign that something that has been suppressed for a long time – usually anger. Take constructive action to release your anger.

Leaping   (See *Jumping*)

Leather

• This is a sign of strength. Is there a situation in your life where you need to be tough as leather?

Leaves

• Leaves are a sign of growth, abundance and achievement, especially if they are green, vibrant and healthy. Yellowing leaves or leaves on the ground are signs of completion, letting go and releasing.
• Are you considering leaving someone or something? This may be a sign saying that this is the time to go. Is someone about to leave you?

Leech

• Do you feel that something is sucking away your strength or property? Or are you taking advantage of someone?

Left

• Your left-hand side is usually thought to symbolize the receptive forces of the universe, as your right represents the projecting forces. This is especially true if you are right-handed. Do you need to be more receptive and open in your life?
• Do you feel left behind or left out? Affirm to yourself, 'I am always exactly where I need to be in my life for my evolution and growth.'

Leg

• Legs represent your foundations. Weak legs may mean a lack of firm foundations or a lack of feeling centred. Strong legs may suggest being well supported. Do you feel like you do not have a leg on which to stand?
• Are you willing to step forward in life and make a stand?

Lemon

• Lemons are considered a cleansing and purifying agent. Go on a cleansing diet. In addition to cleansing your body, purify your emotions and mind as well.
• A 'lemon' colloquially can mean that something is poorly constructed. Be warned, the purchase you are considering may be a 'real lemon.'

Lens

• Focus your attention. Take time to focus the direction of your life.

Leopard

• This is a powerful sign of prowess, cunning and stealth. The leopard also expresses ferocity, valour and power. In all your enterprises call upon the qualities of the leopard to attain strength and success.

Letter

• Information or news is coming your way – watch the mail! Check other signs to see if the news will be good or bad.
• A letter can also mean an indirect communication from someone.
• In almost all ancient cultures, individual letters of the alphabet had mystic symbolic importance. This sign can refer to the individual letters and their corresponding meanings. This most likely has its roots in the ancient tradition of pictograms, as well as the idea that every component of a linear sequence has a corresponding meaning. The science of letter symbolism is important and worth pursuing, however it would take greater space than is available here to examine the meanings for each individual letter.

Library

• This sign signifies your inner knowledge and your own inner resources.

Lifeguard   (See also *Water*)

• A lifeguard can symbolize safety while you are moving through an emotional crisis, or it can be a sign to say you are safe to express your emotions freely.

Light

• Light traditionally is associated with spirit or God. This can be a sign of the spiritual light within you.
• There is light at the end of the tunnel. There is hope.

Lightning
• This is a very potent symbol that connotes great power and a break-through ahead. In native tradition lightning was the Sky Father impregnating Earth Mother. This can be a very powerful sign of speed, strength and the awakening of the inner life force within you.

Lily
• The lily is the sign for transformation through life, death and rebirth. White lilies are used at funerals to signify life after death. If there is some part of yourself or your life that seems to be dying this sign is reminding you to have faith. Truly there will be a rebirth.

Lion/Lioness
• The lion symbolizes majesty, power, bravery, and leadership, for the lion is the 'king of the jungle'. This is truly the time in your life to take control with absolute confidence and strength.
• Jung felt that the lion in the wild represented our latent passions. Is this the time to explore and unbridle your passions, and live life fully and courageously?
• This can also be a sign of a test of courage. For some African tribes, part of the rite of manhood concerned pitting one's strength against the lion's. You may be tested in an area of your life. Garner your inner strength and you will be victorious.

Little Finger
• This can be a sign of manipulation. Do you feel like you are being wrapped around someone's little finger?

Liver
• This almost always is a sign representing anger, for the liver is thought to be the seat of anger. Affirm to yourself, 'I feel deep peace and accept myself unconditionally.'
• This could also be a sign that you need to pay attention to the physical health of your liver.

Lizard
• The lizard stays in the shadows during the heat of the day and is thus considered the keeper of the shadowlands and the dreamtime, as well as the keeper of dreams. If this sign appears for you, pay particular attention to your dreams. They will contain some very important messages.
• This sign can also signify your subconscious mind and your inner shadowlands. Identify your recurrent fears and concerns. Confront them and bring them into the light.

Lock/Locking

• Locking a house or structure can be shutting yourself away from the realities of the world or locking out other people. Do you feel locked out of someone's life? Is there someone you wish to lock out of your life?

• This can also indicate a need for being more self-accepting in your life. Are you locking something up within yourself that you find undesirable?

• A canal lock, which metes out the river's water, can be a homonym for the lock which requires a key, or it can indicate measuring out your flow of psychic and emotional energy.

Lost

• Are you unsure about who you are and where you are headed? Meditate and ask for personal guidance from within.

Lotus

• This flower can be a sign of spiritual awakening. Just as the lotus comes out of the mud, you are coming up out of the darkness and into the light.

Luggage

• This may be a sign of the desire or need to travel. Pack your bags and go. Take a risk. Life is meant to be experienced.

• This can also be a sign of old habits, patterns and conditioning that you need to get rid of.

Lungs

• Lungs represent the breath of life and taking in life, as well as taking charge of your life. Are you living life to full capacity?

• Lungs are often associated with grief. Is there a situation that you are grieving over? It's important to allow yourself to grieve rather than repressing your grief.

• Do you need more breathing space in your life?

Machine

• Are you acting in a rote or machine-like way? Be more spontaneous.

Machinery

• The symbolism will depend on if the machinery is working in perfect order. Are all the parts of your body and your life functioning in harmony with one another?

• Are you feeling out of touch with the organic process of life?

• This can be a sign to pay attention and give maintenance to the machines under your care.

Magic

• There is a mystical power beyond your normal reality. Listen to your inner magic. There is magic in the universe. Believe!

Magician

• Magic comes from the ancient word 'magh', meaning power. The magician symbolizes channeling power from the inner to the outer realms. The Tarot meaning for magician is realizing aspirations by utilizing inner resources. This card, one of the most powerful in the entire deck, is the symbol of transformation and manifestation. If you can dream it, you can become it. Your dreams can come true.
• The magician has the ability to create illusion out of that which is not real. Something in your life which appears real may in fact be an illusion.
• The magician may symbolize the sage or the wise old man.

Magnet

• Is there someone or something to which you have an irresistible attraction?

Mail   (See also Letter)

• This is an obvious sign for messages. It is also a homophone for male.

Man/Male

• This is the male part of yourself. It usually represents that linear, rational, practical part of yourself. It is the focused, conscious part of you, as opposed to the diffuse awareness which comes from your subconscious. Do you need to step more into your male energy? This can occur even if you are a woman, for we all have male energy within ourselves.
• Depending on other signs this could refer to a male in your life.

Mandala

• A mandala is usually either a circle or a square surrounding a central point, with spiritual geometric forms or sacred paintings within it. Mandalas represent the whole self and the entire universe. They are often used as a visual aid in meditation and religious worship. Carl Gustav Jung suggested that they are so spiritually powerful that they are 'a kind of nucleus about whose intimate structure and ultimate meaning we have no direct knowledge'. Any time a mandala appears in your life this is a very, very powerful sign of harmony, beauty, and balance.

Mansion   (See *Home/House*)

Map
• It's time to plan your journeys, both inner and outer.

Marriage
• This can be a sign of uniting the male and female sides of yourself and integrating various aspects of your being.
• This can be a sign of the uniting or coming together of ideas or people.
• Are you considering getting married or are you making some choices in life that will affect your marriage?

Mars
• Mars was originally the god of farming, fertility and prosperity of the harvest. Later, after the Romans came into contact with Greek culture, Mars became the Roman god of war. This sign can represent the small disharmonies in your life. It can also be a sign to use your focused and directed power, and to use it for prosperity.

Marsh   (See also *Water, Earth*)
• A marsh is an area of soft, wet, low-lying land, characterized by grassy vegetation. It forms a transition zone between water and land. If the marsh is stagnant, this can be a sign that you are stagnating and unsure of yourself emotionally. A healthy marsh provides food and shelter for many kinds of birds and animals and is a vibrant ecosystem. This is a sign that your emotions and the physical aspects of your life are in balance.
• Are you getting bogged down in life? Purify yourself. Cleanse body and soul to be on solid ground again.

Martyr
• This is a sign of a complete lack of personal power. Are you feeling that you are a victim of life's circumstances? Work with self-acceptance. Accept responsibility for the circumstances in your life. Affirm to yourself, 'I am in control of my life and I am responsible for the circumstances of my life.'
• This sign can pertain to giving to others and feeling resentful when you do not get enough appreciation. If you can't give freely, then don't give.

Mask

• Masks were traditionally used in native cultures during initiations. The metamorphoses that initiates went through during these rituals were so completely mysterious and awesome that these transformations needed to be hidden beneath a mask. Depending on the kind of mask, this can be a powerful sign that you are indeed in the midst of a personal transformation.

• Masks can represent different aspects of yourself. You might have one mask or persona that you use at work, another that you use with your parents, and yet another that you wear with your friends. Almost everyone has different personas. However, it only creates difficulties where the personas are at odds with each other. Are you happy with your persona, or it is time to see yourself in an entirely new way?

• A mask can be a way to conceal one's real personality, character, or intentions. Or it can be a face having a blank, fixed, or enigmatic expression. Is there someone in your life who is not what they seem, or who is concealing their identity and not showing you their true face? Do you feel the need to conceal who you really are?

Massage

• This can be a sign to pleasure yourself and take care of your body's needs.

Match

• A lit match can mean your inner light beginning to shine forth. Unlit, a match is potential as yet unrevealed.

• A match can be a competition. Are you in a competitive situation with someone?

• A match can be a connection such as a 'good match' or a 'match made in heaven.'

Maze

• Are you feeling lost and confused, unsure what direction to go in life? Stop and tune in to your intuition. You actually do know the way out. Listen to your inner voice.

• This can be a homophone for maize, which was the staff of life for the Native Americans.

Meadow

• A meadow is a sanctuary of great beauty and spiritual harmony and balance. It is a place of rest that is rejuvenating and nurturing. It can also be a magical realm filled with fairies and unicorns. Create an inner sanctuary within yourself. You can do this by imagining that you are feeling strong and healthy as you walk in a meadow.

Mean

• If you perceive that people are being mean to you, ask yourself if you are being mean to others, or to yourself. Are you caught in the illusion of victimhood?

Meat

• Meat is the edible part of an animal or of a fruit. It is also the essence, the substance, or gist of something. This is a sign to get to the real meat of the matter in your life.
• This can be a homophone for 'meet'. Is there someone you need to remember to meet?

Medicine

• This is a sign of healing and balance.
• It can also mean that you need to get some medicine for a condition that you may be experiencing.
• This can also be a sign of karmic retribution. Are you getting a 'taste of your own medicine'?

Meditation

• This may be a sign that your guide desires to speak with you but your mind is too busy to listen. Take time to be still and connect with your own inner voice and the Creator. Meditation is as simple as being quiet and listening to your heart.

Melons

• Melons round and full of seeds are a sign of wholeness and opportunity.

Melt/Melting   (See also Water)

• Are you melting down the barriers between yourself and other people, or between yourself and other parts of yourself?
• Are you melting the old structures to create new dimensional understandings?
• This sign can herald the advent of a dramatic inner change through letting go of personal form and structure.
• Melting ice can mean repressed emotions are being freed and opening the way for love, self esteem and forgiveness.
• Metal melting by fire can symbolize form being transformed into spirit.

Menstruation

• This is a good sign for releasing the old and embracing a new beginning.

Mercury

• Mercury was the messenger of the gods and the bearer of messages. He was also the god of trade, commerce, gain, luck, travel and good gifts. A good message will be arriving for you.
• Mercury is quick, changeable in temperament and volatile. Are you mercurial with rapidly changing moods?
• This can pertain to having the characteristics of eloquence, shrewdness, and swiftness attributed to the god Mercury. Do any of these adjectives apply to you in your life?

Mermaid / Merman

• This can be a sign of a magical and spiritual commune with the sea, with your emotions and with the depths of your being and your subconscious mind.
• Do you have a temptation or attraction towards an unattainable lover?

Merry-Go-Round

• Do you feel like you are going around and around without making any progress?
• This symbolizes your inner childlike joy. Who says you need a destination? Just enjoy the ride!

Metal

• This is a sign of your strength.
• Metal could be a homophone for 'mettle' or your basic character. What is your mettle?

Microscope

• It is time for some intense self-examination.

Middle Finger

• This is an obvious sign of anger or sexuality.

Middle Path

• Anytime that you are given a sign of a middle path the message is very clear. Take the middle path in life. Don't go to one extreme or another. Take Buddha's course of moderation in all things.

Milk

• Milk is a sign of the nurturing sustenance of mother's milk. If the milk is fresh, this sign can mean the milk of human kindness. Sour milk can be a nurturing person or a situation that went sour. Take time to nurture yourself.

Mine   (See also Hole)

• There are inner treasures as yet undiscovered in you. You are so much more than you seem.
• This can refer to your personal possessions, as in 'This is mine!'

Mirror

• This is a powerful sign with a multiplicity of meanings. A mirror can mean your imagination and your conscious thought in the way that it reflects the world of form around you. It can also be a sign of self-contemplation and the need for you to turn your thoughts inward. Some psychologists associate mirrors with hidden or unconscious memories. In China mirrors are used to reflect or dispel unfavourable influences. Locate other associated signs to discover the meaning of this sign in your life.
• In folklore and in fairy tales the mirror has a magical association. It is an entrance point or a mythic door between this world and other realms. Explore the magic in your life.
• A mirror can allow you to step apart from reality to gain perspective in your life.
• Do you need to see a reflection of what is really going on in your life and to see who you really are?
• This can be a sign to confront yourself and see yourself as you truly are.
• A mirror allows you to see yourself as others see you.

Miscarriage

• Has there been a miscarriage of justice in your life?
• Beware of future plans that may be aborted or not fulfilled.
• If you have had a miscarriage of a foetus in the past, this sign could be bringing any unresolved emotions to the surface to be healed and released.
• If you are pregnant this could be a sign to be more careful with yourself for a while.

Missing the Boat/Plane/Train

• Are you feeling a lack of progress in your life? Are you feeling left out because of your circumstances in life? Affirm to yourself, 'Where I am in my life is exactly where I need to be to gain the greatest evolution.'
• This sign can signify a lost opportunity. Remember when one door closes another will open.
• Are you not really making enough of an effort in your life? Take time to reassess your goals and pursue with passion and focus those goals that are most important to you. Never give up.

Mist   (See also *Fog*)

• The mists are symbolic of the mystical inner realms. Believe in magic!
• The mists can represent your subconscious mind and something that you are not coming to terms with in your life. Do you feel lost in the mists of your mind?

Mole

• Is there something beneath the surface in your life that you are not willing to let others see? Affirm to yourself, 'I am perfect exactly as I am, and who I am is a unique miracle of creation.'

Monastery

• This is a sign saying that it is time for inward spiritual retreat and withdrawing from the world.

Money

• If the sign is coins or small change, this can signify a change coming in your life.
• If you keep finding money this can mean your finances and your abundance is on the upswing.
• This sign could be reminding you to pay attention to your money and your financial affairs for a while.

Monkey

• This is a sign to loosen up and embrace the wild, carefree, mischievous part of yourself. Be willing to be silly and spontaneous. Play! Don't take life so seriously.
• The expression 'Monkey see . . . monkey do,' means someone is imitating another person. Are you imitating someone else? It can be a valuable exercise to model after someone. However, eventually find your own direction and follow it, even if it isn't conventional.

Monster

• A child's hidden fears will appear in the manifest form of a monster. Is there some unacknowledged part of yourself that you fear?
• Really examine your inner monster(s). The greatest fear is that which is unknown. Become familiar with your inner demons. Ask yourself what parts of yourself they represent. You might even imagine the monster and ask it what it represents. If you are confronting a threatening monster, instead of being victimized go back and fight it, or make friends with it.

Moon

• The sun and the moon powerfully represent the two opposing yet harmonious forces of the universe. The sun represents the outward, projecting, male, warm, light force in the world, while the moon is the quintessential symbol for the receptive, feminine, cool, dark aspects of the world. Pay particular attention when the moon comes to you as a sign. It is saying to delve into your inner realms. Listen to your dreams. Take time to be still to receive the gifts of the universe. You do not need to exert so much effort in life. Just be.

• The phases of the moon indicate different states. A full moon represents wholeness and creativity from an intuitive base. It is a time to go for it. A new moon or a crescent moon indicates a time of deep inner reflection. It is a time to listen to your own inner voices and your own inner magic.

• The moon is a particularly good sign for romance, poetry and inspiration.

• Since ancient time the moon has been associated with fertility. It rules the tides, germination of seeds, and a woman's moon-time (her menstruation cycles). Some ancient traditions even believed that the moon made women pregnant.

Moth

• Moths will beat themselves against a light until they die. Do you have perseverance beyond reason? Do you keep working at something without ever achieving results? Look at the situation from a different perspective and know that you can attain results without striving so hard.

• Moths eat holes in clothes in dark closets. Is something being eaten away without your attention?

Mother

• Mother symbols usually are indicative of a nurturing quality of nature, Mother Earth and the Divine Mother. The mother is the wise woman who dwells inside you. (Even if you are male there is a female energy within you.)

• The significance that you project onto this symbol may reflect that part of yourself that your own mother represents.

• Jung states that the mother is symbolic of the collective consciousness and of the inward or nocturnal side of life, as well as the source of water.

Mountain

• A mountain is a sign of an attainable goal or opportunity. Going up the mountain means you are progressing towards that goal; going down that you are moving away from the goal.

• A mountain can be a spiritual uplifting experience. Monasteries and lamaseries are in the mountains because the mountain is a place of spiritual retreat.

• Are you making a mountain out of a molehill?

• A mountain can be viewed as a sign of a coming obstacle or an opportunity, depending on the other signs that present themselves to you in conjunction with this sign.

• If you feel like you are struggling to attain insurmountable heights, just remember that you can do it. And don't forget to enjoy the journey as much as the destination.

Mourning

• Mourning can be a sign of an external loss, such as the loss of a relationship, of your possessions, of your position in life, or the loss of a friend or family member. Mourning can also reflect an inner loss due to releasing parts of yourself, such as habits and attitudes that no longer serve you in order to make way for more appropriate ways of being. This is not necessarily a bad sign. Often when we release an old negative behaviour, even though it created barriers, there is a period of mourning because we have lost part of our identity.

Mouse

• Do you feel insignificant or 'mousy'?

• This can be a sign of temerity and fear.

• Do you feel a need for quiet, or a concern about being quiet? Are you being too quiet in your life? Is it time to let people know who you are?

• Mice have been associated with paying attention to the details in life. Attend to the small matters in life and the bigger things will take care of themselves.

Mouth

• Mouth is usually an obvious sign of communication and verbally expressing yourself. Even in ancient writings such as the Egyptian hieroglyphs the mouth symbolizes the power of speech. Are you speaking your truth? Is there something you want to tell someone about which you have been hesitant? The mouth is the transition point between the inner world and the outer world. It is a vehicle that gives form to your thoughts, feelings and ideas. Are you willing to express yourself freely and openly? If not, affirm to yourself, 'I communicate freely, easily and effortlessly with courage and strength.'

• 'Mouthing off' is speaking with a lack of respect. Are you mouthing off too much? Or do you need to speak up more?

• Someone who is a 'big mouth' is a gossip. This might be a sign that someone is gossiping about you. Are you gossiping inappropriately about someone else?

• A mouth can also connote sensuality, sexuality and kissing.

Movies

• Are you observing life instead of participating in it? Take action today. Live life fully and passionately instead of watching from the sidelines.

• Are you becoming bound up in the drama of life?

• This sign might be referring to the different roles you play in life.

• A movie is a sequence of photographs projected onto a screen with sufficient speed so as to create the illusion of motion and continuity. Is it time to look between the frames of your life and enter into the silence between your thoughts?

• Movie signs could also mean it's time to make a 'move.'

Mud

• Are you feeling stuck and as if you are not moving or growing in your life? Affirm to yourself, 'I move freely and easily in all aspects of my life.' Spontaneous dance and free-form movement can often help us to become unstuck emotionally. As you dance with wild abandon, this creates a template for movement in other areas of your life.

• Do things seem muddy in your life, not clear? Take time to view life from a different angle. Consider eliciting the aid of others to gain their perspectives on the situation in your life.

• 'Mud, mud, glorious mud,' elicits the wonderful realm that a child enjoys. It connotes a childlike joy.

• Be willing to roll up your sleeves and get dirty. Live life fully.

• Mud can symbolize the union of the most basic aspect of earth with the transformative energy of water. It is out of this primordial medium that life has emerged. This can be a powerful personal sign that out of the base primordial soup of your life will come new life and new awareness.

Mule

• Are you being stubborn about a situation in your life? Loosen up. See the other person's point of view. In their personal universe they are just as right as you are in your personal universe.

• A mule has the ability to carry a heavy load. Do you feel that you are carrying too heavy a burden?

Murder   (See *Killing*)

Museum
• A museum can be a sign for knowledge. It is now time to bring wisdom from the past and assimilate it into the present.

Music
• The symbolism for music is incredibly varied and complex. For example in ancient times individual notes were thought to be intimately connected to the different celestial planets. One ancient philosopher assigned different notes to different animals and gave each note an associated meaning. Another philosopher thought that the shape of the instrument that created the music signified the meaning of the music.

Basically, to interpret what signs mean in regard to music, notice the way that you are relating to the music. This signifies how in rhythm you are with your life. Beautiful, harmonious music can signify uplifting spiritual alignment and inner harmony. Music that is out of tune can signify feeling at odds with your life.
• Music is a very powerful reflection of your inner states. Your responses will change according to your inner state. You can find out where you are in life by observing your reaction to music. Notice your emotional response to music. Do you feel sad, tragic, angry, delicate, loving or some other emotion? Do you feel soothed or bored by ambient music? Do you feel energized or irritated by rock and roll?
• Listen carefully to the words within the music around you. There will always be messages in the words that draw your attention to them.

Musical Instruments
• This symbolism depends on the particular instrument. A piano might be the keys to life. A flute can connote nature, freedom or the pure child within. Drums can indicate primitive or primordial instincts, staying with the beat, or marching to a different drum. An organ can be a homonym for the male organ or the body's organs. A harp might suggest celestial alignment and angels. A harmonica is the wandering minstrel, symbolizing time with friends, enjoyment and contentment. Bagpipes are cultural fellowship. The sitar can symbolize Eastern culture, mysticism and inner peace.

Nail
• A carpenter's nail can represent the details of the support for a larger structure. Nails bind the components of the project together. Are all the details in place for the larger projects in your life?
• Are you getting to the essence of your problem by 'hitting the nail

on the head'? If not, it may be time to redirect your aim in life.
• This might symbolize getting 'nailed' or getting caught. If you are involved in any clandestine activity, this sign is reminding you to beware. You might get caught.
• The term 'spitting nails' refers to being incredibly angry. Is there an issue in your life that is making you very mad? Take a breather. Cool off. Get some objective advice.
• Nails can be a homonym for fingernails. Chewing your fingernails represents anxiety. Remember that your life is divinely guided and there are no accidents in life.

Nakedness

• Nakedness can be a sign of total freedom and honesty. It can express childlike exhilaration when you run around naked.
• This can also be a sign of extreme vulnerability. Are you feeling exposed in your life? Begin to create personal boundaries so you have a sense of personal confidence.
• For some, nakedness is associated with shame because of repression regarding the body or past personal trauma. If this is so, affirm to yourself, 'I accept and honour all parts of myself, including my body and my past.'
• Nakedness can be a sign of exposing a situation and baring your soul. Be willing to be open and frank with others and yourself.
• This can also be a sign of sensuality and revelling in your passions and in your body.

Names

• Pay attention to the names of people and places around you. Often these carry powerful messages for you.
• In some esoteric traditions there is great power in one's name. In ancient Egypt it was believed that personal names were a reflection of one's soul and helped determine one's destiny. It is valuable to examine the root and meaning of your name (both your birth name and the name you use as an adult) to gain an understanding of your personal destiny path.

Narrow

• Are you feeling limited and restricted? See the bigger picture.
• This sign might also represent focused attention and the discipline necessary to reach your goal. Do you need to restrict and narrow down your options in order to optimize future choices?

Nausea

• Something is making you sick to your stomach. It's essential to stop and examine all situations and relationships in your life to see if there is something that you can't stomach.

• This can be a sign that you need to get rid of what isn't wanted or needed in your life.

• Nausea can be a sign to change your diet. Explore your diet to see if there is a food that you are eating that doesn't agree with your body.

Navel

• The navel is the point where the umbilical cord connected you to your mother in the womb. This sign can be giving you a message regarding your relationship with your mother.

• The navel is the origin of the silver cord that connects your astral body to your physical body. Are you ready to dance through the universe?

• In the Orient, the navel is thought to symbolize the centre of the universe. Return to your centre.

• Navel oranges are orange-coloured which is the colour related to the emotions. They are spherical-shaped which equates with well-being, so sometimes navel is a sign of emotional well-being.

Neck

• 'Sticking one's neck out' is taking a risk. Is this the right time for you to do this in your life?

• There is an energy centre in your neck that is linked to communication. Are you open to speaking your truth?

• Are you or is someone in your life being a pain in the neck?

• The neck is the connection between your head (intellect) and your heart (emotions). Do you need to balance your emotions with your intellect or vice versa?

• This sign can also symbolize necking or kissing.

• The neck can be a sign of flexibility, as the neck can represent being willing to see both sides of an issue. Being 'stiff-necked' means being immovable. Are you being immovable in your life? Do you need to loosen up a bit?

Nest

• Nest is a sign of incubating ideas or projects.

• When you are nesting you are creating a warm, cosy, safe space within your home. This is an excellent sign for congenial family life and domestic affairs.

• A nest can be a sign that it is time to pull inward for rejuvenation. Go into your inner nest and incubate there for a while. There are times in life when you need to be still and inward and times when you need to be outward and expansive. If you see a nest this could be a sign for you to withdraw into yourself for a time of renewal.

Net

• This sign can represent feeling caught in a web or net of your own perception. Take time to still your mind and allow the myriad of other realities to become apparent to you, so that you can choose one that is more in alignment with who you truly are.

• A fishing net or a butterfly net may be a sign of catching things that are needed or wanted in life.

• Do you feel the need for a safety net because you are taking some risks in life?

Night

• Night is the realm of the feminine principle. It is the domain of dreams, ancient mysteries and the subconscious mind. Ancient Greeks held that night and darkness preceded the creation of all things. Hence night was symbolic of germination and fertility. Experience the inner spaces within yourself. Drink deep of the inner magic inside yourself. Find and follow your dreams.

• Night can also be a sign of obstacles or delays, or of not seeing things clearly and not being in touch with your inner knowing. Affirm to yourself, 'I see clearly my personal path in life.'

• If it is a clear night with visible stars or moonlight, then this sign can be a symbol of your intuition and your inner magical realms.

Nightmare

• Nightmares are powerful messages and should be valued for the information they can impart to us. They allow us to deal with unresolved issues in our waking life that we are not allowing into our consciousness. These unresolved issues affect every aspect of our life, including our health and relationships. The nightmare is our subconscious way of healing these unresolved issues. Celebrate your nightmares!

• If you have a recurring nightmare, listen to the messages in the dream and then imagine going back into your dream and play it through in your mind a few times. Change the circumstances so that there is a positive outcome. This will assist healing the unresolved area of your life that was the source of the nightmare in the first place.

North

• If you live in the northern hemisphere the north represents cold and darkness. To the Native Americans of North America the north was the realm of the ancestors, the spiritual elders and the realm of death and rebirth. If you live in the southern hemisphere north can represent warmth and light.

Nose

• This can be a sign that you or someone in your life is being 'nosy' or a snoop. Mind your own business.
• Is someone 'nosing' in to your business?
• The nose is the most prominent protruding feature on the face. It can be a sign of needing or wanting self-recognition.
• Pinocchio's nose grew when he wasn't being honest. Are you being honest with yourself?

Nudity   (See *Nakedness*)

Numb

• This can be a sign that you are cut off from your feelings or that you are suppressing something that is fearful to you. It can also be that you are in emotional shock. If this sign persists take direct action and see a therapist.

Numbers

• Since the beginning of time, numbers have been viewed as signs which have held mystic significance. The following system is based on the ancient Pythagorean system (upon which modern day numerology is founded). If a number keeps appearing for you in various forms pay attention to the associated meanings for that number. For example, if the number five keeps appearing for you, consider travelling or getting involved in something that entails physical movement and change.
• One: The essence of number one is independence, new beginnings, oneness with life, self-development, individuality, progress, and creativity.
• Two: The essence of number two is a balance of the yin and yang energies (the polarities) of the universe. It is self-surrender, putting others before yourself. It is dynamic attraction one to another. Knowledge comes from the balance and marriage of the two opposites.
• Three: The essence of number three is the trinity: mind, body, and spirit. It is the threefold nature of divinity. Three is expansion, expression, communication, fun and self-expression. Three also relates to giving outwardly, to openness and optimism. 'Third time's the charm.'
• Four: The essence of number four is security and foundations. It is the four elements and the four sacred directions. Four is self-discipline through work and service. It is also productivity, organization, wholeness and unity.
• Five: The essence of number five is feeling free. Five is self-emancipating, active, physical, impulsive, energetic, changing, adventure-

some, and resourceful. It is associated with travel and curiosity. Five is the number of the free soul, of excitement and change.
• Six: The essence of number six is self-harmony, compassion, love, service, social responsibility, beauty, the arts, generosity, concern, and caring. It relates to children, balance and community service.
• Seven: The essence of number seven is the inner life and inner wisdom. It is a mystical number symbolizing wisdom, the seven chakras, and the seven heavens. It is a symbol of birth and rebirth, religious strength, sacred vows, the path of solitude, analysis and contemplation.
• Eight: The essence of number eight is infinity, material prosperity, self-power, abundance, cosmic consciousness, reward, authority and leadership.
• Nine: The essence of number nine is humanitarianism, selflessness and dedicating your life to others. This is a number of completion and of endings. It is a symbol of universal compassion, tolerance and wisdom.
• Master Numbers in Pythagorean tradition were thought to have a special power and significance of their own: 11: The essence of this number is developing intuition, clairvoyance, spiritual healing, and other metaphysical faculties. 22: The essence of this number is unlimited potential of mastery in any area, not only spiritual but physical, emotional and mental as well. 33: All things are possible.

Nun

• This can be a sign to pull your energies inward and isolate yourself from the material world.
• This can also be a sign to gain spiritual attunement through celibacy and denial.

Nurse

• This is usually a sign of healing, of caring and nurturing.

Nut

• Just as a nut has the potential for creating an entire tree so this sign points to new life and potential yet to unfold.
• The gathering of nuts for the winter is a sign of harvest and abundance.
• Are you being a hard nut to crack?
• Is someone driving you nuts?

Nymph

• Nymphs (mystical maidens who dwell in the mountains, waters and trees) were minor divinities of nature in mythology. Jung felt that nymphs symbolized a fragmentary expression of the feminine aspect of the subconscious mind. The nymph was an undeveloped stage of the process Jung called individuation of the being.

• Nymphs are immature insects. Is there an area of your life that is incomplete in its development or metamorphosis?

• This can also be a sign of joyous sexuality.

Oak

• Many traditions throughout history, including ancient Russian, German, Greek and Scandinavian cultures, have assigned meaning to the mighty oak. It is thought to be a world axis, as well as symbolizing powerful strength, solidarity, and steady progress.

Oar

• Oars can mean feeling in control in the midst of emotional imbalance. A boat without an oar may signify you are feeling adrift within an emotional dilemma.

Oasis

• An oasis is a refuge and a place of rejuvenation. This sign is telling you to find a place for personal retreat, where you can replenish your inner reserves before the journey that lies ahead in your life.

Obituary

• This sign can signify the release of old ideas, thought forms and beliefs.

• Very rarely, but occasionally, this sign can mean that someone you are acquainted with might pass over.

Observatory

• Do you need to get the bigger picture and see the deeper meaning in life?

Obstacles / Obstructions

• Constant physical obstacles (such as brick walls, locked doors, traffic jams, fences or even bad weather) that block your way, or personal or business obstacles (such as contracts that don't go through and phones that are out of order) are all strong messages that it is time to withdraw into yourself and re-evaluate your life. Questions to ask yourself during times like these are: 1) Are you subconsciously sabotaging yourself because you are afraid to take a risk and step beyond personal limitations? Are you afraid to leave your comfort zone? 2) Are you going in the right direction in life? Sometimes obstacles are a way of saying go another way. 3) Obstacles can be telling you to withdraw and go within. Spend less time on your outer life and more on your inner life.

Ocean   (See also *Water*)

• The ocean represents the sea of life, your subconscious mind and the tremendous intuitive power within you. This is the time to delve deeply into the ancient primordial wisdom within you. Trust your intuition.

• The meaning of this sign varies according to the condition of the water. A calm ocean connotes great inner power and emotional and spiritual balance. A rough or choppy ocean indicates the need for courage to allow you to move to calmer waters amid emotional upheaval.

Octopus

• An octopus has eight legs, which invokes the power of eight while propelling to the depths of the subconscious emotions. It is thus a powerful symbol of transformation. In Cretan art the octopus represent the mystic centre of the universe and the unfolding of creation.

• Does someone in your life seem tenacious and even grasping towards you? Are you tenaciously trying to grasp many different concepts or projects at the same time?

• Are attachments in life keeping you from free movement?

• In nature the octopus is shy and retiring. Are you shy and afraid to show your true colours?

Office

• This sign can represent production, linear thought processes and organization. Is it time to get yourself organized and create a structure for your business or in your life?

Officer

• Are you feeling the need for protection and for guidance from an authority figure?

• Are you feeling guilty in regard to something that you could be punished for? Sometimes this sign can mean your conscience is bothering you and there is a part of you that wants to be punished.

• This can be an affirmation of accepting authority for your own life.

Oil

• Oil is the lubrication which smooths over difficulties. Sometimes situations that seem a bit sticky only need just a little politeness or negotiation to soothe over misunderstandings.

• Anointing with oil is a blessing. This can be a sign that you are blessed.

• Is there someone in your life who has a 'greasy' or 'oily' personality?

• To oil someone's hand or oil someone's palm is to offer a bribe or tip. Are your trying to bribe someone or is someone trying to bribe you?

Olive

• This can be a sign of peace. Are you offering the olive branch of peace to someone?

One   (See also *Numbers*)

• Being Number One is a sign of success, being first, or being ahead of the pack.

Onion

• This can be a sign of potential sadness.
• This can also be a sign of many layers of consciousness.

Open

• Be open to life and open to new possibilities. The way will open for you. Open to spirit!
• Are you being too open with others? There are times to be completely open and times to be guarded with your self and your energy. Are you opening at the right time to the right people?

Orange

• Orange is a warm, stimulating colour but lighter and higher in vibration than red. Orange is a happy, social colour, used by clowns the world over. It stimulates optimism, expansiveness, emotional balance, confidence, change, striving, self-motivation, changeability, enthusiasm and a sense of community. Orange is flamboyant and warm-hearted, tolerant and sociable. Orange appearing to you as a sign can mean that you are entering into an outward social time in your life.

Orchard   (See also *Garden*)

• This is a great sign for bearing the fruits of your labour and being fruitful in your life.

Orchestra

• This can be a sign of synthesis, harmony, and synergy. If the orchestra is in tune it can signify that all the parts of your life are in harmony. A discordant orchestra can mean that there is inner discord within you.

Orgasm

• This sign depends on the feelings associated with orgasm and whether you physically reached the orgasm or not. It can be a powerful indicator of the alignment with your inner male and female energies and a connection to your life force energy, which is the creative energy that coils at the base of your spine. In addition, orgasm can be a sign of achieving completion and great joy.

Orgy

• This is a sign that your creative force may be dissipating. Focus on your life goals.
• This may indicate a desire to break the norm and step out of the limitations of society's morals.
• This sign can indicate an over-indulgence in food or sex. Take time to centre your life force energy to avoid affecting your health and draining your energy.

Orphan   (See also *Abandoned*)

• Are you feeling isolated and alone? Do you feel that you are without family? There is a sacred place within you where you are not separate from the world around you. As you connect to that place within you, you will feel connected and not abandoned.
• Are you feeling guilty about abandoning someone or something? Take appropriate action. Either clear and release the guilt or don't abandon that person.

Ostrich

• Is there something that you are avoiding looking at in life? Do you have your head in the sand so that you cannot see what is truly going on all around you?

Otter

• The otter is capricious, playful and fun-loving. Get ready for fun! Enjoy life in the moment!

Oven

• An idea or project is incubating within you.
• This can also indicate pregnancy, such as when a woman has two children and 'one in the oven'.

Owl

• This is a very significant sign as the owl is a powerful symbol of transformation. If this sign appears for you there is the probability of a coming transformation in your life.

Most cultures with an esoteric background honour the owl as a revered (and sometimes feared) sign. The owl was feared because it was the sign of darkness and the unknown. Since the beginning of time humanity has been afraid of the dark and the owl has always been associated with the unknown dark dimensions. An Australian aborigine elder explained to me that men were afraid of the owl because it was a woman's totem and it represented the darkness of the unknown.

Owls were also thought to be associated with death as well as rebirth. Some Native American tribes thought that owls housed the spirits of the dead. In Egyptian hieroglyphs the owl symbolized death, night, cold and passivity. When one aspect of you dies there is the opportunity for new growth in another area of your life. It is a universal law. The owl sign represents death and rebirth within your life.

The owl is also the symbol of ancient wisdom born from the inner realms. For within the darkness are dreams, visions and mystic insights. Athena, the Greek goddess of wisdom, was depicted as having an owl on her shoulder which revealed inner truths to her. Merlin, the old Celtic magician who helped the legendary King Arthur, used an owl to gain entrance into the unseen dimensions. The owl sees in the darkness what others cannot see. If this sign appears to you, you are being given the gift of being able to see and perceive the truth. You will gain the ability to see clearly where things may seem dark. Your insights will be keen and the transformations around you will be profound.

Oyster

• This sign can indicate hidden beauty or beauty developing unseen, just as the pearl develops within the oyster.
• A pearl is created when a grain of sand becomes imbedded within the interior of the oyster shell. The oyster surrounds the grain with calcium carbonate to protect itself from the abrasive edges of the sand. This sign can mean that even the small irritations in life can be transformed into something of beauty.
• Oysters can also be sexual symbols representing the vagina.

Pacing

• A pacing back and forth can mean you have uncertainty as to your life's direction. Take time to be still. Actively thinking about the situation isn't always the best solution. As you take time to quiet your mind, the correct solution will gently bubble to the surface.

Pack

• Carrying a pack can mean that there is something, someone or an idea that you are carrying around with you that may not be necessary. You can let it go.

• Carrying pack might also indicate that you have all your essential provisions with you and that you are self-contained.
• Packing can symbolize preparation for a change in your life.
• 'Packing it in' can be concentrating lots of activities into a short period of time. Are you packing too much into your life? Slow down, take a breath and know that you have enough time.

Package

• Sending a package can signify letting go of some attitude or pattern in your life.
• Receiving a package can be acknowledging an unrecognized part of yourself.

Pain

• Pain isn't necessarily a bad sign. Pain is usually a message sent to us by our bodies letting us know that there is a problem so that we can attend to it. If you are given a sign regarding either physical or emotional pain, it means that there is a problem or a disharmony in your life and you need to take care of it.

Palace　(See also *Home/House, Castle*)

• In ancient Cabalistic tradition the sacred inner palace was located in the centre of the six directions and was called the silver palace. It symbolized the origin of creation. In fairy tales throughout the world the palace contains magical rooms and inner dimensional doorways. A palace can represent your true, inner, magical kingdom and your magnificence.

Pan

• Pan was the Greek god of shepherds and hunters who originated panpipes. This sign symbolizes joy in nature. Is this the time to step into the joy that comes from being in nature?
• Panning, as with a movie camera, can mean getting the bigger picture. Do you need to get a wider perspective on a situation in your life?
• Panning for gold can symbolize looking for the true essence of something.
• Pan can mean that the critics don't like it. Is there something that you are criticizing yourself for? Is there someone who is criticizing you?
• A pan or a pot can represent cooking up an idea, or the coming together of different items for something nourishing and sustaining. Do you have an idea or project brewing?

Panda

• The panda bear is associated with the qualities of tranquillity, as well as being cuddly and lovable.

Panic

• Panic occurs when you feel that you don't have the resources to deal with a situation, or when you feel out of control. Be still. Stop. Breathe. Relax and garner your inner strength. Affirm to yourself, 'Fear is an illusion.' As you begin to take control of yourself this feeling will radiate outwards into the situations in your life.

Parachute

• Let go! You are protected and safe.
• Take a risk. Trust that there will be something to catch your fall.

Parade

• Are you willing to be recognized, particularly for your community efforts?
• A parade is a public show of pride. Is this the time to let others know that you are proud of yourself?
• Each of the participants in the parade is an aspect of yourself.

Paradise

• Paradise is a place of perfect peace and love. The kingdom of paradise is within you.
• This sign can also indicate innocence, or the fall from innocence. The Garden of Eden represents a perfect paradise of beauty and peace, however, it was fraught with temptation. Are you facing a temptation that you are afraid will threaten the peace in your life?

Paralyze

• Are you feeling completely immobilized in one area of your life? Dance, run, move your body. As you move, you create an energy template for movement in your life.
• Do you have conflicting feelings or impulses? For example, you might want to quit your job and travel, but you are afraid of losing your security and stability. Or perhaps you are torn between your desire to succeed and your fear of success. This sign can mean that you are experiencing a lack of confidence to make a move and a lack of confidence to go forward in your truth. Affirm to yourself, 'I am decisive. I easily and appropriately choose my direction in life.'

Parasite

• Is there something draining your energy? Is there something internal within you that is eating away at you? Is there someone in your life who feels like a parasite or is draining your energy?

• This could be a sign that you actually have parasites. Get a medical check-up.

Parents

• Family members' roles are changing dramatically. But despite these fortunate changes, our soul memory still retains stereotypical images of parents. This soul memory associates fathers with authority and the linear, rational thought processes. Father can be a sign of your projecting force and your inner authority. This can also represent your own father or your fathering skills to your children.

Mothers stereotypically represent the female principle of receptivity and the inner realms of intuition, feeling and nurturing. This sign can represent your own mother or your own mothering skills.

• Parent signs can pertain to your own experience of your parents, your parenting skills, or the mother/father energy that dwells within you.

Parrot

• Parrot can be a sign for insincerity and speaking another's words without thinking. Are you parroting or imitating someone else? Find your own individuality and express it.

• Parrot can also be a sign of the jungle, colour and expression.

Party

• This is the time to celebrate!

• Is it time to get out and socialize? Are you socializing too much?

• A party, such as a political party, can be people coming together for a common cause. Is there a cause in your life where you yearn for mutual understanding and support from others?

• Are you being a party to something that you don't want, or are you reluctant to be a party to something that you feel that you should?

Passenger

• If you are the passenger, you are along for the ride. You are not deciding the direction; someone else is. Is there an area of your life where you don't feel in control?

• Sometimes it's good to let go of control and go with the flow. Is there an area where you need to just sit back and be the passenger?

Passport

• Opportunities for travel and change are just around the corner. Get ready for change. (You might consider updating your passport just in case unexpected travel is around the corner!)

• This is your ticket for change and for creating what you want in

your life.
• A passport is a means of identifying yourself. What is this sign saying about your self-identity? Are you happy with your identity? Is it time for some changes?

Path

• A path can be a sign for your path in life. Notice the width, direction and straightness of the path. A straight and narrow path going upward can mean you are making progress. You are in alignment with your life's goals and purpose. You are staying on the path. A crooked path can mean that you are wandering off course or that you are not quite sure which direction to go. Affirm to yourself, 'No matter what direction I go in life, I know my path is guided in accordance with my highest good.'

Pattern

• A sewing or an embroidery pattern can connote your usual reality system or the one in which you are comfortable. Changing patterns can mean breaking out of old patterns. Are you happy with the patterns in your life?

Pavement

• New pavement can be a sign of new direction in life.
• To pave is to make your way easier or smoother. This can be a sign that someone or something is paving the way for you for future opportunities.

Peach

• This is an uplifting sign. Life is peachy. Life is good. Enjoy it and live life fully.

Peacock

• This can be a sign of pride and vanity. Are you being cocky? Is someone you know preening like a peacock?
• This can also be a sign of confidence to the extreme. Are you ready to show your true colours?
• In many ancient traditions the peacock has been revered and has been assigned various exalted meanings. In Hindu mythology the peacock was said to represent the stars and the firmament because of the patterns on the iridescent feathers. In Roman times the peacock symbolized the deification of princesses. Some Christian art forms depicted the peacock as the symbol of immortality. In Persia two peacocks on either side of the Tree of Life represented the polarity of man being sustained by the cosmic unity represented by the tree.

Pearl

• The pearl can represent you. A grain that began as an irritation becomes great beauty. You can transform all life's irritations into beauty.

• Pearls are associated with the moon, water, and the shell, which are all symbols of the feminine principle in life. This is a sign to embrace the feminine side of your being. (You can do this even if you are male, for feminine energy dwells within all of us, men and women.)

• In China the pearl represented genius in obscurity because the beautiful pearl was hidden in the coarse oyster shell. The Moslems referred to the pearl as a symbol of heaven. In some mystic traditions the pearl represented the true centre of life.

• Sometimes a pearl can represent pregnancy or a future pregnancy.

Pedestal

• Are you putting someone or yourself in a position of elevation or seeing that one as above you? This detracts from your inner power, because when you experience yourself within all things, nothing is higher or lower.

Pegasus

• This is a wonderful sign for freedom and inner magic.

• This is your soaring strength. This is your time truly to fly high!

Pen

• This is a sign to express yourself with fluidity. Perhaps this is the time to take pen to paper to communicate with someone else or to express yourself.

• Are you feeling all penned in and restricted?

Pencil

• This is a sign to express yourself. However, it is less permanent than a pen. Are you feeling tentative about things in your life?

Pendulum

• This is a sign of uncertainty in your life. Are you weighing several choices? Do you need to find a balance in your life?

• This sign could be an inner suggestion to begin to use a pendulum for divining, as a way to tap into your subconscious.

Penis/Phallus

• This is usually an obvious sign of the male principle, power and potency, especially if it is erect. In some cultures the religious icono-graphy of the penis depicts the divine, virile, propagating energy in the

universe.
- A deflated penis can suggest feeling impotent, or having unfulfilled potential.
- This sign might also suggest childhood memories surfacing.

Penny   (See also *Money*)
- This can signify a small change in your life.

Pepper
- This can be a sign of spicy, heated or stimulating emotions. Have you become bland and boring? Do you need to pepper up your life?

Perfume
- Smell has a very powerful effect on the way we perceive our environment. Though it might seem subtle, nevertheless smell can invoke more powerful emotional responses than sight or sound. Note your emotional response, as well as associated memories, to the perfume that you smell.

Periscope
- This is a sign of a subconscious observation of conscious reality. Do you need to be an objective observer? Have you been the objective observer for too long? Is now the time to start to participate in life instead of observing it?
- If the periscope is in water, it is a sign of observing your conscious reality from the perspective of your emotional intuitive self.

Perspire
- This can be a sign that you are afraid or nervous. Is there something or someone that makes you nervous or afraid?
- This can also be a sign of exerting yourself. Do you need to exert yourself more in your life? Have you been exerting yourself too much? Do you need to slow down and 'work smarter not harder'?

Petal
- Petals falling from the flower can signify sadness.
- Pulling petals off a flower can be saying, 'She/he loves me, she/he loves me not.'
- This could be a homophone for 'pedal'. Are you 'backpedalling' in life? Do you need to pedal faster?

Phone   (See *Telephone*)

Photograph/Photography
• This is a sign of an objective observation of a situation. Do you need to stand back a bit from the situation and observe it, instead of being directly involved?
• Photographs can also represent memories from the past.

Physician
• This can be a sign to see the doctor for a check-up.

Piano   (See also *Musical Instruments*)
• If the piano is out of tune, you are not in tune with yourself.
• This can be a sign of creative expression through sound.

Picture   (See *Photograph*)

Pie
• This can be a sign of a future opportunity. You will be 'getting a piece of the pie.'
• The roundness of pie suggests wholeness combined with nourishment. A pie symbolizes a whole capable of being divided into shares.

Pig   (See also *Hog*)
• This can be a sign of selfishness and over-indulgence.

Pill
• This can be a pill of something unpleasant or repugnant that must be endured.
• Is there someone disagreeable or tiresome in your life who is a 'real pill'?
• This sign can also indicate healing.

Pillar
• Are you feeling the need to be strong to help others? Do you need to be a pillar of strength, or a pillar of the community? If so, will you be happy in that role?
• A pillar supports a structure. Are you feeling supported in your life?

Pillow
• A pillow can represent your intuitive inner realms and your dreams.
• This can be a sign of relaxation and letting go. Do you feel the need to rest? Perhaps you need to put your head down and relax.

Pimple
• This is a sign of bringing things to a head. Is there a situation in your life that is about to come to a head?

Pin
• A pin fastens separate articles together, or is a support that allows one article to be suspended from another. Are you the pin that is the connector between people in a situation in your life?
• Do you feel pinned down, held fast or immobilized in your life?
• Do you need to pin yourself down and make a commitment?
• Is someone trying to pin you down to a date or a plan?

Pine
• Pine is an excellent cleanser and purifier. Pine emits negative ions which create a healing electrical charge in the air. This may be a sign that it is time to purge your body and purify your life.
• Are you pining away or longing for someone or something?

Pioneer
• This is a sign that you are about to expand into new areas within yourself.

Pipe
• As a musical instrument, a pipe connotes joy and freedom.
• As a kind of tube for conducting liquids or gases, a pipe represents the flow of energy within yourself and the universe. Is your life flowing easily and effortlessly? If there is a blockage in the pipe this may indicate a blockage in your life.
• The peace pipe of the Native American was an object of holiness and reverence. It symbolized unity with spirit. This is time to make peace with yourself and with others in your life.
• Psychologists say the pipe is a sexual symbol representing the penis.

Pirate
• Are you or someone you know having unauthorized use of another's product, conception or creativity? Feel your own authority; find your own creativity in life.

Pit   (See also *Abyss, Hole*)
• The void within a pit represents the dark night of the soul. It is time to uplift yourself. Shift gears and view yourself from a higher perspective. If the sign is at the edge of the pit, it's time to re-evaluate the direction in which you are going in life.

Planets
- The planets can represent heavenly bodies and illumination.
- The planets are the quintessential essence of the rhythm of the universe. The earth is associated with grounding and nurturance. Jupiter can mean expansiveness and vastness. Mars can mean aggressiveness, passion. Mercury was a Greek messenger of the gods and signifies communication, speed and swift change of mood. Neptune was the god of the sea and connotes psychic awareness and mysticism. Pluto, although small and concentrated, can be a spiritual unfolding. Pluto can also be seen as capricious joy, as depicted in the Walt Disney character of that name. Saturn can be sardonic and slow to act, with a feeling of coldness. Uranus denotes hidden abilities. Venus calls forth images of beauty, harmony, femininity, gentleness.

Plastic
- This sign can mean flexibility and your capacity to be moulded or shaped, to be pliable in a situation.
- When something or someone is called plastic it can refer to it being artificial or fake. Are you acting in an insincere and plastic manner?

Platform
- Are you willing to take a stand?
- A platform can mean that you are willing to state your beliefs and make a declaration of your principles.

Play
- Children at play symbolize joy and spontaneity. Are you playing enough in your life?
- 'All the world's a stage . . . ' Your life is your script and you can choose to become involved in the drama or not. You write the lines and decide how you want to play the parts. It's all up to you.

Plumbing   (See also *Water*)
- The plumbing in your home can represent your emotions. Backed-up plumbing can signify that you are feeling emotionally backed up in your life. If your plumbing is overflowing, are your emotions overflowing? Frozen pipes can signify that your emotions are frozen. Take time to centre and allow your emotions freedom of expression.

Pocket
- A pocket is a place of safekeeping. It can be a cavity containing something of value, a receptacle or a container. Are you safekeeping the things of value in your life?

Poison

• This is a sign of something destructive or harmful in your life. Most often, it is pointing to an attitude about self, a fear or a judgment. Are you feeling poisoned by someone or something? Affirm to yourself, 'All that I take into my life strengthens and supports me.'

Poker

• Are you gambling with something that you can't afford to lose? If you don't hedge your bets or only bet on a sure thing, this is not a good time to take risks.

Police   (See also *Officer*)

• This can be a sign of protection and guidance. Help is at hand. You are being protected.
• This can be a sign of guilt. Are you afraid your secret will get out? Are you guilty of a legal or moral lapse? Is there an illegal situation in your life that you feel guilty about? Do you have something on your conscience that makes you afraid of punishment? No one has lived a completely moral and legal life, and if they have, they probably are completely boring. Cease your illegal activities. Or if you don't stop, then at least release the guilt that you are feeling and accept responsibility for your actions. Guilt is a way of not feeling and acting responsibly for your actions in life.

Pollution

• This can be a sign of inner stagnation. Consider a cleansing fast.

Pond

• As with any area of water, a pond represents emotions and intuition. A calm and clear pond suggests calm, clear emotions, as troubled water suggests an emotional difficulty.
• The boundaries of a pond are smaller than those of an ocean or lake indicating less of an emotional concern.

Pool

• A pool is suggestive of intuition and the deep inner realms of self.
• A swimming pool suggests relaxation and healthy exercise and training.

Popcorn

• Popping corn can indicate lots of creativity and new ideas that are moving into manifestation. The kernels (ideas) are expanding.
• Stale popcorn can indicate an unsatisfactory ending.

Porch

- An added-on part of yourself; an extension of yourself.
- That which is not a part of your basic nature, yet is something you consider in relation to yourself.

Porcupine

- Is there a prickly situation in your life? Or is there something you want or need to stay away from?

Porridge

- Porridge is warm and comforting. It can symbolize memories of childhood and Goldilocks and the three bears. This is the time to reunite with the child within and to allow that child free rein.

Port

- A port can be a sign of emotional safety and seeking refuge from a particular problem or situation. Notice the water nearby. Is it rough, clear, cloudy? The nature of the water can give you signs about your particular concerns and emotions.
- Port can mean good wine and thus represent enjoyment with friends. Take time to appreciate the finer things in life, to enjoy your senses to the fullest. Live fully and passionately.

Portrait

- This sign relates to how you see yourself or how you think others see you, but it is not necessarily your true nature.

Postman

- A message is on its way to you.

Pot

- A pot contains the food or the sustenance which you are cooking. It can be of various materials, usually pottery, metal, or glass. The pot is the context or the container for that which sustains you. What meaning do you hold that contains the ingredients of your life?
- Pot can also mean marijuana which can signify a different level of consciousness. Are you dependent on outer stimulation rather than your inner resources?
- Potting a plant is placing the plant in a container where it can take root and grow in a contained way. If there is a project that you are working on, this is the time to initiate its growth. However, the growth will be contained for a while.

Pottery

• This sign concerns moulding your life, your attitudes, your beliefs. You can mould and create a life that empowers you.

Praise

• If you are aware of praise all around you, even if it isn't directed at you, this is a sign that you are to be congratulated. You have done well.

Pregnancy

• This is a fantastic sign that there is something you are about to give birth to as a new idea, new relationship, or new way of viewing the world. This can also be a sign of a new creative project or going in a new direction.

• This sign can also signify a subconscious desire to be pregnant or an indicator that you are already pregnant.

President

• This sign can mean that you are your own authority. It can be a sign of control and leadership. It is time to take authority for your life.

Prince

• A prince can signify the most divine masculine part of yourself. Even if you are a woman there is a masculine energy within you. This sign can be saying touch the divine masculine within.

Princess

• A princess can signify the most divine feminine part of yourself. Even if you are a man there is a feminine energy within you. This sign can be saying touch the divine feminine within.

Prison/Prisoner

• This sign can mean self-imposed bars and self-imposed confinement. The key to let yourself out is within you. The only person who can imprison your spirit is you.

Profanity

• If there is profanity all around you, check to see if this is an external reflection of emotions inside you which are either unprocessed or unexpressed.

Prop

• Is there something or someone that is temporarily supporting you until you step into your own wisdom, your own judgment, or your own strength?

Prostitute

• Are you prostituting yourself or using your energy inappropriately?
• This can also be a sign of a latent draining of sexual energy.
• Have you been prudish for too long? Is it time for you to revel in your sensuality?

Prune

• Are you feeling shrivelled and does your energy feel dried up?

Pump

• You are getting your life-affirming energies pumped up!
• This can be a sign of sexuality and sensual potency.
• Water, free-flowing from a pump, indicates easy, free-flowing emotion. To pump without results indicates emotional constriction or restriction. Priming the pump connotes opportunity ahead.

Puppet

• Do you feel manipulated, or are you are manipulating others?
• Are you giving away your power and forgetting that you are in control?

Purse

• Are you tied to another's purse strings?

Puzzle

• Each part of your life is a different part of the puzzle. A completed puzzle indicates unification. Are you not seeing the whole picture?
• This sign can indicate feeling puzzled and unsure, lacking clarity. Step back to get the whole picture before you make any decisions. Take time to concentrate or focus your energy. The answer will be forthcoming.

Pyramid

• This is a symbol of initiation. You have moved to a new level of awareness, a new level of understanding within yourself. This is also a powerful symbol of inner unification and alignment.
• You are open to guidance from those higher energies around you and from your higher self.

Python

• This sign, like all serpents, symbolizes that potent life force within you, just as the caduceus, or the two intertwined serpents, represents the healer's staff of life.

Quail

• The bird called quail can be a homonym for quail which means to fear or to recoil in dread. Is there something in your life which you are shrinking back from? Are you cowering in fear?

Quaker

• Members of this sect generally represent a balanced and peaceful life, as well as family unity and harmony. Do you feel the need to belong to a peaceful society of friends?

Quarantine

• Are you feeling isolated or in a state of isolation? This can be a sign of feeling separate from your true nature.

Quarrel

• If there are quarrels going on all around you, even if you are not personally involved in them, this is a sign that there are different aspects of yourself at war within you. A valuable technique you may use to resolve this difficulty is to imagine that the different parts inside you all have personas. Imagine all the personas talking together, each in turn, until they reach a resolution.

Quartz

• This is a symbol of clarity and spiritual attunement. The clarity and naturally faceted shape of the quartz crystal have contributed to this exquisite stone being a tool for spiritual attunement for mystics and shamans since the earliest times. In addition to the beauty of the stone, quartz crystal has piso-electric qualities which are thought to be helpful in meditation and for inner journeying. Crystal has the physical capacity to be a transmitter and magnifier of energy. The base component of quartz (silica) is the material used for the silicon chips that are used for electrical impulse transmission in computers. Quartz can be a very powerful sign to attend to your spiritual path and to focus your spiritual energy.

Queen

• This is your feminine power and authority. Even if you are a man you have a feminine energy within you. Is this the time to honour and own the power of the divine goddess within? This sign has more strength and power than 'princess'. It is the wisdom of womanliness rather than the purity of girlhood.
• Is someone in your life overbearing and acting like a queen, or are you being haughty and queen-like to others? Remember, all our cosmic shoelaces are connected. You might be a step ahead today but

tomorrow (or in your next life) you may be the one lagging behind. So it is important to treat every human being with respect and dignity.

Quest

• This usually signifies a spiritual journey. Do you have a spiritual yearning within you? Remember the answers are within you. The inward quest is just as powerful as the outer quest.

Quicksand

• This sign can signify fear and the feeling that you are being pulled under. The way to deal with quicksand in your life is to be still. Stop struggling against the circumstances of your life. Expand your horizon; expand your perspective. There is a way out of the difficulty in which you are involved. Instead of fighting against the quicksand become one with it, so that all possibilities are open to you.

Quilt

• A patchwork quilt is created from different components (sometimes different pieces of fabric that are unusable by themselves), which together create something beautiful and useful. You can combine seemingly useless parts of your life into something completely new and beautiful.
• Quilts traditionally were made by a number of women working together at quilting bees. It was a time of conversation, warmth and sharing for the women. Is this a good time to work together in community with others towards a common goal?

Rabbit

• The rabbit is very prolific so it sometimes symbolizes prosperity. It is used at Easter in conjunction with eggs as a symbol of fertility and abundance because of its ability to produce so many young.
• The rabbit is often associated with temerity and fear. Is there a situation or a person that inspires fear in you? That which you fear is often what you create in your life, so face your fears instead of running away from them. Affirm to yourself, 'I have the resources that I need within me to confront any fear in my life.'
• This sign can also pertain to an inner gentleness and softness. Have you been projecting your energy outwards and as a result feeling tired? Perhaps it is time to burrow into your nest and feel gentle, soft and receptive.
• Rabbit is also a symbol of going fast with no organization, in other words hopping from one thing to another. Are you running around with no direction? Stop. Breathe. Relax, and tackle one thing at a time. Access your true goals and prioritize. Choose the thing that is most

important to you and pursue it with laser-like focus. Affirm to yourself, 'I have all the time that I need in my life to accomplish all my goals.'

Race

• Are you in a race against time? Are you racing around in your life? Slow down, smell the daisies. Remember the story of the turtle and the hare. Sometimes you can achieve your goal faster by going slowly and deliberately than by racing around. The only person with whom you are competing is yourself.

• Is someone in your life competing with you, or do you feel that you are in a race with someone? Measure your own worth against yourself rather than against someone else and you will ultimately feel much happier about your life.

• If your race is against yourself, enjoy the process as well as the ultimate end reward and you will experience greater poise.

Radar

• Put your personal radar on. There are messages all around you but you need to use your intuition to hear them. Meditate. Be still and listen.

Radio

• There are a multitude of dimensions and experiences available to you. All you need do is tune the inner dial within you to experience them. To do this, take time to meditate and tune in.

• This can also be a sign of communication and guidance from another source.

Rage

• If you are aware of rage around you, this most likely is a reflection of a deep inner rage within you. Allow the anger that has been held in for so long to be expressed. However, rather than expressing blame and shame, communicate what emotions you are feeling.

Rags

• Rags is a word used to describe threadbare or tattered clothing and can be a sign of feeling poverty of spirit. Are you feeling materially or spiritually poor? There is always some area of your life that is abundant. Perhaps you are abundant in friends or in good health or in a particular skill. Focus on the areas of your life that are prosperous and this feeling will expand into other areas of your life.

• To 'rag' can be to tease or taunt, or to berate and scold. Are you ragging someone inappropriately, or are you feeling that someone is ragging you? If you are ragging someone, remember that your judgments of others usually reflect back on you. If someone is ragging you, remember that their ragging is demeaning to them. Find your inner magnificence to understand and have compassion for their imbalance.

Railings

• A railing is a structure made of bars or rails that is used as a guard or barrier, or for support or creating boundaries. Are you aware of your personal boundaries? Do you need to create more clear boundaries between yourself and others?
• A railing gives you something to hold onto for support. Do you need to have something to hold onto for a sense of security in your life? Affirm, 'I am always supported by life around me no matter what the circumstances of my life are.'

Rain

• Water represents emotions and rain cleanses the air of impurities. Rain means that perhaps you are going through an emotional time and a cleansing process. It can symbolize intense emotional purification. This is a symbol that is cleansing as well as emotionally refreshing.
• Rain can also symbolize the shedding of tears. Is there a situation or person where you have unresolved grief?
• This potentially can be a sign of growth and fertility as the rain brings life to the plants below. This can be a sign that you are entering a fertile time in your life.

Rainbow

• Throughout the world the rainbow is one of the most universal signs of blessing. A rainbow blesses your ventures, your relations and you. It is a message from spirit to you that you are going in the right direction and that your path is blessed and guided. It is a very powerful sign signifying joy, celebration, completion. If you have been involved in a difficulty this is a sign of a completion and new hope. It signals the end of despair and difficulty.

Ram

• Ram is the symbol for the astrological sign Aries. As the ram charges forward it symbolizes the pioneering spirit. It is also the symbol of initiation of new projects and ideas.
• This can also be a sign of masculine thrusting strength. If this sign appears for you, take life by the horns and charge forward. The time is right!

Rape

• This is a very powerful sign. Are you feeling emotionally or energetically raped? Are you in a situation where you feel like a complete victim in your life? Are you accepting someone else's reality as your own, or are you losing energy to someone or something? This can be a sign of an incredible loss of power and self-esteem and a feeling of being ripped off or feeling emotionally penetrated. Affirm with intensity, 'I am a strong and powerful human being and I create my own destiny. So be it!'

• Symbols of rape can occur at a time when early childhood memories of abuse are beginning to emerge. If the signs continue, consider going into therapy to tackle potentially deep-seated emotional issues.

Rat

• The rat can be a sign of the betrayer or the wrongdoer. Are you ratting on someone? Either release the guilt and take responsibility for your actions or stop ratting. This can be a sign that someone is ratting on you. Watch your back.

• Are you letting things gnaw at you? Take action on the things that are bothering you and affirm, 'I am not concerned with the small things in life. My focus is on the bigger and more important things in my life.'

• Is your home or office a rat's nest or a real mess? Clean it up or quit judging it and your energy will soar.

• Rats can also be a symbol of those things inside yourself that you are initially disgusted or appalled by. It's important to integrate and accept those parts of yourself. In the story of the Pied Piper of Hamelin, when the rats left the town so did all the children. The parts of yourself that you reject are also the parts of yourself that have great potential, just as children have potential. Love and honour all parts of yourself and you will become whole.

Raven   (See also *Crow*)

• Raven can represent delving into the unknown darkest parts of yourself. Are you willing to journey to the darkest part of your being to find the truth? This is the time to travel inward.

Rebellion   (See *Revolution*)

Recipe

• This sign can symbolize combining the ingredients of your life in such a way that there is unity. It's time to bring together all the various parts of your life to create something fulfilling.

Record

• Do you feel like you are going around and around? Are you stuck in a rut or a groove with the same old attitudes and the same old feelings? It is time to step off the treadmill.

Red

• Red is a powerful colour that symbolizes passion, physical strength, anger, sexuality, sensuality, aggression and danger. It is also the colour of blood, so in some cultures it is a favoured colour. The Chinese looked favourably upon it and painted their banners red as talismans. The Mother Goddess in India is painted red because she is associated with creation; red symbolizes life and creation because a child is born amidst blood. Even in prehistoric times individuals associated red with life. They would stain with blood any object they wished to bring to life.

Red Cross

• This is a sign of healing and self-healing. The cross is a sacred symbol that goes back even before the advent of Christ. It represents wholeness and unity.

Refrigerator

• Are you emotionally feeling closed off from others? Are you emotionally frozen and not feeling enough warmth in your life? Affirm to yourself, 'I share my emotions and my feelings easily and effortlessly with others.'

Repair

• Is there is something in your life that you feel needs mending or needs to be repaired? This might mean emotional or spiritual repairs are in order. However, it can also relate to repairing physical objects in your life. When you repair a physical object there is a corresponding meaning in another area of your life. For example, if your repair your bicycle you are increasing your mobility in other areas of your life as well.

Rescue

• Are you are feeling out of control of your life and like you need to be rescued? Do you feel there are others in control of your safety and destiny? This point of view comes from the point of view of the victim. Remember, there are no victims. There are only volunteers. In the deepest sense you are the only one who can rescue yourself. Begin to become more responsible for your life and your experiences.

• If you are constantly rescuing others, sometimes this can be a dysfunctional behaviour pattern. Look at how your emotional needs are met by constantly rescuing others and see if there are other more constructive ways that your needs can be met.

Restraint/Restriction

• If this sign appears to you, examine both your internal and your external circumstances for physical and emotional limitations and restrictions. Restrictions sometimes have the value of allowing you to explore new areas of your life. For example, if you become physically restricted because of a foot injury and aren't as mobile as usual, your disability can help you gain a slower, softer perspective of life. However, if you are not gaining anything positive from your restrictions, then it is time either to accept them with grace or change them.

Revolution

• Are there different aspects of yourself at war? Usually a sign of this kind suggests a coming time of change. Take time to discover and be aware of the different parts of yourself. Find resolution of the internal rebellion or the revolt that is occurring within you by getting to understand the needs of each individual part of you. For example, you might have one part of you that wants to be carefree and wants to live for the moment. You might have another part of you that wants to have stability and security. If you deny or judge one part of yourself, that part will most certainly rebel and cause physical and emotional problems. Find the middle path of compromise so that the carefree part of you can have times of wild abandon, while the responsible part of you can retain a stable base.

Revolving Door

• Do you feeling like you are moving around and around with old attitudes, old ideas? Affirm, 'I am ready to step forward into greater and greater opportunities in my life.'

Rhinoceros

• This can be seen as a sexual symbol as well as a sign of power. The rhinoceros is a powerful, forceful animal, charging ahead at full steam without stopping.

Rice

• This is usually a sign of domestic happiness, weddings, joy and celebration.
• This is an excellent sign of a good harvest for the projects you are working on in your life.

Riding

• If a person is riding an animal, this can be a sign of mastery and moving in alignment with nature.
• If the sign indicates that you are riding in a vehicle and someone else

is driving, do you feel that you are not in charge of your life? Do you feel that someone else is guiding you? Affirm to yourself, 'I am in control of my destiny.'

• Are you being taken for a ride or being deceived? Affirm to yourself, 'I see the inner truth in all situations.'

Ring

• The ring is a powerful sign of the continuous circle of life. The ring can be a sign of completion, wholeness and unity.

• This has long been a sign of friendship, engagement and marriage. If this sign appears to you it can be the sign of a coming engagement or commitment. It can also be a sign of eternal love.

River

• The river has many powerful, symbolic meanings. It has been called 'the river of life', 'the flowing waters of life' and 'the river of time'. It always is a sign of movement and the rhythm of change. The expression, 'Don't push the river, it flows by itself,' means that to get into a flow of life you don't need to work so hard. Quit trying to swim upstream. Allow the river to carry you. Don't fight the current so much in life.

• A river can also represent an emotional barrier you are having trouble crossing. Make yourself a new route or look at your situation in a new way in order to resolve it.

Road

• The road is your direction in life. Look carefully at this sign. Is it rocky? Crooked? Straight? Does it go uphill? Downhill? Is it clear? This represents your destiny, your direction in life. Look for forks in the road, forks representing major decisions to be made. The condition of the road suggests the way that your life is running at this moment. Affirm to yourself, 'My destiny unfolds easily and effortlessly for me in every moment.'

Robber

• This can be a sign of tremendous fear and insecurity. Do you feel like a victim of life? Do you feel at the mercy of life's twists and turns? Accept responsibility for your life and live it the way you want to. Find areas of your life where you do have control. Practise living fully there, so that you can gradually expand that feeling to a greater and greater proportion of your experience.

• This can also be a very pragmatic sign to take extra precautions with your home security.

Robot

• Are there people around you who seem uncaring, unfeeling or who seem to have mechanical feelings? Are you feeling shut off from your emotions? Affirm to yourself, 'I express my feelings easily and effortlessly and I honour all my emotions.'

Rock

• All around the world, the rock is a symbol of strength, permanence, and solidity. Are you as sturdy and strong as the rock of Gibraltar?
• A rock can also be a sign of grounding. This sign could be reminding you to get more grounded. A good way to ground yourself is to sit or stand with your back to a tree. Relax and feel a deep connection to the tree. Know that you are truly a child of Mother Earth.

Rocket

• This sign can mean soaring to spiritual heights. You have unlimited potential and power.
• Some psychologists (usually male) suggest that the rocket is a symbol for the penis, due to its shape and its thrusting power.

Roof   (See also *Home/House*)

• This sign can refer to your general protection in life.

Room   (See also *Home/House*)

• Room is an aspect of yourself.

Rope

• A rope can be a lifeline, or it can be an attachment to a person or place or thing.
• A rope that is neatly coiled can represent organization, inner twining and a balance of mind, body and soul. A rope that is frayed or knotted can represent disassociation.
• Are you feeling tied up or restricted, as if you are all in knots? Affirm to yourself, 'I'm relaxed in all areas of my life and I know my life is unfolding according to a greater plan.'

Rose

• The rose is a universal sign of love and beauty. In various cultures the rose is also the mystic centre of the heart, the emblem of Venus and the mystical sign of the divine being.

Row/Rowing

• Rowing across water can represent moving through an emotional situation.

- Row can mean a fight or having an argument.
- Row can also represent organization, such as soldiers in a row or a neatly laid out garden.

Royalty

- Depending upon whether it is male or female, this sign can pertain to the divine aspects of self: the divine feminine and the divine masculine.
- This can also be a sign of feeling a sense of your own royalty, and your own divinity.

Running

- Are you running away from a situation or are you running from something for which you are not yet ready? Are you are unsure of yourself and afraid of a situation or experience that you are not willing to acknowledge? Stop! Turn around. Face the truth. Face that from which you are running and you will begin to dissolve that barrier.
- Running away in slow motion can mean the time is coming soon when you will have to face an inner difficulty.
- Running towards something means you are in a time of great acceleration within your spiritual life. Celebrate!
- This could be a sign that you should consider jogging as a form of exercise.

Rust

- This can be a sign that your talents are not being used. You are a bit rusty in your skills. Polish up those abilities.
- This can be also a sign of deterioration. This can mean that it's definitely time to rejuvenate your body and your mind.

Sack

- A sack can suggest hiding or self-concealment. Or perhaps it refers to future events yet to be revealed.
- This can be a sign of getting sacked or losing your power. If this is a possibility, you should begin to check your options and plan ahead.

Sacrifice

- If you are aware of sacrifice as a sign or if you are constantly sacrificing yourself, it is possible that you have a martyr complex. This is very dysfunctional behaviour and it's important either to work with a therapist to resolve this negative conditioning or reprogramme your subconscious mind by affirming to yourself, 'I accept and honour myself. I am a valuable human being.'
- This sign can signify that you are feeling at the mercy of circum-

stances rather than in control of them. Affirm to yourself, 'I choose my life and I choose it completely. I am in control of my life. I have chosen my life's circumstances.'
• Giving of yourself to others and for the good of the community is different from sacrificing yourself. The actions might be the same but the energy behind the actions is different. When you give generously and fully without expecting anything in return, you gain emotionally and physically. When you sacrifice yourself, usually there is a subconscious expectation of being appreciated. When this doesn't happen (which is usually the case), your energy is depleted.

Saddle
• To saddle is to load, burden or encumber. Are you feeling bound or saddled by a situation that you wish you could be free of? Affirm, 'I am free to journey in any and all directions in my life.'

Sailboat   (See also *Water*)
• This sign can signify navigating through emotional change. If the boat is moving quickly and easily, you are soaring through emotional change with ease.

Saint
• This symbol is usually associated with a message from your guardian angel or your higher self. Listen very carefully to the messages surrounding this sign.

Salmon
• This sacred fish of the Celts can be a sign of moving ahead against all odds.

Salt
• Salt can be a powerful sign of strength and stability. Salt has been prized by ancient people from the dawn of time for its great uses as a medicine, a preservative, and as a link to the spirit world. In ancient times salt was considered so valuable that it was traded ounce for ounce with gold, and in early China salt cakes were even used as currency. Throughout the centuries salt's presence has permeated many aspects of language and culture. It is reported that Cabalistic tradition considers salt a sacred word because its numerical value is the same as God's name of power, Yahweh, multiplied three times.
  In ancient times, salt was thought to be a substitute for the Mother Goddess' regenerative blood. In both the Jewish and Christian religions, salt was considered a substitute for blood on the altar as it came from the womb of the sea and had the savour of blood.

The Bible speaks of a 'covenant of salt' (Numbers 18:19), which is a covenant as binding as blood that can never be broken. Semitic visionaries talked of 'salt of the earth' to mean the true blood of the Earth Mother. Even in present days when we want to say that someone is truly trustworthy, we say they are 'the salt of the earth.' Salt can be a sign of wisdom, stability and strength.

• Salt can also be a powerful symbol of purification and of dispersing negativity. Salt has remarkable purifying properties. In the ocean it acts as an antiseptic to destroy bacteria. Even though the sea is subjected to the same destructive pollution as the land, salt water rejuvenates itself more quickly. The salt in the ocean is able to neutralize and destroy some of the biological pollution which plagues our planet's coastlines. This sign can be saying, cleanse and purify every aspect of your life.

Sand

• A house built on sand doesn't have a permanent foundation. Nothing is permanent. Everything is an illusion. Are your dreams built on the shifting sands of time? If this sign appears for you there is a possibility that there will be changes coming in your life.

• Sand can represent the irritations and small annoyances in life.

Saw

• A saw might symbolize cutting one down to size. Or it could refer to the construction of something new. In this sense, it is a very positive sign having to do with building, creating, making and doing.

• A saw can be used for pruning. Are there areas of your life that need to be thinned out in order for new fresh growth to take place?

• This sign might relate to an emotional wound from the past that is healing but is still not forgotten. Check the other symbols, people and situations to help identify the emotional scarring that still needs to be healed.

Scissors

• This is a sign for cutting away, releasing that which is unnecessary in your life.

• Are you feeling cut off from others, and from yourself? Affirm, 'I am not separate from the world around me. I am one with all things.'

Sea (See Ocean)

Seam

• A seam is that which binds things together. Are you coming apart at the seams? Affirm to yourself, 'No matter what external form my life takes, I know that there is a greater plan for my life and that plan is unfolding in perfection.'

Seeds

• Great things grow from small beginnings, provided they have the right environment. This is a great sign for a new beginning.
• 'As you sow, so shall you reap.' The seeds of consciousness and kindness that you plant will germinate and sprout in the time ahead.

Seesaw

• Do you feel as though you are going up and down but not getting anywhere? Get off the seesaw. Make a choice, even if you are not sure of the outcome. There is power in decisiveness.

Sex

• If you are aware of sexual innuendoes, sexually oriented material and sexual signs all around you, this can be a reflection of a subconscious sexual energy brooding within you. Your libido is high. If you find others interested in you sexually and you are, on the surface at least, not interested at all, there is a possibility that you are subconsciously broadcasting sexual signals. Take time to tune in to your inner wisdom to discover the source of these signs. Listen to yourself and figure out what you really want.

Shadow

• Your shadow is the unknown part of yourself. Locate and bring to light the parts of yourself that have remained hidden and unseen to become a more fully integrated person.
• This can also be a sign of fear. Remember a shadow is an illusion. It disappears in the light.
• This can be a sign of the latent potential of an individual. Delve into your shadow to find forgotten yet potent aspects of yourself.

Shark

• The shark can be an omen of danger.
• This can also be a sign of hidden fear. Explore your inner and outer world to discover the source of the hidden fear.
• Someone who is called a shark usually is taking advantage of others. Are you taking advantage of others or is someone taking advantage of you?

Shave

• Did you have a close shave or a close call? Take precautions if this sign keeps appearing for you.
• Shaving is grooming and bolstering your opinion of yourself.

• Monks will shave their heads to show humility and renunciation of the worldly path. Do you feel the need to withdraw into a more reclusive meditative period in your life?

Sheep

• This can be a sign of following without using your own judgment, of non-thinking trust. Objectively examine your choices in life. Are you making choices based on the views of others, or based on your own intuition? Affirm, 'I listen to my own inner wisdom and follow my inner guidance in every moment.'
• This sign can also pertain to being taken advantage of monetarily, or being fleeced.

Shell

• Pulling into your shell can be closing off from the outer world. Is this the time for you to enter into a less active period for a while?
• Shell can also connote emptiness, as in the expression, 'He was just an empty shell of himself.' Are you feeling empty and unfulfilled? Push yourself into activities and events that aren't necessarily consistent with the way that you view yourself to begin to break old patterns and to establish new ones.

Shepherd

• This sign can connote the guardian of your spirit and the guardian of your inner way.

Shield

• A shield is your protection allowing you to stay balanced and centred amid change.
• A shield can also be a defence mechanism. Affirm to yourself, 'I am always safe. My guardian angel is always looking over me, even when I am not aware of it.'

Shoes

• There are steps to be taken in your life. Take these steps now. Every step takes you a little closer to your goal.
• Shoes are your connection to the earth. They allow you to be grounded and at the same time protected from the elements.
• 'Don't judge another until you walk in his shoes.'
• Are you filling too many shoes, or trying to play too many roles in your life?

Shooting

• Shooting at a target can mean focusing energy for a particular goal in your life. Be certain of what you are aiming for in your life because you are on target.

• Shooting can also mean that you want to kill off an aspect of yourself. It's healthier to integrate unwanted parts rather than resisting them.

• Shooting can also signify feeling penetrated, and feeling the victim in life. Gather your inner resources and affirm to yourself, 'I am in charge of my life and I make decisions that empower me in every aspect of my life.'

Shoulder

• Are you shouldering your responsibilities? Do you need to put your 'shoulder to the wheel?' Do you feel like you are carrying the burdens of the world on your shoulders? Life was not meant to be a struggle. Lighten up. Enjoy your life. Take time to have fun.

Signs

• Notice street signs and billboards and random advertising signs that you see. Often there are messages hidden in the words in the signs that catch your consciousness.

Skunk

• The skunk can be a sign that something stinks. Is there a situation in your life that just plain stinks?

• Everyone gives the skunk a wide berth because of its penetrating odour. Do you have body odour to which others are responding but not telling you?

• The skunk walks tall and proud with the knowledge that even though small, he has an inner power of protection within him. This symbol can be reminding you to, 'Walk tall. There is an inner strength available within you that will protect you and keep you safe.'

Sky

• The sky is the limit. Reach to the heavens. There is no limitation to your success. You are free to expand in all directions.

Slave

• Are you being a slave to old habits, old ideas and old beliefs? Are you feeling like a slave to other people, other situations? Affirm to yourself, 'I am my own master and I am in charge of my destiny.'

Sleeping

• This can be an obvious sign that you need more sleep.

• This can also be a sign that you are stagnating and not willing to change. Affirm to yourself, 'I am awake and aware of myself and all of life around me.'

Slide

• Are you feeling out of control? You can either be sliding out of control and feeling frightened, or you can just enjoy the ride. Let go and see where you are taken.

Smoke

• Where there is smoke, there is fire. This can be a warning of danger in your life. Is there a situation that is about to go up in flames?
• Smoke can also indicate a lack of clarity. Things are confused and smoky. Take time to clear your thoughts.
• To Native Americans, smoke was the vehicle on which prayers could travel to the Creator, and through which the Creator's blessings could journey back to earth. Sacred smoke can carry your prayers to the heavens.

Snail

• Are things moving slowly? Is there something in your life that is going at a snail's pace? This can be a sign to get going.

Snake

• This is a very significant sign. It is not a sign to be feared. The snake has long been a symbol for healing. An example is the two intertwined snakes on Hermes' staff which is used as the symbol of the medical profession. In India, Hindus believe that at the base of the spine there is incredible life power energy which is symbolized by a coiled serpent. When this snake arises (called the rising of the kundalini energy) it is said that there is a spiritual awakening and even spiritual healing.
• This sign can represent temptation, as in the serpent in the Garden of Eden. Are you feeling tempted, or are you wanting to tempt someone? Affirm to yourself, 'I am guided to whatever is best for me in accordance with my highest good.'
• The snake is a powerful sign of transformation and resurrection. For just as the snake sheds its skin as it grows, this sign can indicate that you are shedding your old persona and old beliefs to embrace a new path in life.
• The snake may also be a sign of sexuality, representing the male's penis.
• Is someone in your life being a snake in the grass?

Snow   (See also *Water*)

• This is a sign of purity and cleansing. It is now time for a fresh start and a new look at the world. A new beginning is just around the

corner.
- Snow can also represent frozen emotions.

Soap
- Soap is an obvious sign of cleansing and purification. Do you need to clean your body or the objects in your life?

Soldiers
- Is there an inner war going on inside you?
- Soldiers can represent organization and discipline. Is this the time to incorporate more discipline into your life?

Sole
- This can be a homophone for soul which is the true heart of a matter.

Speedometer
- Are you going too fast or too slow in life?

Spider
- The spider's weaving of its web has been a symbol of the creative forces in the universe. The spider's web spirals into a central point and has been considered a representation of the world. The Hindus talk about the web of illusion.
- This can be a sign of a trap or entrapment. Do you feel like you are getting caught in your own web? Do you feel that you are being caught in someone else's web of manipulation and deception? Take time out to view the situation from a higher perspective.

Spiral
- This is a very powerful transformational sign. It can represent the intricate component basic to all life – the DNA helix. It can be an image of evolution, as an upward spiralling movement can symbolize progress and achievement. A downward spiral may be a sign of spiralling into despair and negativity.

Sponge
- Are you soaking up everything? This can be valuable, as there are times in life when it is valuable to store information and knowledge. However, are you learning indiscriminately? Are you soaking up everything without taking time to figure out which things you actually need in your life?
- Are you 'sponging' off other people? Are you feeling others are sponging off you?

Spring

• Spring can be a sign of new growth, new possibilities and new life.

Spy

• Do you feel unsafe? Are you being intruded upon or intruding upon others? Are you involved with another person rather than involved with your own development? Affirm, 'I am involved only in my own evolution. What others think of me is none of my business.'

Square   (See also *Mandala*)

• A square can be a sign of stability. It gives the psychological impression of foundation, firmness and stability.
• The square contains the four elements, the four sacred winds, the four directions and the four seasons. It has the power of the mandala.
• If someone is square, they are old-fashioned and not in touch with the times. Are you out of step with others?
• Do you feel boxed in or controlled?

Squirrel

• This can be a sign of frugality, and of comfort through patience. The squirrel gathers nuts and foodstuffs for the winter. This sign can be telling you to make preparations for the leaner times in life by stockpiling and storing. This can also pertain to stockpiling your energy, or creating a reserve of energy within yourself. Be prepared.

Stag

• This sign can connote sexual vigour and powerful potency. The stag has also been associated with the tree of life because of its powerful antlers. In some cultures in Asia the stag is a symbol of regeneration because of the way that the antlers are renewed every year.

Stage

• This sign can signify the stages of your life. What role do you play in life? How do you feel you appear to others?

Stairs

• Note the direction the stairs are going. Ascending stairs can indicate a rise in status and success. Descending stairs can point to a loss of recognition or loss of confidence.

Star

• This is a very significant symbol representing light, guidance, and insight. As the star shines in the darkness it is a symbol of light and of the spirit within. You are your own star. You are your own light. Your star is rising.

Statue

• Are you feeling immobile, as if you can't move? This sign can indicate frozen feelings and emotions. It can even indicate a feeling of lifelessness. Are you not operating out of your own strength and your own energy? Now is the time to work on self-confidence. Affirm to yourself, 'I move easily and effortlessly and I express myself with energy and joy!'

Steel

• This is a sign of strength and determination. It can also be a sign of immobility and inflexibility.
• Steel can be a homophone for steal. Is someone stealing from you? Is your energy being stolen? This can also indicate the subconscious recollection of something that you have stolen. If this is the case, make reparations. If you can't repay the person or institution that you stole from, make reparations to someone or something else, equal in value to what was stolen.

Stomach   (See also *Nausea*)

• Do you feel like you just can't stomach something in your life?
• The stomach holds nourishment. What in your life is helping you digest attitudes, ideas, feelings?
• This sign could be pointing to an inability to assimilate that which is new. Do you feel fear of the new? Affirm to yourself that you can assimilate new experiences in your life without threatening those things which are already important to you. Without new experiences, you will grow stagnant and stop growing.

Stones   (see also *Rock* and individual colour definitions)

• Each individual stone has its own energy and its own symbolism. For example, a diamond can be a sign of clarity and brilliance. The lustrous green colour exhibited by jade makes it a sign of growth and abundance. Notice the feelings which arise in response to a particular stone to interpret what this sign means to you.

Stork

• This is a sign of a new arrival or a new birth of a project within your life. It can signal a conception or the birth of a new idea. This sign can also herald a child coming into your life.
• The stork is also an omen of domestic happiness and contentment.

Storm

• A storm can indicate an internal conflict. It can also indicate that the air is clearing in regard to a situation in your life.

Suicide

• This sign is a warning. Don't give up. Know that you are never given anything in life that you can't handle, that you can't do or accomplish. You are not alone. There is always help available for you from the inner realms. Pray. Ask for help. Reach out to those around you. You can do it.

• Suicide can sometimes be a sign of wanting to kill off aspects of yourself. Instead of killing off parts of yourself, it's better to have compassion and understanding for those unwanted parts. Integrate them into your personality rather than try to destroy them.

Summer

• This can symbolize maximum fulfilment, confidence, happiness and contentment.

Sun

• This can be a sign of the source from which all things flow. In numerous cultures throughout the world the sun was the symbol for God, Great Spirit, Christ, and for the god within.

• This can also be a sign of power, strength, and clarity, as well as your own inner light.

• The sun was thought to be the masculine aspect of spirit because it was a projecting energy while the moon was the feminine aspect because it was reflective. If the sun appears to you as a sign, this is the time in your life to project your energy forward and just go for it! The signs say you will be successful.

Sunflower

• This is a great sign of joy, of embracing the fullness of life.

Swamp

• Are you feeling completely bogged down, with absolutely no clarity and no way to get out? Are you feeling overwhelmed or swamped with work? Breathe. Relax. Shift gears. Do something completely unexpected to change inner behaviour patterns that are playing out in your life.

Swan

• The white swan is the sign of the white goddess and beauty. If this sign appears to you, plan on gliding to new heights with freedom and grace. A black swan can allude to the inner mysteries of life and your intuition.

• Some have suggested that the swan is a sign of the balance of male and female energies because its rounded soft body suggests femininity and its long outstretched neck suggests the male phallus.

• Apollo, the god of music, was aligned with the swan because of the mythic belief that the swan would sing with exquisite beauty at the point of death – the swan song.

Swastika

• This symbol of power has been found in almost every ancient culture in both its clockwise and anti-clockwise forms. It has been found in Indonesian, Asian, Celtic, Viking, Native American, pre-Columbian, and Germanic cultures. It has been discovered in Christian catacombs, in Ireland, Britain, Mycenae, Gascony, and among the Etruscans. It is a symbol that far predates Hitler's abuse of it. This symbol has been interpreted to mean the masculine and feminine aspects of God. Clockwise represents the masculine and anti-clockwise the feminine aspects of divinity. It has also been seen as the symbol for the creation of the universe in motion because of the rotating arms.

Sweets

• Are you ready to receive the sweetness of life? Honour yourself by making sure that you take time to nurture yourself.

Swimming

• Do you feel like you are swimming against the current? Go with the flow and life can become fun instead of a great effort.

• Do you feel that you are having trouble staying afloat amidst emotional changes? Relax and let the current carry you to the centre of your soul.

• This could be a sign that you should take up swimming as a form of exercise.

Sword

• The sword is a powerful sign that can connote several meanings. It can mean power, truth, and honour. The Knights of the Round Table used their swords for the honour and service of truth and for the good of all people.

• Swords can also be a sign of defence. Do you feel that you need to defend yourself and those you love from physical or emotional attack? Sometimes there is more power in strengthening yourself than focusing your attention on attack and defence.

• The sword is also the means of slaying the ego and cutting through the veil of illusion of life. In folk tales the monster or dragon is usually slain with a sword. The monster can represent your own inner demons or the illusionary world that exists within you.

Syrup

• Are you overly sentimental and overly emotional to the point of insincerity? Is someone around you buttering you up with insincere flattery and syrupy sentiments? Get straight with your communications, with yourself and with others.

Table

• Are you putting off making a decision? Are you tabling a decision or emotion? Put your cards on the table and let people know how you feel.

Tap

• Water usually represents your emotions, hence a leaky tap may mean leaking emotional energy. A stuck tap can mean you can't turn on your emotions. A rusty tap may mean being out of touch with your emotions.
• Do you need to tap into your inner resources?

Tape

• Do you keep playing the same problems over and over again? Are you stuck in the same pattern? Break the mould. Attend to the inner source of the pattern and heal it at its source.
• Taping things together can also represent unity or unification. Are there some areas in your life that you need to tape together?

Tapestry

• Each part of the tapestry represents a different part of you. The tapestry is the complex weaving of your life.

Target

• This is your direction. This is your goal. With self-focus and self-discipline you can reach your goal.

Tax

• Are you being taxed to your limit, emotionally and physically? Are you taxing your strength? You need to rebuild your resources and reassess your capabilities.
• This can be a very obvious sign that you need to get your financial taxes in order.

Tea

• This can be a sign of friendship and relaxation.

Teacher

• Each person we meet in life is our teacher. The greatest teacher of all is within you. Listen to yourself.

Teeth

• Do you need to chew your food more thoroughly to aid digestion?
• Chewing can be a sign of really biting into a problem. Get right to it. The time is now.
• Chewing the fat means talking and discussing something. Is there some situation that you really need to discuss with someone?
• If the sign is teeth falling out, this can mean talking too much or scattering your energy. Or it could mean that you do not understand a problem or situation.
• Teeth stand for decisiveness. Loss of teeth symbolizes loss of the power of decisive action. Loss of teeth can also reflect a loss of face and a spoiling of your appearance in some way. Do you feel a loss of power in your life? Do you need to keep your mouth closed because you are talking too much? Loss of teeth as a sign can mean careless speech. The loss of teeth can also symbolize growing up, moving to a new stage of development, or a new stage of life, as baby teeth are replaced by permanent teeth.
• Sometimes a sign of teeth or loss of teeth can indicate dental problems. Check with your dentist.

Telegram

• Expect a message from someone far away.

Telephone

• A ringing phone can indicate that someone is trying to get your attention or that your subconscious has something to tell you.
• A phone that you are afraid to answer can indicate that there are hidden messages within your unconscious mind that you are afraid to hear. It can also indicate that there are people with whom you are afraid to communicate. Face your fears. Come to terms with them and resolve them. Don't let your fears eat away at your vitality.

Telescope

• You might be looking from afar at a situation but not all is revealed.

Temple

• The word temple comes from the root word *tem* which means 'to divide'. In ancient times the temple was the intersection or division between the heavens and the earth. In fact it was thought that an earthly temple was a recreation of a heavenly temple. If this sign appears to you, take time to establish an inner temple or inner sanctuary within yourself.

Tent

• Any structure that one lives in is usually symbolic of one's self. A tent can be a sign of a feeling of impermanence. Are you feeling temporary within yourself? Is your image of your self not yet solidified? Affirm to yourself, 'I am home within myself. No matter where the outer circumstances of my life lead me, I am always at home within myself.'
• This can also be a sign saying, 'Go camping! Get out in nature!'

Thread

• Thread is an ancient symbol. It can be a sign of the umbilicus, which in turn is connected to the thread of karma, or fate, that weaves its way through your life. Look for the thread of truth throughout the circumstances of your life.

Throat

• A positive aspect of this sign can be an indication that you are willing to speak your own truth. A negative aspect can be that you are afraid to speak your truth, or that you are feeling emotionally strangled in your life.
• Is there something in your life that you just can't swallow?

Thumb

• Thumbs up mean go ahead. Thumbs down, forget it!

Thunder / Thunderbolt

• Thunder, along with the accompanying lightning, represents fire from the heavens. It has the power of illumination and contains the creative forces of the universe. Connected with Aries, which is the first sign in the Zodiac, lightning is associated with the springtime, initiation and the initial stages of any project. It is a sign of bringing the fire of creative energy to any project.

Jupiter, the Roman god, used three thunderbolts containing the energies of chance, providence and destiny to mould future destinies. Thunder and lightning pierce the darkness like a flash of illumination, revealing truth and giving clarity. In Tibet the *vajra* is the symbol both for thunderbolt and for diamond. If this sign appears to you, you are at an exciting point where you are about to pierce through the darkness into the light.

• This sign can also indicate an enormous release of suppressed emotions and feelings. This can indicate the advent of anger, hostility, rage, or the aftermath of a powerful, emotional-psychic release.

• Thunder can also be the warning voice of the gods. Pay attention to the messages and the signs around you.

Tidal Wave   (See also *Water*)

• This sign indicates a huge emotional upheaval.

Tide

• This indicates ebbing and flowing in life, as well as the ebbing and flowing of your emotions. Life is always in movement. There are times of projecting your energies outward and times of withdrawing. There are abundant times and there are lean times. Doors in life open and doors in life close. It is just change, you are safe.

Tiger

• This is a powerful sign of energy, strength, and prowess. The words, 'Tiger, tiger, burning bright,' from William's Blake's poem provide vivid images of the incredible dynamic energy that the tiger exudes. This energy can be used constructively or destructively. Affirm, 'I always use my energy in a positive, constructive manner.'

• Get up and go for it, you tiger!

Tightrope

• Are you feeling tense, as if you have to walk a tightrope in life? Are you under great pressure and stress? This sign can be telling you to take time to relax and re-evaluate. Stress can make mountains out of molehills and can exaggerate your problems until they seem overwhelming. When you unwind, breathe and relax you can begin to see your life's difficulties in perspective.

Toad   (See also *Frog*)

• The toad has similar symbolism to the frog, although the frog is more connected to feelings and emotions because of its aquatic environment. Also the toad is more aligned with the grounded, fertile energies of the earth.

Toilet

• This sign represents elimination of that which isn't needed in your life. Let it go. You don't need it any more.

Tomb

• This sign can symbolize transformation, death and resurrection. For example, in Celtic tradition the burial mound was considered to be a womb of Mother Earth. Hence the tomb was seen as a kind of womb, as a place of preparation for rebirth.

Tower

• This sign can represent isolation. Do you feel as if you are being locked in an ivory tower or cut off from different aspects of yourself? Affirm, 'I participate fully and passionately with other people and I enjoy my interpersonal interactions.'
• This sign can also represent a spiritual point of clarity. In ancient Egypt the tower is a sign designating rising above the rabble of common life. It is a sign of ascending to a new and higher level of spiritual awakening. It is for this reason that in the Tarot falling from the tower can represent personal emotional upheaval.
• Freudian therapists suggest that a tower is a phallic symbol.

Toys

• Play more. Enjoy yourself. Allow your inner child to play and have fun.
• Do you feel like you are being 'toyed with'? Garner your inner strength and state your truth clearly and assertively.

Train

• This sign can be telling you that you have the power to accomplish your goals. Remember how in the children's story, 'The Little Train that Could', the little train knew that with determination and effort he could ascend to the top of the highest mountain. You too have the power to reach your goals.
• Missing the train can mean missing opportunities in life. A freight train carrying a heavy load can indicate that you are carrying too heavy a load in life.

Trash

• This sign indicates emotional junk that you are carrying around with you. Let go of it. Eliminate it and release it.

Treadmill

• Do you feel like you are putting out energy in life, but you are getting nowhere? Affirm to yourself, 'All the energy that I put out in life is valuable and moves me further along on my path in life.'
• This can be a sign that you are stuck with the same old beliefs, the same attitudes, the same old thought forms. Affirm, 'I am open to new

experiences and new opportunities in my life.'

Treasure

• This can be a sign of inner gifts and inner wealth from spirit. In fairy tales the treasure is often hidden in a cave which can be a symbol of the unconscious mind. Jung states that the treasure in the cave that the hero attains after great effort is, in fact, a kind of rebirth in the womb-like cave.

• This is an excellent sign for the possible future attainment of valuable or precious possessions of any kind.

• You are treasured. You are especially precious and valuable.

Trees

• Trees represent one of the most common and traditional signs throughout the world, hence, the Tree of Life and the Tree of Knowledge. Trees can be a personal symbol of your life's development. The roots of the tree that go deep into the earth can be likened to your earthly life, while the branches rising into the sky symbolize your higher consciousness, allowing you to feel rooted and grounded within the earth plane, yet soaring to spiritual heights.

Each tree has its own properties. Is the tree straight or crooked? An old gnarled tree can represent wisdom, strength. A slender willow tree can mean being able to bend with circumstances. The meaning of a tree can vary depending on whether the tree is just beginning to leaf, is in full leaf, is losing its leaves or has no leaves. An aspen can represent fear, as in quaking with fear. The oaks, which were sacred to the Celts, represent strength. A pine can represent spiritual clarity and purification. A palm tree can represent warmth and freedom. A fruit tree can mean bearing fruit in life.

• A tree can pertain to family matters, as for example, your family tree. Examine other surrounding signs to understand how this sign relates to your family.

Triangle

• This sign holds the power of integration through the trinity: of body, mind and spirit, of mother, father and child, of past, present and future, of the Holy Trinity. You are now in a time of integration in your life. It also embodies the power of the pyramids. It is an active symbol for spirit and aspiring to higher realms. Two triangles – one in the normal position and one inverted and superimposed on the first – form a six-pointed star (called Solomon's Seal), which constitutes a symbol for the human soul. The triangle also has the power of protection. This sign says, 'You are safe and you are being protected.'

Tunnel

• The tunnel is an inner passageway to self. Going into the earth is often a metaphor for going into the unconscious mind. This is the time to turn your awareness away from the outer world and to explore your inner world.

• A light at the end of the tunnel can signify that you will make it through this difficult time. The circumstances in your life will improve. You are going to make it.

• Do you have tunnel vision? Are you being too close-minded? Expand your personal perimeters so that you can see the situation from all angles.

• When someone has a near-death experience, they almost always report going down a tunnel towards a light. This image resides in the collective subconscious as a powerful metaphor for changing realities and changing levels of consciousness. You are in the process of shifting gears and attuning to different frequencies in life.

Turtle

• This is a powerful symbol. The Native Americans call their continent Turtle Island. The legend goes that once there was only water and there wasn't anywhere that people could live. Turtle made a very great sacrifice and let everyone live on her back. Thus she became the spirit keeper of the earth. When Native Americans enter into the darkness of a covered dome structure for the sacred purification ceremony called the Sweat Lodge, they believe that they are entering into the turtle, into the very essence of the Mother Earth. It is a time of spiritual death and rebirth.

• This can also be a sign of slow but steady progress towards reaching a goal, or completion through diligence.

• A turtle pulls into its shell when frightened. This sign may signify a wish to withdraw from a problem, or a need to withdraw and go inward to gather forces.

Tyres   (See also *Car*)

• This is a sign of your mobility, your ability to move in life. Often a car is symbolic of the way we perceive ourselves.

A flat tyre can mean you are not balanced. An over-inflated tyre can mean that your ego is over-inflated, or perhaps you have over-inflated a situation in your life. A tyre without much tread can mean that you can't really get a grip on things in life.

UFO

• There are two directly opposed meanings for this sign. A UFO sign can signify the quest for personal integration and higher intelligence. Its round shape suggests a sign of unity, completion and wholeness. UFOs hovering in the skies suggest the heavens. Hence UFOs can be powerful signs of spiritual, personal integration.

• UFOs can also be a sign of fear of the unknown. Numerous reports of UFO abductions, whether actual or anecdotal, still give credence to this being a sign that signifies tremendous fear. Are you afraid of the unknown realms within yourself? Affirm, 'I am a courageous, strong individual. I accept all aspects of myself.'

Umbrella

• This is a sign of protection and being sheltered from life's storms. Know that you are safe and protected always.

Uncle

• This sign depends on the relationships that you had with your uncles. Was your uncle a friend to you? Then this sign represents a reliable friend. If your uncle terrorized you, then this sign can symbolize fear.

• To 'cry uncle' is to give up. Are you ready to give up? If not, fight like hell.

• Have you been feeling foolish? Are you being a 'monkey's uncle?' Enjoy all the parts of yourself, even your foolishness. It's a part of your magnificence. Without it you wouldn't be who you are.

Underground

• Anything that is underground is related to your subconscious mind. Notice the other signs to determine what part of your unconscious mind needs attention or is repressed.

Undertaker

• Are you undertaking an unpleasant situation or experience? Either don't do it, or find a way that you can gain value and joy from your participation.

Undressed

• Are you feeling exposed? Are personal secrets about you being revealed? Do you feel too vulnerable and open? It is time to create some personal boundaries for yourself. Find a balance between being too open and being too closed off. Find the middle path.

• This can also be a sign to free yourself from inhibitions. Free yourself from your outer persona. You've outgrown it. Let go. Be wild and madcap. Live life fully and passionately.

Unicorn

• Traditionally the unicorn has been a symbol of Christ. It represents spiritual unfoldment, chastity and purity.
• Psychologists allude to the unicorn as a symbol of sexuality because of the unicorn's single protruding horn.

Uniform

• Are you experiencing too much rigidity and inflexibility? Is everything too uniform in your life? Creativity often occurs through chaos and disorder. Create some disorder in your life. Make a mess. Play in the mud. Have fun!
• Uniforms can be a sign of authority. Do you have problems with authority figures? If you do, usually this is a sign that you need to take more authority in your own life.

Upper Lip

• This sign signifies carrying on in spite of difficulties, keeping a stiff upper lip.

Urn

• An urn can be a closed metal vessel which is used for warming or serving tea or coffee. Because of its round, hollow, containing shape, it can be representative of female energy.
• As urns are often used to contain ashes of the dead, they can be a sign of death or of the dead. Are you subconsciously dwelling on someone who has passed over? Are there any undelivered communications with this individual? Even if someone is dead you can still communicate with them. This can be healing for them as well as you.

Vacation

• This might be an obvious sign that you need a vacation. If you can't leave town to get away, at least make time for some enjoyment and relaxation.
• Take a vacation from your old way of thinking. Let go and release old beliefs about who you are and what you can be in life. Take a new look at your ideas and your goals and the way that you define yourself.

Vaccination

• This sign can signify that you need emotional protection or it can mean that you actually need a vaccination. Get a health check-up.

Vacuum

• Do you feel as if you are living in a vacuum? Are you feeling isolated and not very creative? Get out. Join a club. Take a walk.

Participate in charity work or do some volunteer work. Participate in life to get back a feeling of vibrancy again.

• To vacuum is to clean or remove that which isn't needed. This is the time to eliminate the negativity in your life.

Vagina

• This is a powerful symbol of womanliness, openness, acceptance and receptivity. It is the inner valley of spirit.

• If you have had any negative sexual experiences where the vagina was involved (either your own vagina or the vagina of another), this sign can be bringing repressed memories to the forefront for release.

Valley

• This sign can signify a low point in your life. Every life has mountains and valleys. The challenge is to be able to enjoy your life whether you are on the mountain heights or in the depths of the dark valley of the soul. All life is precious. Every experience is valuable, even those experiences that you feel are negative, for they all allow you to grow spiritually and become more whole.

• This can also be a sign that says it's time to pull inwards.

• This sign can also indicate sexual desire.

Vampire

• Are you feeling exhausted and drained of your vitality by others? Each person is responsible for his or her own energy level. In truth, no one can drain anyone else. However, if you are feeling that there is someone in your life who is draining your energy, affirm to yourself, 'My energy is my own. I create my own reality in every moment, and I am free.'

Velvet

• This can be a sign of sensuality, or of desire. Embrace your sensuality. Revel in your senses. Experience life fully.

Ventriloquist

• Are you voicing someone else's opinions and not your own? Find your own truth and speak it. You will never be happy only voicing someone's opinions.

• What you hear might be the wrong source of information or inaccurate. Your information may be coming to you secondhand. Check the source.

Vineyard

• If the grapes are round and ripe, it is now time for harvesting the fruits of your experience.

Virgin

•   This is a traditional sign of chastity, of Mother Mary, and of the female aspect of God.

•   Virgin is also a sign of newness, as in virgin wool or a virgin forest. If this sign occurs for you, you are entering a fresh phase of life where everything will be new and pure.

•   The myth of the virgin as being the most desirable partner in marriage is a damaging one. However, fortunately it is a myth that is changing. Unity grows out of maturity and understanding within relationships.

Volcano

•   This is a powerful sign that represents an enormous explosion of suppressed emotions and passion. The volcano symbolizes a primal force of nature from within the depths of Mother Earth (which often is a symbol of the subconscious). This is not necessarily a bad sign, for it can be very healing to allow that which is repressed within you to come to the surface, even if it comes in an explosive manner.

Vomit

•   This is a sign that connotes getting rid of that which you don't need. Get rid of old ideas, old attitudes, old beliefs. This is the time. Do it now!

•   Are you needing to express and communicate that which you are holding back or that which is making you sick? This is the time to get things out in the open.

Vulture

•   Vultures feed almost exclusively on carrion. They perform a very useful function, in that they are eliminating potential sources of disease, although people often think that they are unclean birds because of this. However, they are very clean. In Egyptian hieroglyphs, the vulture was depicted along with mother symbolism which, according to Jung, was because Mother Earth contains both death and life. The Parsee placed their dead where the vultures could consume them, believing that this would allow them a rebirth.

Is there a potential problem that you are being asked to clean up? Are you always putting yourself in positions where you are asked to clean up messy situations? Look within to discover if there is an underlying pattern that is drawing these situations to you.

•   Do you feel a need to clean away something that you may consider complete or dead?

• Is there someone is your life who seems vulture-like? Do you feel there is a competitor waiting for you to make an error, or someone who has ill feelings towards you?

Waiter/Waitress

• Are you being asked to be of service to others, or of service to yourself? Make sure that you are offering service and not sacrifice, since the latter will drain your energy rather than uplift it.

Walking

• Your goals will be met through a slow but sure pace.

Wall

• This sign can indicate an obstacle or a blockage currently in your life or upcoming in your future. There is more than one way to obtain a goal. If you find yourself blocked by something, go around it or over it. Where there is a will, there is always a way!

• Are you feeling walled off from others? Make an effort to get out into the world and participate with others. Even if it feels forced in the beginning, you are creating a template of socializing and participating that will eventually become a new pattern in your life.

Wallet

• A wallet represents the personal beliefs and thoughts that you hold privately. It can also represent your identity. Loss of your wallet can be a loss of identity. Are you happy with your current identity? If there are things that you would like to change, begin now.

Wand

• This sign says yes, you can change things instantly. It is an excellent sign of transformation.

War   (See also *Battle*)

• This is a powerful sign of inner conflict and aggression. Spend time delving within yourself to ferret out any unresolved inner issues.

Warehouse

• This is your potential. All that you ever need is within yourself. Go for it. You have all the internal reserve that you need.

Washing

• Are you ready to release the past, old attitudes and beliefs, and go on? It is time to wash away the old and embrace the new.

Wasp

• Are you feeling threatened by stinging thoughts or stinging words from others?
• This sign can also pertain to White Anglo-Saxon Protestants (WASP).

Watch

• This sign pertains to the passage of time. Time is passing. Do you feel that time is running out? Affirm, 'I have all the time that I need to accomplish my goals in life.'
• This can also be a sign that says that you need to watch for the signs around you, or perhaps you need to watch out for yourself.

Water

• Water is one of the most universal signs throughout the world. Though it varies in richness of meaning from culture to culture, it usually is connected to emotions, feelings, intuition, psychic perceptions and the subconscious mind, as well as the mysterious realms of the archetypal female energy. As the spring rains bring new life to the lands, water can also represent fertility, new life and new creative potential.

The Chinese considered water to be the source of all life. In the Vedas, water is referred to as matritamah (the most maternal) because at the beginning of time everything was like water and without light. In India water was considered to hold the secret of the preservation of life. In Christian baptismal rites water represented life, death and resurrection. When one was submerged underwater the old person disappeared and a new person emerged. The birthing process is accompanied by uterine fluid, providing another analogy between water and life. There are many, many associations between water and fertility and the feminine nature of life, going back to ancient times.

• Flowing water can represent flowing emotions and feelings. Blocked or dammed water can mean that your feelings are blocked.
• Crystal-clear spring water can symbolize clarity, being in tune with life around you and connected to the inner feminine energy of receptivity and intuition. Stagnant water can mean you are stuck emotionally and it's time to shift gears, to step out of your emotional quagmire.
• Floods and tidal waves can indicate complete emotional chaos or being overwhelmed emotionally. This is not necessarily a bad sign, as sometimes it takes a huge upheaval to release old belief patterns.
• Check and see the quality of the water, whether it is clear or murky.
• Water also relates to spiritual alignment and attunement. This is your unconscious self, the waters of life, the source of your vitality.

Waterfall (See also *Water*)

• This sign can signal a complete emotional release and healing, as well as a complete emotional recharging.

Wave

• An ocean wave suggests surging forward, great emotional strength and power.
• This can also be a sign of waving at someone or someone waving at you. It can signify love, personal connection and acknowledgment.

Wax

• A situation you are involved in can be changed or easily moulded.
• Waxing can make a surface shiny, like new. Is there something in your life that has become dull that needs to be waxed?
• To wax means to increase gradually in size, number, strength, or intensity, or to show a progressively larger illuminated area, as the moon does in passing from new to full as it waxes and wanes. Are your energies waxing right now? It is time to go for it! You have the energy and the inner light to succeed in your endeavours.

Weasel

• Weasels are incredibly quick. They are expert and voracious hunters with speedy reflexes. Is there a situation in your life that needs quick action? Take action now!
• Do you feel someone is pushing you out of the way or weaselling in on your territory? This sign can pertain to treachery and betrayal.

Weather

• Weather signs can signify your emotional state. Stormy weather can reflect an inner storm. Rain can connote grief or emotional purification. Fog can indicate feeling that you can't see your life clearly.

Weaving

• This sign indicates the pattern or the tapestry of your life. Every experience you have is an important part of the great weaving of your life.

Web

• Are you feeling caught or entangled in a situation not of your own making? Beware of a trap, or of being ensnared in a web of deception.
• Native Americans have many traditions regarding the weaver and the web. Grandmother Spider is said to have brought the people the gift of fire. She carried it from the other side of the world in her woven basket. Some say that she wove the webs that form the very foundation

of the earth. Other traditions say that her webs are the threads of life. The web can be likened to the pattern of your life. It is now time to rebuild and reweave the web of your life. 'You are the weaver. You are the web. You are the flow and you are the ebb.'

Wedding

• This is a wonderful sign of a union of your conscious and unconscious mind, of your body and spirit, of the male and female energies within you.

Well

• The well contains refreshing life-giving waters. In many cultures the well was the centre of life. It was a place where women would gather around to share the news of the day. This can be a sign of community and emotional *well*-being.
• The well can also be a sign of a depth of wisdom and inspiration accumulated from past experiences.

Whale

• The whale uses sonar to tune in to the surrounding environment. The whale can be a sign of perception and intuition. Use your intuition to tune in to the situations in your life. This is a sign to connect with your instincts, your creative intuition and your psychic perceptions.
• The whale has tremendous power and strength and yet is gentle and considered non-aggressive. You can access the inner strength within yourself and yet still be gentle and loving.
• This sign may concern the size of something, as in a whale of a job.
• This sign may be a homophone for wail. Are you grieving or crying for help?

Wheel

• The 'wheel of life', the 'wheel of fortune' and the 'wheel of karma' all refer to the ever-turning, ever-changing nature of reality. Everything changes. That is the nature of life. Yet there is always stillness in the centre of the wheel, where nothing ever changes. That is the nature of spirit. Together you have the great wheel of life which encompasses mystery and form, life and death, inner and outer – the continuous interplay of the two opposing yet harmonious forces of the universe.

Whisper

• Are you unwilling or unable to communicate and say what is in your heart and mind? Are you feeling held back? Examine why you feel that you can't communicate. Work on resolving any inner blocks to speaking your truth loudly and clearly.

Whistle

• This can be a warning sign. Someone or something is trying to get your attention. Be aware and alert.

Willow

• Willows are extraordinarily graceful and fluid. Are you able to bend and move with the circumstances of your life? Learn to be more flexible.

• Willow is often a sign of grieving or sadness because of its name, weeping willow, called thus because of its long, hanging branches which appear to some people as though they are drooping over with sadness.

Wind

• Air is the element that represents thought and intellect. It can also represent spirit or the celestial breath of God. In Arabic and in Hebrew the word for wind also signifies breath and spirit. Wind can vary from a gentle breeze on a warm summer afternoon to a violent hurricane, and can signify either a subtle or a dramatic shift in consciousness, particularly through the power of higher thought.

• In many native traditions throughout the world it is felt that the wind carries messages from the realm of spirit. Each directional wind carries it own meaning, which varies from tribe to tribe. For example, in some traditions the north wind carries messages from our personal ancestors. Whenever you feel the wind, it's valuable to be still and imagine what the wind is trying to tell you. Every breeze, every zephyr, every gust carries personal messages for you. Listen and you will hear the whispers of the universe.

• Changing winds can mean that there are changes ahead for you.

Wine

• Wine can symbolize prosperity, abundance, celebration and relaxation. Are you ready for 'wine, women [men] and song'? Even if you don't drink, this sign has collective consciousness energy suggesting the good life.

• This sign can also symbolize spiritual attunement as wine representing the blood of Christ or that spiritual energy within.

Wings

• This is a great sign for personal freedom. It is your time to soar. You are free. Transcendence and liberation are at hand.

Witch

• In the past, witch came from the word 'wica', meaning wise woman. This sign can represent that wise female energy within you. This is your latent inner wisdom. (Even if you are male, there is a feminine energy within you.) For some, witches are a malevolent symbol. This view has been perpetuated in modern times by writers of children's fairy tales who aren't aware of the horrific Christian persecution of witches in the Middle Ages. These witches were basically benevolent herbalists, healers and midwives. Their persecution grew out of the Christian tendency to separate God from nature and to worship a god based in the sky rather than an indwelling earth deity.

Wolf

• Wolves have a very strongly developed sense of family and community. They act together to hunt and raise their young, and they have a very strong sense of social hierarchy in the pack. There has never been a case of a wild wolf killing a human being in North America (though there are several reported cases in Europe). As a rule wolves are non-aggressive and very rarely do they engage in violence among themselves. Do you feel supported by your family? Do you need to balance your personal needs with the needs of your family? This is a powerful sign that speaks to you of your relationship to your personal family and your sense of family.

• Are you eating too fast? Are you 'wolfing' down your food? This sign may indicate a need for more affection or emotional support.

• For some, this can be a sign of fear, especially concerning being pressed for something without the resources to meet the need, as in the saying, a wolf at the door.

• This can also be a sign of inappropriate flirtatious behaviour. Are you being a real wolf?

Womb

• This is a sign of nourishment, of safety, of protection.

• This sign may be telling you to pull in and regroup your energies before your next endeavour.

Worm

• This can be a sign of hidden preparation or work beneath the surface. Beneath the surface of a situation there is work that needs to be done to prepare fertile soil for your project.

• This sign can indicate someone in your life who is a low life or someone with no backbone.

• Is someone intruding upon you or is someone worming his or her way into your life without your agreement?

X-Ray

- This is a sign of seeing what is within with more clarity, with deeper understanding. Perhaps there is a situation in your life that requires that you look beneath the surface to see the true reality. Go deep within yourself to access inner depth and understanding.

Yawn

- This is an obvious sign of boredom. You need another outlet for your creativity.
- This sign may be telling you that you need more sleep.

Yo-yo

- Do you feeling like you are going up and down, repeating the same patterns? Affirm to yourself, 'I pursue my life goals with clarity and focus.'

Zero

- This sign is saying it's the zero hour. It's time to blast off and initiate that goal that you have waited for so long.
- This may also be a sign of feeling that you are nothing and are feeling empty. Affirm to yourself, 'I am a valuable human being. My life makes a difference.'
- A zero can be a sign of absolute wholeness and completeness, because the physical representation of a zero is a circle, which is a universal symbol of unity, wholeness and infinity.

FURTHER INFORMATION

Denise regularly conducts seminars in many English-speaking countries around the world and also teaches in a number of non English-speaking countries, working through an interpreter.

For information about her seminars in the Northern Hemisphere contact:

New Life Designs
Arnica House
170 Campden Hill Road
London W8 7AS
UK
Tel: 0171-938-3788

In the Southern Hemisphere contact:

New Life Designs
Suite 2
4 Belgrave Street
Manly
Sydney NSW 2095
Australia
Tel: 61-2-977-1200

For information about where to obtain Denise's audio tapes contact:

QED Recording Services
Lancaster Road
New Barnet
Hertfordshire EN4 8AS
UK
Tel: 0181-441 7722